From Yellow Dog Democrats to Red State Republicans

USF LIBRARIES' FLORIDA STUDIES CENTER

UNIVERSITY PRESS OF FLORIDA

Florida A&M University, Tallahassee
Florida Atlantic University, Boca Raton
Florida Gulf Coast University, Ft. Myers
Florida International University, Miami
Florida State University, Tallahassee
New College of Florida, Sarasota
University of Central Florida, Orlando
University of Florida, Gainesville
University of North Florida, Jacksonville
University of South Florida, Tampa
University of West Florida, Pensacola

From Yellow Dog Democrats
to Red State Republicans

Florida and Its Politics since 1940

David R. Colburn

University Press of Florida
Gainesville · Tallahassee · Tampa · Boca Raton · Pensacola
Orlando · Miami · Jacksonville · Ft. Myers · Sarasota

To Claire, Caroline, James, Alison, and Benjamin,
for their faith in us. May we measure up to it.

UNIVERSITY OF
SOUTH FLORIDA

Published in cooperation with USF Libraries' Florida Studies Center

12   11   10   09   08   07   6   5   4   3   2   1

Library of Congress Cataloging-in-Publication Data
Colburn, David R.
From yellow dog Democrats to red state Republicans : Florida
and its politics since 1940 / by David R. Colburn.
p. cm.
Includes bibliographical references and index.
ISBN 978-0-8130-3155-2 (alk. paper)
1. Florida—Politics and government—1950- 2. Florida—
Politics and government—1865-1950. 3. Political culture—
Florida—History—20th century. 4. Political culture—
Florida—History—21st century. 5. Political parties—Florida.
6. Politicians—Florida. 7. Florida—Ethnic relations—Political
aspects. 8. Florida—Social conditions. I. Title.
F316.2.C58   2007
975.9'063—dc22
2007007776

The University Press of Florida is the scholarly publishing
agency for the State University System of Florida, comprising
Florida A&M University, Florida Atlantic University, Florida
Gulf Coast University, Florida International University, Florida
State University, New College of Florida, University of Central
Florida, University of Florida, University of North Florida,
University of South Florida, and University of West Florida.

University Press of Florida
15 Northwest 15th Street
Gainesville, FL 32611-2079
www.upf.com

Contents

Acknowledgments

They are several great pleasures in writing a book, not the least of which is completing it. Expressing appreciation to those who have greatly aided this process certainly ranks among the most important and gratifying.

I have benefited particularly from the generous support, wise counsel, and goodwill of many people. Their friendship and professionalism cannot be overstated. At the University of Florida, Jeffrey Adler, who had his own book project nearing completion, read the entire manuscript. I badgered him further for advice about revised chapters on several other occasions. He never complained, although I am sure he is as pleased as I am that the book is finished. Near the final stages of the manuscript, I asked David Lawrence, former publisher of the *Miami Herald* and now president of the Early Childhood Initiative Foundation and University Scholar for Early Childhood Development and Readiness at the University of Florida, to read it. Few people understand Florida or Florida politics as well as David Lawrence. He said that, if I could send it to him soon, he thought he could get to it in a couple of weeks. Three days later he called to tell me he had finished and would be sending his extended comments shortly. Two days later they arrived. Dave's comments were instrumental in helping me polish the manuscript's prose and in adding several sections to provide greater clarity and fuller explanation of key political developments.

Outside the University of Florida, Cynthia Barnett, senior writer for *Florida Trend* magazine—who was also in the final stages of publishing her own book on Florida's environment—read the entire manuscript. She gave me a short course on what it takes to tell this story to the general reading public. I am not sure I have got it right yet, but Cynthia and Dave Lawrence provided me with as good an education as one can get in writing for a general audience. Readers will have to judge for themselves whether

I learned my lessons well. I also want to express my appreciation to Jane Healy, executive editor of the *Orlando Sentinel*, who has been a friend and wise counselor on state political developments.

Gary Mormino, friend and Frank Duckworth Professor of History at the University of South Florida, also read the entire manuscript and prevented me from making several historical errors of omission and commission as well as offering me his insight into some of the important events of the post-1940 period in Florida that warranted further analysis. Gary's wonderful book on Florida, *Land of Sunshine, State of Dreams: A Social History of Modern Florida*, is a model of historical writing about this unique place and its people. It has established a standard for the rest of us to emulate.

Julian Pleasants, director of the Samuel Proctor Oral History Program at the University of Florida, helped identify interviews that would assist me greatly in this process and gave me a copy of his book *Hanging Chads, The Inside Story of the 2000 Presidential Recount in Florida*, which was extraordinarily useful in understanding the unique and frequently bizarre election developments in the state. This book deserves much more attention from readers and political writers than it has so far received. Two other colleagues—David Chalmers and Michael Gannon—each wrote extensively on Florida's racial past, its Spanish heritage, and the events of World War II that defined and redefined Florida. Together with Samuel Proctor, distinguished state historian and director of the Oral History Program that now bears his name, these three served as mentors to many of us as we began our scholarly careers at the University of Florida and were of great help to me in grappling with Florida politics and culture. Charles Frazier, a distinguished sociologist at UF, proved a great sounding board for some of my ideas and a good friend throughout.

I also owe a great deal to James Button and George Pozzetta, two close friends and colleagues who died much too young. Before their untimely deaths, I had the privilege of teaching courses with both of them and writing with them, and learning a great deal in the process about what it takes to pursue serious scholarship. From Jim, I learned much about local politics in Florida and about the influence of senior citizens on state political developments. From George, I gained a fuller understanding of and insight into the diversity of the state and the ways that diversity was redefining Florida. Both men were models of the teacher-scholar that all of us who are privileged to teach at universities seek to be.

Susan MacManus, Lance deHaven-Smith, Rick Foglesong, and Richard Scher are four political scientists who have written extensively, insightfully, and fervently about Florida, and whom I am privileged to call friends. Each of them has taught me a great deal about political developments in the period since 1940. I coauthored my first book with Richard Scher, *Florida's Gubernatorial Politics in the Twentieth Century*, and still draw on that research to assist me in understanding state politics today. Lance coauthored two books with me and remains a thoughtful and passionate critic of Florida politics.

Over the years, I have been privileged to work with, write with, and learn from many other scholars whose writings about Florida, southern politics, and southern and American race relations have shaped my own thinking. From Steven Lawson to Jane Landers, James Clark, Maxine Jones, Larry Rivers, Jim Cobb, Elizabeth Jacoway, Bill Chafe, Tony Badger, Raymond Mohl, Daniel Schafer, Brian Ward, William Rogers, and Thomas Dye, this Rhode Islander has learned a great deal about the state's southern heritage and about its evolution during and after World War II. All have taught me a great deal about our nation's recent past and enhanced my knowledge of southern culture and politics. Brian Ward was a wonderful colleague, who added much to the intellectual life of the department and who, through his research and writing, gave me great insight into southern culture and race relations.

During the past twelve years, I have had the extraordinary opportunity of directing the Reubin O'D. Askew Institute on Politics and Society at the University of Florida. The institute, named for former Governor Reubin Askew, introduced me to many of the key figures and issues that shaped Florida in the modern period. Most importantly, it allowed me to develop a professional relationship and personal friendship with one of the great governors of the twentieth century—Reubin O'Donovan Askew. He remains a remarkable person who continues to inspire others about the true meaning of public service. I have tried to employ my professional detachment as a scholar in writing about him and his influence in this modern period, but it has not been easy. Foremost of the many things I have learned from Reubin Askew is that he particularly values personal and professional integrity. It is in that spirit I have written about him, his service as governor, and his influence on state and southern politics. I also want to acknowledge my colleagues in the Askew Institute, Lynn Leverty, who is also a member of the Political Science Department, and Lynne Holt, who also assists the Public Utility Research Center. Both have brought remarkable professionalism and dedication to the Askew Institute and to assisting Floridians in understanding the critical issues confronting their state. I have been fortunate to work with and learn from both of them.

I would also like to acknowledge the staff at the University Press of Florida and express my esteem for them, their professionalism, and their guidance in producing this book. The press has come a remarkable distance in the last fifteen years, under the watchful eye and careful leadership of Directors Ken Scott and Meredith Morris-Babb. Together they have assembled a superb professional staff, and I thank them all for their assistance with this project.

Throughout my work on this and other books, my wife, Marion, has been patiently supportive as only a partner can be. She knew when I was struggling with the writing and research and when I was not, and she knew how to support me in either circumstance. It may sound trite to say that I have been blessed in marriage, but trite or not, it is true. Normally, I dedicate my books to her or to her and our children. But in this instance, we both would like to dedicate this book to our grandchildren: Claire, Caroline, Alison, James, and Benjamin, each of whom has enriched our lives in ways that even we did not anticipate, and each of whom represents in a small way the future of our country. Being grandparents has been one of the great joys of our lives, and we have been privileged to have this opportunity. My wife and I dedicate this book to them in the hope that this history and others will give them an appreciation of our past, the struggle of Floridians and Americans to live up to the ideals of our nation, and the fundamental importance of an engaged citizenry.

Introduction

On election night in 2000, CBS television news anchor Dan Rather announced emphatically, "Florida is the whole deal, the real deal, a big deal."[1] In Rather's view, Florida was critical to the outcome of the 2000 presidential election. But his comments also suggested that the state had taken on greater importance. Indeed, by the end of the twentieth century, Florida not only stood at the center of one of the closest elections in American history, it had become a megastate and the demographic future of the nation.

Florida's rise to a place of national prominence took less than a lifetime, beginning with the onset of World War II. For much of its history, it had been an isolated, impoverished, southern frontier outpost. Whether it was under the Spanish, British, United States, or Confederate flag, Florida was an afterthought to the aspiration of each. Floridians struggled to carve a place for themselves out of the piney woodlands of the Panhandle, along the lush coastline, and in the flatlands and swampy interior of the Peninsula. The state historian Michael Gannon wrote expressively of its traumatic early history: "Failure followed failure as a long succession of Spanish captains, beginning with Ponce de Leon, carried their proud lances into this wilderness only to see them broken by outrageous fortune."[2] What the Spaniards encountered typified the experiences of other Europeans and Americans who followed in their footsteps.

Despite Ponce de Leon's discovery of the Florida Peninsula at Eastertime in 1513 and the establishment of a small Spanish settlement in St. Augustine by Pedro Menéndez de Avilés in 1565, it took most of the intervening years up to World War II before Florida awakened an interest in others to invest their lives and their fortunes there. And it took until 1950 before one could be confident about either investment.

On the eve of World War II, Florida remained little more than an intriguing footnote in the history of the United States. It was the place of both the oldest European settlement and the oldest free black community, but Americans not only failed to celebrate that history, most did not know it. And most Floridians themselves were as oblivious to it as the rest of the nation. But as the historian Gary Mormino has written, "The march to and fro across Florida was irresistible and irrepressible, as orange groves became gated communities, small towns were transformed into cities, and big cities sprawled into metropolises and boomburbs."[3] Between 1940 and 1980, Florida gradually abandoned its southern past and its racial traditions and became a place where the northern and southern regions of the Western Hemisphere intersected culturally, socially, and economically.

During this period and the years that followed, Florida rose from being one of the poorest states in the nation and one of the least developed, with the smallest population in the South, to the most dynamic state on the east coast and, alongside California, the most diverse state in the nation. Leading this change was a massive wave of migration and immigration that saw the state's population increase from 1.9 million people in 1940 to approximately 17.4 million people by 2005. The Hispanic population grew from less than 1 percent of the population in 1945 to 19.6 percent of the population in 2005, while the population of senior citizens over sixty expanded from 6.9 percent to nearly 21.8 percent.[4]

John Shelton Reed and his colleagues at the University of North Carolina concluded in 1990 that, as a result of this population infusion from the Northeast, Midwest, the Caribbean, and Latin America, all of peninsular Florida had dropped out of Dixie, and by 1990 only a very small segment of the Panhandle could still be called southern. A few pockets of the state's southern past remained across the Panhandle and down through the center of the Florida Peninsula.[5] But so many new people had moved into these areas after 1990 that they altered the image of residents in these pockets of Dixie. A Cracker culture could still be identified there, evidencing itself mostly in cultural events, but seldom did it influence state politics after 1990. The sociologist Richard Peterson may have captured it best when he observed about the persistence of this Cracker culture and its political influence: "To call oneself a redneck is not so much to be a redneck by birth or occupational fate, but rather to identify with an anti-bourgeois attitude and lifestyle."[6]

Race relations in the state and region, which were so pivotal in making the South distinct from the rest of the nation, had also changed to such an extent by 1990 that, according to Reed, few could claim that racial differences persisted between the South and the North.[7] Even fewer would contend that race defines Florida today, or that it remains a southern state. Alongside the tremendous demographic changes that persisted throughout the 1950s, the civil rights developments and massive resistance of that era redefined Florida and its politics. These dramatic developments splintered the state Democratic Party, helped pave the way for the emergence of the Republican Party in Florida, and made the state a centerpiece in the battle between the two parties for state and national dominance.

No state changed more than Florida during the post–World War II period. The populations of Texas and California grew larger in total population, but Florida's population increased at a much faster rate. In fact, Florida looked a great deal like southern California by 2000. Thirteen million new residents descended on the Sunshine State between 1950 and 2000, an increase only slightly less than the nearly 15 million who resettled in southern California.

Both places attracted a peculiar mix of the profane and the mundane. Alongside working-class and middle-class families, the rich and famous, speculators, and con artists arrived, seeking a piece of paradise, easy money, and innocent prey. Political essayist and humorist Carl Hiaasen was frequently perplexed by human behavior in his native state of Florida. Perhaps too much sun affected the synapses of the brain, or perhaps this had something to do with the increasing mix of Yankees and Rebels. From flim-flam artists to mobile-home salesmen hawking their products during hurricane season to indiscreet politicians freely accepting cash bribes, many like Hiaasen and writer Michael Paterniti found it hard to take Florida seriously. "If you're a Floridian, there's a certain sort of rueful but good-natured pride in the state's notoriety," Hiaasen noted drolly. "It's a camaraderie born of being part of the freak show. You gotta laugh, because what the hell else are you going to do?"[8]

Florida holds a particular fascination to Americans because of the romantic attraction of the sun, beaches, and gentle sea breezes as well as the glamorous and bizarre characters that frequent the place. What also makes Florida particularly fascinating to this writer are the ways it has changed in a lifetime, from 1940 to 2006, and the way Floridians have changed with it. From one of the least appealing, most racially polarized, and poorest states to one of the most desired, most diverse, and most prosperous; from a state that had been anything but a bellwether of the nation to one that Dan Rather asserted is "the whole deal, the real deal, a big deal." Certainly Rather was embellishing the story of the 2000 election. But few would deny that Florida reflected the new America, a nation of young and old, immigrant and native, rich and poor—all searching for a place in paradise that would afford them opportunity, freedom, and a better quality of life.

Beneath the sensational headlines, many decent, hardworking people found their way to Florida. Their experiences were not the stuff of the designer Versace or former Florida Secretary of State Katherine Harris or young Cuban refugee Elian Gonzalez. They were largely everyday folks in search of good jobs, new beginnings, political freedom, a healthy and extended retirement, and political stability. Their stories did not help sell newspapers or provide the grist for best-selling novels. Yet, in less than a lifetime, they fundamentally altered the face and complexion of Florida, and they reshaped its politics in the process.

The demographic changes—approximately 17.4 million people as compared to 1.9 million in 1940—have made Florida a vastly more complex state in 2005. Only one-third of Florida residents were born in the state; nearly 46 percent of Floridians were born in a different state; and 17.6 percent were born in another country. What had been in 1940 essentially a biracial state has become, by 2005, one of the most demographically diverse states in the nation. Hispanics, attracted by Miami's diverse culture and economic opportunities, increased their numbers in Florida to over 3.4 million, up by over 2 million in only fifteen years, and they constituted 19.6 percent of the state's population. Moreover, their numbers only hinted at the ethnic complexity they brought to Florida.[9] As one Hispanic woman observed about the growing population, "They're from all over Central and South America."[10] More precisely, Hispanics came in large numbers from most island nations in the Caribbean and in lesser, but still significant numbers from Mexico, Brazil, Nicaragua, Colombia, Peru, Venezuela, and Honduras, so that by 2005 non-Cuban Hispanics outnumbered Cubans in Florida. Sandra Cortes, who moved to Miami from Colombia in 2000, said most of her friends in the city are from that South American country. "I don't seek them out," she commented, "but we gravitate to each other because we share similar cultures."[11]

Less visible but equally significant, the black population increased as a percentage of the total population, from 13.8 percent in 1990 to 15 percent in 2005, after having declined steadily throughout the twentieth century.[12] The growth and consequential economic expansion of the state together with the rejection of the racial policies of the past convinced African Americans to join the throngs of whites and Hispanics who descended on Florida, reversing the outward trend of black Floridians for much of the twentieth century. Broward County attracted more black residents than any other county in the nation between July 2004 and July 2005. Immigrants from the Caribbean sparked this trend, but African Americans joined them in this increasingly polyglot area of southeast Florida.

As with most others who migrated to Florida, African Americans came in search of opportunity and freedom. Salaries in the service sector, which dominated the state economy, were low, but opportunity was not limited by one's race, gender, or ethnicity. And this was no small factor for African Americans as well as Hispanics who relocated to Florida. Numerous small businesses emerged to cater to the needs of megatourist companies like Disney, SeaWorld, and MGM. By 2000, Florida's African American–owned businesses ranked fourth nationally, Hispanic-owned businesses ranked second in the nation, and women-owned businesses ranked third.[13]

As word spread about the opportunities in the state and the decline of racial discrimination, the total number of black residents grew from 1.8 million in 1990 to over 2.6 million in 2005. Middle-class and well-to-do black newcomers found the state's diversity an asset in gaining acceptance in companies and in upscale housing developments in and around Orlando, Tampa, and Fort Lauderdale. Despite a racial heritage marked by violence and discrimination, Florida offered a dramatically improved racial climate by 2000, and black residents seldom encountered racial discrimination in these new neighborhoods in central and south Florida. Further aiding racial progress, both political parties actively courted black voters, appointed black leaders to major state offices, and even apologized for the state's racist past.

Joining the influx of Hispanics and African were senior citizens—those retirees over sixty—who longed for cloudless days, the freedom and invigoration of the outdoors, and a prolonged life. The gray wave descended on the state in search of Ponce de Leon's Fountain of Youth, and many contended that they had found it. They first came in dribs and drabs in the 1950s, but as word spread about the quality of life and the longevity that seemed to follow from it, others followed en masse. By 2005, those over sixty constituted over 21.7 percent of the population, or nearly 3.8 million people, making them the nation's largest and most politically influential retirement group. But their numbers only hinted at their political influence as they tended to vote in much larger percentages than any other age, ethnic, or racial group in the state. Aided by the American Association of Retired Persons (AARP), seniors let their interests and political views be known, and they reshaped the state socially and politically as much as any ethnic or racial group.

This book seeks to provide readers with an understanding of the political, demographic, and social developments that dramatically transformed Florida in just sixty-five years, from 1940 to 2005. In doing so, the book focuses on the way Floridians of all ages, from a variety of backgrounds, and from all sorts of places, altered the state and its politics—from an undemocratic and chaotic political system in which the Democratic Party elected nearly all candidates and set the political agenda for much of the twentieth century to a highly partisan and hotly contested political environment in which the Republican Party wrested power from the Democrats.

For much of the period prior to 1940 and throughout a good bit of the post-1940 era, Florida's political environment was defined by the politics of personality and race. The state's decision to join the Confederacy in the nineteenth century and its post–Civil War racial traditions linked it to the Democratic Party for most of the ninety years that followed the Reconstruction era.

By the end of the twentieth century, however, the elimination of segregation that had been championed by elements within the national Democratic Party and supported by Florida Governor LeRoy Collins in the 1950s undermined the state's one-party politics. Yellow Dog Democrats—those who voted religiously for Democratic candidates and who, it was said, would vote for an ugly yellow dog before a Republican—wavered and then abandoned the Democratic Party.

These developments, alongside the massive social and demographic changes, drew Florida voters increasingly to a politically and culturally conservative Republican Party in the last third of the twentieth century. The political transition proved less than felicitous, leading to allegations that the state had become a "banana republic" like its neighbors to the south and to charges that, like those so-called banana republics, it favored the wealthy at the expense of the poor. Hiaasen was one of many who reflected this view when he wrote: "The Sunshine State is a paradise of scandals teeming with drifters, deadbeats, and misfits drawn here by some dark primordial calling like demented trout. And you'd be surprised how many of them decide to run for public office."[14]

What resulted in Florida may not have been a democracy that satisfied all. And it may have been messy at best, as the 2000 presidential election made obvious. But Florida was a dynamic democracy of newcomers, immigrants, natives, seniors, rednecks, evangelicals, and, yes, flim-flam artists and mobile-home salesmen. All of whom came to the state looking for ways to improve their lot in life.

In examining the events of this era, I have detailed particularly the role of state governors in influencing the evolution of postwar Florida. Gubernatorial leadership proved crucial in giving direction to the state, recruiting new businesses and residents, persuading voters to accept the racial and ethnic changes, and launching a political dialogue with voters over "rights and responsibilities" in the late twentieth century that sparked the resurgence of the Republican Party.

Some may take exception to this book being a top-down study of Florida, and certainly its attention to gubernatorial leadership lends itself to that concern. Post-1940 Florida is a complex story, and an analysis of state governors and their role in responding to and shaping the political environment tells only one part of the story. Governors, after all, did not operate in a political vacuum, nor did they or could they impose their will on voters. But state governors in Florida played a central role in shaping the political discourse with voters and in giving it direction, most notably during the era of massive resistance in the 1950s and especially after the constitutional changes of 1968 strengthened the powers of the state's chief executive and allowed governors to succeed themselves. Governors were, in fact, at the center of every postwar development from Cracker to Sun Belt politics, from segregation to integration, from boosterism and modernization to ecological and environmental crisis, from the dominance of the Democratic Party to the emergence of the Republican Party. In many cases, governors responded to voter pressures; in others, they anticipated them; and in still others, they influenced and gave direction to voter concerns. This approach does not tell the entire story of Florida's postwar development. Indeed, I have injected extended sections about civil rights, immigrant, ethnic and racial developments, and religious trends to flesh out this study and to give readers a better understanding of Florida's emergence as the most vibrant and politically influential state in the nation.

As in other states and particularly in neighboring states, Florida politics were influenced significantly by developments at the federal level and by the policies of the two national parties. Both Democratic and Republican parties in the state, for example, felt the effects when the national Democratic Party opted to support civil rights reforms in the 1950s and 1960s, and later, in the 1980s and 1990s, when the national Republican Party championed a rights, responsibilities, and values ideology. Significantly, both these political developments were linked to one another, with Republicans capitalizing on public concerns over integration, school busing, and the social discord of the 1960s to reach out successfully to middle-class voters in Florida and in the nation.

But the Florida story is more complex than those that unfolded in other southern states. Race and racial developments, for example, did not cause Floridians to flee straightaway to the suburbs or to abandon the Democratic Party, as the historian Kevin Kruse argues occurred in Atlanta. Race was certainly a significant factor in Florida politics and in political developments that occurred in the 1960s as a result of the civil rights revolution, but it did not redefine Florida politics or give rise to Republican leadership in the 1990s. Nor did developments in Florida parallel what the historian Matthew Lassiter claims was a "class ideology" that sparked the political transformation of the region. Indeed, the political motivations of immigrants, migrants, and retirees in Florida typically extended beyond class concerns.[15]

Florida's racial politics were fundamentally transformed in the mid-1960s by federal action and by the migration of retirees, northerners, and Cuban émigrés. Seniors, who lived in massive condominium complexes and voted in substantial numbers in local and state elections, were largely unaffected by school integration and busing because their children and grandchildren resided in other states. Together with most newcomers from the North, the Midwest, and Cuba, they had little interest in or commitment to segregation. Additionally, retirees and Cubans were less class-driven. Retirees were most concerned with quality-of-life issues, taxes, and health care, while Cubans focused on resettlement issues and developments in their homeland.

During the period from 1970 to 1994, Democratic governors, led by Reubin Askew, Bob Graham, and Lawton Chiles, successfully forestalled the Republican rise to power in the state by advancing a progressive and populist appeal to natives and newcomers that highlighted equal rights and equal opportunity, economic advancement, environmental protection, tax fairness, honest and responsible government, and the health and well-being of Floridians. These issues proved much more important to newcomers, business leaders, and retirees than preserving the racial traditions of the past or advancing and protecting class interests.

Neither race nor class should be dismissed as factors in the political transformation that occurred in Florida, however. They were clearly factors, and, at times, they influenced political developments. But people coming to Florida, no matter their class, race, or ethnicity, saw Florida as a land of opportunity, an emerging economic frontier, where they had a chance to get ahead and where they could live a good life in a place of pristine beauty. President Ronald Reagan, former governor of California, recognized that race and class did not necessarily motivate voters in his state. He was convinced that Californians were more concerned about such issues as taxes, economic development, crime, quality of schools, and property values. These issues were also of great importance in Florida, which shared many of the same demographics and where residents had aspirations similar to those of Californians. Newcomers to both states sought new beginnings in paradise, not social reform or class conflict. Economic and social instability posed a direct threat to their aspirations and to the quality of life they sought for themselves. Reagan's understanding of their interests helps explain why voters in both states enthusiastically supported him when he ran for president.

The Republican tide that ultimately engulfed Florida grew out of state and national developments and focused on the issues mentioned above. The state's wealthy and middle-class voters, Cracker and Cuban voters, religious conservatives, and many suburban residents gradually embraced the Republican Party during the last two decades of the twentieth century. Despite the popularity of Democrats Bob Graham and Lawton Chiles, they believed that the Republican Party would address their concerns more effectively than the state and national Democratic Party. Seniors remained less certain and thus remain conflicted about the two parties. Even without a political consensus among seniors, this union of voters formed a powerful new political coalition in Florida. Together with the reapportionment of the state legislature and the emergence of Jeb Bush, who gave the party statewide recognition and star appeal in the 1990s, Republicans seized political control and ended Democratic hegemony in the process. How this political revolution unfolded in the second half of the twentieth century said a great deal about Florida's place in the region and in the nation.

Despite the seeming collapse of the state Democratic Party, no one could predict confidently its demise or the state's political future. Change was the one constant in the state—change resulting from the massive migration. Three hundred thousand people entered Florida every year from 1970 to 2006, increasing both its ethnic and racial complexity (so that by 2005 nearly 35 percent of the population was either Hispanic or African American) and its retirement population (so that over one in every five Floridians was over sixty in 2005).[16] Mobility within the state added to the social and political instability, as natives and newcomers searched anxiously for new beginnings and new opportunities. Other than California, no state was as complex as Florida or experienced change on such a continual basis. Although these developments were more intense in Florida and California than elsewhere, they presaged what was happening in the nation as a whole, where population growth, population movement, ethnic diversity, immigration, and senior longevity promised to redefine the nation and its politics. Population trends for both states indicate that minorities will constitute a majority of the population by 2050, and Florida's senior population could well reach 30 percent by 2020. The significance and magnitude of these demographic changes in Florida made astute politicians wary about their future as well as that of their party.

How Florida's demographic, economic, social, and political environment unfolded from 1940 to 2006 is the story of this book. It is also the story of the nation.

1

From Darkness to Sunshine

World War II, Race, and the Emergence of Modern Florida

For most of the twentieth century, Florida was as Blue, politically, as the waters that surround the Peninsula on three sides. But in the 1990s, the state abruptly turned Red. Like so many of its southern and Sun Belt neighbors, Florida came to embrace the Republican Party. But, as opposed to most of these states, the Democratic Party managed to retain a majority of registered voters and the party remained very competitive in statewide races. As a consequence, Florida continued to be one of the most intense political battlegrounds in the nation—and a catalyst, in the year 2000, for one of closest and most confusing presidential elections in American history. During the infamous contest of 2000—which provided a script that even the author and humorist Carl Hiaasen could not have written—its election officials and voters became the butt of jokes and synonymous with political ineptitude of a magnitude not encountered since the late nineteenth century, when immigrant voters and their deceased relatives cast ballots under the direction of urban political bosses of Chicago and New York City. The writer Michael Paterniti observed about the state: "Florida has always been a stage on which its visitors preened and strutted, often briefly and unsuccessfully, perhaps at times hubristically, which may explain our feelings about the state as being somehow alien, or an altogether Otherworld." In Paterniti's view, Floridians were not shocked by the election result because they "have come to expect the surreal."[1]

New Florida Slogans

FLORIDA: If you think we can't vote, wait till you see us drive.
FLORIDA: Home of electile dysfunction.
FLORIDA: We count more than you do.
FLORIDA: If you don't like the way we count, then take I-95
and visit one of the other fifty-six states.
FLORIDA: Relax, Retire, Revote.
FLORIDA: Palm Beach County: So nice, we let you vote twice.

How did Florida find itself at the center of the controversy in the 2000 presidential election? And why did Floridians begin to turn away from the Democratic Party during the late twentieth century? Was Florida simply marching in lockstep with the rest of the South for much the same reasons? Or was something else taking place?

For most of the late nineteenth and twentieth centuries, Florida was a one-party state in which the Democratic Party dominated statewide and local elections, much like it did throughout the former Confederate South. Rooted in native white resistance to Republican Reconstruction and to a biracial society, Floridians embraced the Democratic Party when federal troops were finally removed from the state following the Compromise of 1877. Ironically, the compromise settled the hotly contested and chaotic presidential election of 1876, in which controversy and charges of corruption marked the Florida vote and in which the state's four electoral votes proved crucial in the election of Republican Rutherford B. Hayes. Democrat Samuel Tilden won the popular vote by over 250,000 votes, but Hayes defeated Tilden in the Electoral College, 185 to 184, after an electoral commission appointed by Congress decided the contested votes in South Carolina, Louisiana, and Florida for Hayes by an 8 to 7 vote in every instance. In many ways, the outcome of this election and the subsequent compromise proved more critical to the nation, which many felt was on the brink of another civil war, than the disputed election of 2000.[2]

By the end of the nineteenth century, Florida candidates of all political persuasions ran as Democrats. So many, in fact, ran as Democrats that party affiliation became meaningless, and so did the November general election. As a result of these developments, the party adopted a "white primary system" in 1901 to enable candidates to compete with one another for political office in Florida and to prevent black voters from influencing the outcome. The *Tampa Morning Tribune* observed in 1909 that "the negro has no voice whatsoever in the selection of United States Senators, Representatives in Congress, Governor, statehouse officers, members of the legislature, [and] county offices." The historian Paul Ortiz wrote that African-American resistance to segregation "was continuous over time, but its effectiveness varied" because of economic, political, and legal changes implemented by white politicians.[3]

Democratic candidates campaigned vigorously and even combatively to obtain the party's nomination, but once nominated they were literally assured of election. In many cases, successful Democratic candidates, like those in other southern states, seldom faced a Republican opponent in the general election for much of the twentieth century. When they did, they rarely took it seriously even for the most important office in Florida— governor of the state. In the 1940 Democratic primary, eleven candidates ran for governor, but they faced no Republican opponent in the general election. Millard Caldwell, who was the Democratic candidate for governor in 1948, claimed he "ignored [the] race" in November and met with his staff to discuss plans for his inauguration and pursuit of his gubernatorial agenda. In 1956, Democrat LeRoy Collins ran for reelection as governor and officially spent $292,000, and unofficially much more, to capture the party's nomination against three difficult Democratic opponents. But in the general election, he spent $174 against the Republican candidate and won with nearly 74 percent of the popular vote.[4]

The total dominance of the Democratic Party undermined any impulse toward party unity or party structure. The political scientist V. O. Key Jr. observed in his classic 1949 study *Southern Politics in State and Nation* that Florida was different from its neighbors. Individual ambitions and fiefdoms marked the political landscape in the state, and the Democratic primary encouraged even the ne'er-do-well to throw his hat in the ring in hopes of making the runoff. Fourteen candidates ran for governor in 1936, including several who were barely known in their hometowns; another ten sought the party's nomination in 1960; and most elections up to 1964 had at least six candidates seeking the party's endorsement. Key understandably described Florida politics as "Every Man for Himself," portraying it as the most chaotic political system in the South and, by implication, the nation. Few would disagree.[5] From 1900 to 1950, Florida voted for a Republican only once, and that was to support Republican presidential candidate Herbert Hoover against Al Smith, a member of the infamous Tammany

Hall political machine and an Irish Catholic from New York City, in 1928. Smith may just as well have been nominated by the Devil himself as far as most Floridians were concerned; he represented everything they opposed.

Some political observers contend that Florida remains a one-party state, but it is certainly no longer a Blue one. Governor Charlie Crist heads the Republican juggernaut, and Republicans control all but two major offices in the state; have substantial majorities in the state Senate (twenty-six Republicans to fourteen Democrats in 2005) and in the House of Representatives (seventy-eight Republicans to forty-one Democrats); and control nineteen of the twenty-seven congressional seats. While Democrats continue to hold one of the two U.S. Senate seats and still contest many statewide races, Florida has turned decisively Red at the local level as well. Significantly, it was only briefly Purple in the early 1990s (a period in which there existed some balance between the two parties), before it turned solidly Red in the mid-1990s.

So why did Florida and Floridians shift political allegiances? Was the change as sudden and rapid as the political events of the 1990s seem to suggest? And what does it say about Florida's place in the region and the nation?

It's a long story, former Republican Governor Claude Kirk used to say. And to hear him explain it, it was indeed a long, entertaining, and inflated story. But in the context of Florida history, it really hasn't been that long. Democrats held every major position of political leadership in Florida in 1964. And as recently as 1994, Democrats held most statewide offices, including the governorship and a majority of the seats in the congressional delegation, and competed reasonably well in local campaigns for seats in the state Senate and House of Representatives. By 1996 Republicans seized control of state politics. This political transformation represented a sea change in state politics. It took place in the blink of an eye in the context of Florida's history, which dates back to the founding of St. Augustine by the Spanish in 1565. And although the Spanish did not elect the Republican majority, some of their descendants did. So where and when did this political revolution commence? To understand where this political revolution began, you have to start with World War II and the discovery of the state by soldiers-in-training who came from all parts of the nation.

1900 through World War II

For the first forty years of the twentieth century, Florida was largely a poor, backwater state, with most Floridians, white and black, residing in rural areas within thirty to forty miles of the Georgia border. Often compared by historians to the frontier states of the West, Florida had few cities of any size, and traveling from one place to another posed a significant challenge because of swamps, deep woods, and the absence of good roads. The only tangible wealth in the state was seasonal: wealthy Americans who fled the harsh northern winters to enjoy the warm sea breezes of Palm Beach, Fort Lauderdale, and Miami. Henry Flagler's East Coast Railway had made such visits possible by the turn of the century, and Henry Bradley Plant added Tampa Bay to the tourist list with his South Florida Railroad running from Jacksonville to the southwest coast.[6] But Florida was, despite these developments, one of the poorest states in the nation, and until 1940 its population was the smallest in the South. Even Mississippians were alleged to have muttered, "Thank God for Florida."

Much of northern Florida had been settled in the nineteenth century by the Scots-Irish who migrated down from western North Carolina into South Carolina, Georgia, Alabama, and then into Florida. Those who made the trek all the way to Florida were dirt-poor. And they led a hardscrabble life in Florida on farms that barely kept families fed and in lumber mills and turpentine companies, where working conditions and the weather took a heavy toll on their health. W. J. Cash, in *The Mind of the South*, called them "men in the middle"—dirt farmers, herders, turpentine mill workers, pencil factory workers, and lumbermen. These jobs tended to be so brutally demanding that few ever made it to retirement. Their wives and children also felt the harshness of Florida's environment in their hard lives, with women frequently dying in childbirth or shortly thereafter, and their children perishing with them. The Scots-Irish seldom complained, however, in large part because they had not known anything better. And they were a tough lot. They worked hard and drank hard and were known for their independence and ribald sense of humor.[7] But they and their families also yearned for greater prospects and a better life for their children. In politics, they became known as Yellow Dog Democrats because they tied their fate to the Democratic Party and the party's commitment to segregation.

Florida remained largely unknown territory to most Americans until the land boom of the early 1920s, but the Great Depression soon followed before prosperity extended to the western and northern reaches of the state, where most of the Scots-Irish resided. The land and population boom of the early 1920s, which seemed insatiable, collapsed by 1926, leaving the dreams of Floridians in ruins. Walter Fuller, a land developer in St. Petersburg, explained: "We just ran out of suckers. That's all. We got all their money, then started trading with ourselves. . . . We became the suckers."[8] And the Great Depression was a cruel taskmaster for Floridians, rich and poor, lasting nearly thirteen years, until 1939, and dashing hopes and dreams in the salt water and swamps that surrounded and permeated the state. Key West went bankrupt, and cities that had expanded dramatically during the boom of the early 1920s teetered on the edge of bankruptcy. Two powerful hurricanes ripped through the state in 1926 and 1928, killing over three thousand people, leaving a substantial number of people in south Florida homeless, and sealing the fate of the land boom. The Great Depression and a fruit-fly infestation that destroyed 72 percent of the state's citrus trees delivered the coup de grace. By the time all these disasters befell the state, 45 national banks and 171 state banks in Florida had collapsed, and state banking resources fell from $593 million to $60 million. Annual per-capita income likewise plummeted by 58 percent to $289, and state revenues declined by 25 percent. Desperate for a helping hand, Floridians turned to Democrat Franklin Delano Roosevelt in the 1932 presidential election, and he offered federal support to relieve their circumstances and their anxiety about the future.[9]

President Roosevelt's leadership, his New Deal recovery programs, and his personal optimism kept most Floridians going when all else failed. In his inaugural address, Roosevelt assured Americans, "This great Nation will endure as it has endured, will revive and will prosper."[10] The president's fireside chats built a personal rapport with Americans and restored public confidence and hope. Following his first radio broadcast on March 12, 1933, Mildred L. Goldstein of Joliet, Illinois, expressed the feelings of many Americans and Floridians when she wrote, "You are the first President to come into our homes; to make us feel you are working for us; to let us know what you are doing."[11]

And the Scots-Irish Crackers and other Floridians did not forget the president. Pictures of Roosevelt hung from the walls of many homes in

Florida, alongside those of family members and Jesus Christ. For many, he was the only president they knew when he died in 1945, having served over twelve years in office. But more importantly, he was also the only politician who seemed to care about them and who appeared to understand the impact of the Great Depression on their lives. Already in the Democratic fold, Floridians reenlisted in the Democratic Party because of Roosevelt and the programs he bequeathed them. They certainly did not remain Democrats because of the three governors—Doyle Carlton, David Sholtz, and Fred Cone—who led Florida badly and often ineptly during the Depression years.

The Roosevelt administration endeared itself further to Floridians during World War II, from 1941 to 1945, when it directed the construction of 172 military training facilities in the state. No event in the twentieth century so dramatically changed Florida as World War II. It not only put an end to the Depression but also led to the discovery of the state by the veterans who trained there and their families who accompanied them. From Pensacola to Key West, the military built facilities to train naval, air force, and army troops for war in Europe and in Asia. Nearly 2.2 million trainees, support personnel, and families came to Florida in the war years, more people than the entire population of the state in 1940. Shipyards were constructed in Tampa, Jacksonville, Panama City, and Pensacola, turning out Liberty Ships and landing craft for the invasion of Europe and the islands in the Pacific. The military also built airbases throughout the state as training sites, many of which became the airports for modern Florida after the war. More than 250,000 Floridians also served in the army, navy, marines, or Coast Guard, and nearly 4,700 gave their lives. The demands of the war enriched Florida farmers, who helped feed both Allied soldiers and civilians at home and abroad.[12]

Military men who trained in Florida and their families arrived from all parts of the nation, but particularly from the Northeast and the Midwest, and they liked what they saw. For recruits, Florida had only been a name in their mind's eye. When they imagined Florida, it was an exotic place of palm trees and beaches as well as of intense heat, alligators, and swamps. Those who were destined for military training in Pensacola and Miami thought they had found paradise, and they weren't far off. Assigned to live in local hotels, which were leased by the government while their barracks were being built, they commenced training in an oceanside environment that bore little relationship to that of Europe or Asia or to their home-towns. Hotels and bars filled with American boys brimming with vitality and confidence about the future, despite the devastating depression they had only recently escaped and the possibility of death and destruction awaiting them in Europe and Asia. Their optimism was what Florida and Floridians needed after years of economic and personal depression. The men loved Florida and the sheer beauty and feel of the place. They wrote home to parents and girlfriends, noting the differences between Florida and their home states, and expressing their interest in settling in Florida when the war was over. Dan Moody from Virginia captured the senti-ments of many when he wrote his mother from the Hotel Blackstone on Miami Beach: "This is the most beautiful place I have ever seen. . . . I re-ally think when the war is over, I'll move down here." Almost overnight, the Depression ended in Florida. And in the process, the state would be changed forever.[13]

Florida had been rediscovered. And the natives could not have been more delighted. Although no one knew precisely what being discovered meant, they liked the feel of it. The state bustled with activity, and war mo-bilization brought plenty of business to most parts of the state. The trans-formation in Florida was nowhere more apparent than at Camp Blanding, which went from being a small outpost in a pine forest, just to the south and west of Jacksonville, to being the second-largest population center in the state, with over twenty thousand troops stationed there. The soldiers had money to spend, and their families, when they joined them, had needs from housing to a host of local services. Businesses that had been margin-alized by Florida's stagnant economy during the Depression struggled to meet the demand. But few complained.

Unlike World War I, the importance and the magnitude of World War II was never in question after the bombing of Pearl Harbor. Fighting a war on two separate fronts against two military superpowers, Japan and Germany, steeled the resolve of Americans. Most understood that the war would be very difficult and were grateful for an experienced president and for the oceans that separated the nation from its two enemies. While the long coastline of Florida became a natural place for training military per-sonnel for seaborne invasions, it also provided an inviting target for Ger-man submarines. Florida experienced the tribulations of war more than most states, with German submarines exacting a heavy toll on shipping off its coast. Floridians from Jacksonville to Miami watched the naval war from their homes and nearby sand dunes as American cargo ships, struck by German torpedoes, exploded like fireballs in the night sky. Arnold Harms, a veteran who was trained in Miami, recalled sighting German submarines prowling along the coast while on guard duty and witnessing the destruction of many cargo ships.[14] Floridians worried about German troops and spies landing on its shores and infiltrating the nation; fears quickened when four German saboteurs landed at Ponte Vedra Beach, just north of St. Augustine, on June 17, 1942. But all four were spotted changing their clothes on the beach and were captured by the FBI, tried, and executed. Subsequent fears of an invasion proved baseless, but throughout the war Floridians remained anxious about an invasion.[15] While death, destruction, and anxiety ran high, none of this derailed Florida's economic boom.

Floridians embraced the changes brought by the war as well as the scientific advancements that promised to make the state more accessible to natives and visitors. It was a new world, and Floridians were not hesitant about entering it. Floridians welcomed the use of DDT to control mosquitoes and other insects in the last year of the war without concern about the health and environmental consequences. After all, the elimination of the bugs made the state much more inviting to visitors and more satisfying to natives. And air-conditioning, which came into limited use during the war years, promised to make Florida more appealing year-round. For those who lived through the sweltering summers in Florida, air-conditioning seemed like one of God's miracles. It was not until the middle of the 1950s, however, that air-conditioning became sufficiently widespread to make summering in the state attractive. With new roads provided largely by the federal government and improved living conditions, Florida's appeal promised to reach thousands, if not millions, of middle-class Americans and draw them to the state as visitors and permanent residents.

Postwar Developments

When the war ended in Europe in May 1945, and in Asia that August, Floridians joined with other Americans in embracing veterans who had made the world safe from war and oppression. But Floridians and many other Americans were not fully sanguine about their economic future. Americans feared the nation's economy would collapse in the aftermath of the war—as it had in 1919—and with it the recovery from the Great Depression that had been fueled by the war production. Floridians experienced this anxiety firsthand when many of the military bases closed, and the troops and their families returned to their home states. Local businesses suddenly lost much of their customer base, and many wondered if prosperity would ever return. Many wondered, too, if this would be a repeat of the Florida economic collapse of the 1920s.

They did not have to wait long for an answer. The great migration promised by military veterans Dan Moody and others soon came to pass. Approximately nine hundred thousand people, or nearly two hundred thousand per year, moved into the state from 1946 to 1950, increasing the population by 50 percent. It resembled the massive influx at the start of the war, but this time people came of their own free will. And this time they came to stay. Their sheer numbers would change Florida fundamentally, altering its southern identity over time.

The new arrivals did not relocate throughout the state, and they did not initially alter state politics. Most, in fact, settled in southeast Florida, along the coast between Palm Beach and Miami, following the Flagler railroad line or highway U.S. 1. A smaller but still sizable number located in the Tampa Bay area, following rail lines from the Midwest or highway U.S. 19/27, which went from Chicago to Tampa. These settlement patterns led one pundit to observe that the farther south you went in Florida, the more it began to feel like the North. Few migrants chose north Florida, where opportunities were not as immediately evident as those in the southeast, and where the beauty of the area was not as obvious or as enticing. A smaller number settled in Pensacola, attracted by the huge naval base.

Perhaps surprisingly, the new residents had little impact on state politics in these immediate postwar years. Longtime U.S. Senator Bob Graham attributed this to what he called the "Cincinnati factor" in Florida politics. The Cincinnati factor explained the behavior of most, but not all, of the postwar migrants into the state, who stayed true to political and other loyalties back home. They did not view themselves as Floridians in many respects, Graham observed, choosing instead to subscribe to a Cincinnati newspaper, summer in Cincinnati, send children back north to schools in Ohio, and eventually have their remains sent to Cincinnati for burial.[16] In many respects, Florida became a way station for them in the passage of life.

Thus, despite the dramatic increase in the size of cities in southeast Florida, the new residents exercised remarkably little influence in state politics. Moreover, while many were New Deal Democrats who maintained their loyalty to the party, they found the Democratic Party in Florida to be a different animal from the one they had known back home. This was not the party that embraced the social reforms of the New Deal, recognized the right of labor to organize, and supported educational opportunities for all. Nor was it the well-organized party at the neighborhood level that could turn out large numbers of voters in state and local elections. The Democratic Party in Florida was, in fact, dominated by those in rural north Florida, where residents were concerned about economic development, not social reform or labor unions; where they preferred small state government; and where they remained doggedly committed to preserving the racial status quo.

Joining the throngs of people who traveled to Florida in the late 1940s were many retirees, who first visited to escape the winter weather back home. In the early years, most stayed for just the winter months because the summers were too oppressive and air-conditioning was not widely available. But as the latter became more commonplace, seniors lengthened their stays, and many, especially Jewish retirees, opted to make the move permanent. The historian Gary Mormino writes: "For American Jews, the 1950s signaled the beginning of a great new diaspora. Miami beckoned."[17] Word about the quality of life in Miami quickly spread throughout Jewish communities in the North, and the laid-back lifestyle and tolerance drew Jews by the thousands. Mormino calculates that eight hundred Jews arrived per month in Miami between 1945 and 1960, creating the fifth-largest Jewish community in the nation. Making the transition easier, a transplanted Jewish culture took hold on Miami Beach and in the city of Miami, and Jewish seniors established their synagogues, hospitals, social and cultural organizations, and, of course, delicatessens.

The Jewish resettlement represented the most significant migration for a single ethnic and religious group, but even it was swallowed up by the wave of northern retirees who descended on Florida beginning in the 1950s. In 1950, the percentage of seniors in Florida barely surpassed that in the nation; 8.5 percent of the population in Florida was then over sixty compared to 8.2 percent for the nation, and most were people who had resettled in the state. The number and percentage in Florida escalated significantly after that; by 1960, 11.2 percent of Florida's population was over sixty-five, compared to only 9.1 percent for the nation.

Seniors flocked to Florida because of the weather, the environment, very low taxes, and inexpensive property. They lived reasonably well on their retirement and Social Security checks, and for many it represented Ponce de Leon's fabled Fountain of Youth. All it needed to make it tolerable was air-conditioning and bug spray. By the 1960s, both were plentiful, and summer living in the state became bearable. H. Irwin Levy, a West Palm Beach attorney, observed the wave of seniors descending on the Gold Coast and decided he could capitalize on this migration by leaving the practice of law and becoming a developer. Levy launched Century Village on 685 acres in Palm Beach County, and it became the model for other retirement villages throughout south Florida, providing all the services seniors needed within the village and transportation to local stores, to a concert, or to the theater. In a pamphlet entitled *The Truth about Florida* (1956), a retiree informed fellow retirees around the country that they "can live comfortably, have a whale of a good time and save money on an income of about $40 per week."[18]

The marketing of Florida as a senior haven by Levy and others became a business empire in its own right, and it proved to be highly profitable. Seniors in the 1950s and 1960s had money to spend and a steady income, and they needed services, even when housed in villages. Medical facilities and their staffs as well as pharmacies, social and cultural organizations, and, of course, golf courses developed around retirement communities to meet the needs and activities of senior citizens. Stores like K-Mart and S. S. Kresge's opened nearby and provided the merchandise and other services they needed. Kresge's offered a dinner that included turkey, pumpkin pie, and coffee for seventy-seven cents. Who, among the seniors, could resist such enticements?

But life for retirees was not all sunshine, beaches, and bougainvilleas. Some found the constant interaction with other aging seniors and the deaths of friends and neighbors psychologically draining, and the distance from family and grandchildren, while welcomed by some, was not so appealing to others. Many solved this by returning home during the summers, others by moving back home, and still others by subscribing to the hometown newspaper. Cynics in the media referred to the abundance of seniors residing in condominiums as "God's waiting rooms" or, even more pointedly, "cities of the unburied." Eastern Airlines allegedly staved off its bankruptcy in the 1990s with earnings from transporting coffins from Florida to various U.S. cities, and in 1998 Delta Airlines handled more than forty thousand coffins from Florida alone.[19] But none of this slowed the pace of migration by retirees, which accelerated throughout the 1970s, 1980s, and 1990s, increasing the percentage of retirees from 11.2 percent of the population in 1960 to 18.5 percent in 2000. This was a staggering percentage when one remembers that the population of the state increased by an average of 3 million people for each of the decades from 1970 to 2000. By 2000, those over sixty-five totaled nearly 3 million people in a population of 16 million, and the numbers of retirees showed no sign of lessening in the twenty-first century. Pennsylvania ranked second to Florida with a retirement population of 15.6 percent, and the national average stood at 12.5 percent.[20]

This first wave of seniors was overwhelmingly Democratic in its politics, having come of age in the Great Depression and having been immersed in the events of World War II. Franklin Delano Roosevelt was their president, and while a few did not like him, most revered him. Those who revered him remained avid New Dealers, committed to his memory and dedicated to the social and economic programs that were adopted during his twelve years in office. They acquired the nickname *condo commandos* in Florida as they went to the polls en masse to elect Democrats, especially those who espoused the views and values of the New Deal.[21] Initially their orientation was to national politics and to the politics of their former states and hometowns, as Bob Graham observed, and they tended to ignore state issues.

But as the years went by, and as seniors lived into their seventies and eighties in Florida—or ten to twenty years past their retirement—they began to pay closer attention to issues in their adopted community and to become important constituents in local elections. Financial issues and taxes were of considerable concern to most who retired to Florida in the 1950s and 1960s because they lived on fixed incomes. Subsequent generations of retirees had more time to prepare financially for retirement and had greater financial flexibility, but they too kept a wary eye on taxes and the expansion of local and state government.

These retirees differed dramatically from the traditional Florida Democrat—the so-called Yellow Dog Democrat and Florida Cracker. They largely favored a strong, central government, unions, social and economic programs to protect the average citizen, and investment in education to improve their quality of life, and especially the lives of their children and grandchildren. While they did not embrace integration, they did oppose racial violence and were not prepared to resist the federal government or the federal courts in the desegregation of American society.

Although most seniors voted Democratic at the local level as well, midwesterners in the Tampa Bay area and in nearby St. Petersburg and Sarasota were instrumental in launching the Republican Party in Florida in the 1950s. A *St. Petersburg Times* editorial mused in 1953 that Pinellas County had become as rock-ribbed Republican as GOP strongholds in Maine and Vermont. It was a middle-of-the-road Republican Party that embraced the likes of former Senator Robert Taft, son of President Taft, and ascribed to traditional midwestern values of individualism, hard work, responsible government, low taxes, and education. These retirees differed fundamentally from New Deal Democrats over the size and activism of federal and state governments, and in doing so they stood at arm's length from the New Dealers residing on the southeast coast of Florida. But, significantly, these Republicans shared much in common ideologically with the state's native Democrats. As noted previously, getting beyond race and the historic ties between natives and the Democratic Party were critical to the development of a serious courtship between longtime residents and this "new" Republican Party. If they could clear these major hurdles, they might well recognize that they shared a commitment to individualism, limited government, low taxes, strong family values, and economic development.[22]

Over time, seniors had an impact on the politics of Florida that went well beyond their numbers. Their generation had matured in an era when momentous events made them keenly aware of the importance of voting and when decisions at the ballot box had enormous consequences for the nation. They had witnessed and participated in the tribulations of the Great Depression and World War II. As a consequence, they took voting seriously and showed up at the polls in larger numbers for local, state, and national elections than did their younger counterparts.[23] Few natives and Cracker politicians comprehended what these dramatic social changes meant for state politics and the continuing dominance of the Democratic Party. But they would soon find out.

As they watched these changes unfold, Cracker politicians joined together to ensure that they retained political control of the state. Beginning in the 1950s, they repeatedly blocked efforts to reapportion the state legislature based on the 1950 census. Indeed, throughout the period from 1945 to 1964, political leaders from north Florida ignored this constitutional requirement and stonewalled every effort to reapportion the legislature to prevent south Florida from taking control of state politics. It was a heated political battle that occurred principally within the Democratic Party, and the stakes were high, for the outcome would determine who would control state politics, the future of Florida, and the state's place in the nation.

The famous dictum by Pogo—"we have seen the enemy and he is us"— fit the business and economic policies of rural north Floridians and their political allies. In their desire to strengthen the state's economy and improve opportunities for themselves, north Florida's leaders aggressively pursued northern businesses, tourists, and residents, few of whom shared their commitment to racial segregation or the state's other cultural traditions. During the postwar period, state governors traveled extensively throughout the nation to recruit new companies and new residents into Florida. Governor Millard Caldwell (1945–49) became the first of the state's postwar gubernatorial boosters, visiting Massachusetts, New York, and Chicago during his four-year term in an effort to interest business leaders in the state, while simultaneously blocking any effort to change state racial traditions. The historians James Cobb and Matthew Lassiter observed about this period that rapid economic development in the postwar South undermined the region's racial and cultural differences because "the business agenda of industrial recruitment and regional modernization required a political culture of racial moderation." Like nearly all southern governors, those in Florida were slow to realize this equation until the presidential election of 1948 and the racial crises of the 1950s.[24]

State leaders catered to the needs of northern businesses, offering tax incentives, cheap land, a lush environment, and better and safer roads by fencing cattle in order to ensure that they did not roam onto the highways, endangering the life and limb of tourists. Those businesses that depended on tourism for their financial success also looked to the state and the community to provide social stability, so that tourists enjoyed their visit and were likely to return to Florida. Political and social instability were particularly dangerous to the economic success of the tourist industry, which depended heavily on tourist satisfaction and which had invested considerably in Florida in the belief that it would become a national tourist destination.[25]

Governor Caldwell addressed one of the primary concerns of newcomers by securing passage of the Minimum Foundation Program, which provided a base level of state financial support to improve the quality of public schools throughout Florida. Residents welcomed this plan since funding at the county level varied widely across the state and provided the lowest level of educational funding in the nation. Caldwell, an arch-segregationist and states-righter, had additional reasons for proposing this legislation, however. In the postwar era, federal courts examined the doctrine of "separate but equal" in public education and found, to the surprise of no one, that funding for public schools in the South was anything but equal. In the school year 1939–40, for example, white teachers in Florida earned $1,145, compared to $583 for black teachers. By 1949–50, salaries for white teachers averaged $3,030, while black teachers earned $2,616. The gap between white and black teacher salaries had been narrowed as a result of court petitions filed by black teachers in Florida. D. E. Williams, superintendent of Negro schools in Florida, commented that even with this improvement in salaries, black teachers still earned "appallingly low" salaries, and although their white counterparts supplemented their salaries with other jobs, black teachers generally did not have this option because of racial discrimination in hiring.[26]

The condition of many black schools in Florida was also deplorable, and teachers complained about the deteriorating, and at times dangerous, physical plants; the absence of such essentials as chalk, paper, and pencils for children; and the substantial differences between white and black schools. In an age when many Americans were beginning to recognize the value of education and the tragedy of segregation, the plight of black children and their teachers caught the attention of the federal courts. Caldwell's plan promised to increase funding for all schools but also to keep them segregated by complying with court concerns about equitable funding. Few newcomers complained about the governor's intentions, even when it became obvious that Caldwell intended to block integration, because they too opposed sending their children and grandchildren to desegregated schools.

Republicans, who had only one elected spokesman in the state Senate (J. Houghton) and six in the House of Representatives during this period, offered no alternative to the Democratic position on segregation and on postwar development. The Republican Party was, in fact, only a regional party, with its strength concentrated principally in Pinellas County, and it had yet to develop a structure within which candidates and voters could be recruited into a statewide party. Those who had been Republicans in the North looked chiefly to the national Republican Party and its candidates for guidance on political issues, while those who were politically ambitious cast their lot with the state Democratic Party if they hoped to get elected. The continued migration of midwesterners into the state in the 1950s, however, steadily built a solid base for a state Republican Party. In Pinellas County, home to St. Petersburg, for example, population growth from the Midwest significantly altered the dominance of the Democratic Party in a single decade. Registered Democrats outnumbered Republicans, 47,424 to 13,367, in 1950, but only by 97,269 to 86,798 in 1960.[27] The continued growth of the St. Petersburg–Tampa Bay region throughout the 1960s enabled Republicans to begin competing successfully for legislative offices and to assemble the party infrastructure that eventually mounted a serious challenge to the Democratic Party regionally and statewide during the decade. This political transition was unfolding quietly in one section of the state, and native Democrats had yet to give it much attention.

What did concern natives was the growing prominence of northeastern Democrats who settled in southeast Florida. Many of these newcomers, who were FDR/New Deal Democrats, found the state a peculiar political environment compared with the one they had known back home. Labor union leaders, as previously noted, were nowhere to be seen among Florida's Democratic leaders. And neither were minorities. In fact, the agenda of the Florida Democratic Party focused heavily on race relations, almost to the exclusion of the social and political reforms that these newcomers supported in their native states. In response, the state's newcomers built a local Democratic Party and elected officials who looked and acted much like FDR Democrats back home. They were thus slowly beginning to make their political influence felt, and their notions of party politics, business growth and development, and race relations differed dramatically from those of native Floridians.

The potential divisions in the state Democratic Party and the effects of the massive migration into the state could not be masked for long, especially in national elections. The presidential election of 1948 placed potential political differences in Florida front and center, when Governor J. Strom Thurmond from South Carolina and fellow southern Democrats bolted from the Democratic presidential ticket because of the party's adoption of a civil rights plank in the 1948 Democratic national platform. Incumbent Harry Truman and his aides had tried to forestall a regional conflict over race by proposing a plank that was essentially the same as the 1944 plank on race, but Minnesota Democrat Hubert Humphrey, an up-and-comer in the party, successfully championed an effort to endorse Truman's civil rights initiatives—including anti–poll tax and antilynching legislation, fair employment laws, and an end to segregation in the armed services—as part of the party platform. Although Truman could not deny his racial reforms, he worried that Humphrey's plank would divide the party and handicap him in the general election.[28]

Thurmond, a forceful speaker, condemned both Truman's position on civil rights and the platform, calling the Fair Employment Practices Committee "communistic" and the integration of the armed services "un-American," and denouncing the party's platform on civil rights. The Dixiecrats, as they came to be called, proposed to continue "the segregation of the races and the racial integrity of each race." As the campaign unfolded, Thurmond's supporters confidently predicted that he would win 140 electoral votes and capture a majority of votes in every state of the former Confederacy.[29] North Floridians rallied to his cause and sought to take the state into the Dixiecrat camp, but they vastly underestimated the impact of those who had moved into south Florida from the Northeast.

Most Democratic newcomers in southeast Florida were aghast at Thurmond's candidacy and his extremist comments and worried that their adopted state might support him. While few were racial reformers, they refused to embrace the segregationist views of north Floridians and Thurmond's Dixiecrats. Thurmond campaigned passionately throughout the Deep South and into the Florida Panhandle, where he encountered large, enthusiastic, and vocal crowds. A bulldog of a man who appealed to the worst fears of white southerners, Thurmond seized the podium to decry the positions taken by the president and the federal courts, telling his audiences that the future of the South and the nation was at stake in this election. He called on whites to rally behind him to preserve segregation and the southern way of life, while he simultaneously carried on the lifelong affair with a South Carolina black woman that was revealed after his death in 2003. That Thurmond would champion efforts to deny blacks their rights as citizens while he engaged in a sexual relationship with a black woman might strike many southerners and northerners as repellant or worse, but it was fully consistent with his views of race and white power. Many Democrats in southeast Florida worried that Thurmond's campaign placed the future of Florida and the nation at risk, especially if he was elected or carried their state.[30]

The full consequence of the postwar migration into Florida revealed itself in the November election of 1948. President Truman carried Florida overwhelmingly with 281,988 votes to 89,755 for Thurmond, with south Florida casting huge majorities for the president. Even Thomas Dewey, the Republican candidate from New York, received more votes than Thurmond in Florida. All eight of the state's electoral votes went to support Truman's election. Moreover, a closer examination of the voting revealed that Thurmond secured very few votes in south Florida, while running strongly in the northern areas of the state. The political divisions in Florida as a result of migration patterns were clear for all to see, but what would be their result? No one knew in 1948, but it was certain that there would be a battle for the heart and soul of the state and for its future.[31]

Despite the rejection of Thurmond's candidacy and his racial appeal, however, the battle over race in Florida remained unresolved, and local developments revealed how difficult it would be to settle this issue. From the Panhandle to Orlando, many civic leaders and law enforcement officials joined forces with white militants to preserve segregation barriers. In Orlando and communities to the north, for example, county sheriffs and deputies worked closely with orange grove owners, lumber companies, and farmers in forcing local black residents, who felt emboldened by their service in World War II and in Korea, to return to the groves and fields. Similar incidents also occurred in south Florida. When blacks refused to do so, many were arrested on trumped-up charges and presented with the option of going back to work or staying in jail. In Lake County in

1949, Sam Sheppard was told by deputies to remove his military uniform, which he had been wearing around town, and report to work or the deputies would find work for him. When black activists protested, they were imprisoned and beaten and then delivered to citrus owners who needed black workers. In some places, such as Lake County, where Sheriff Willis McCall followed his own legal standards, deputies occasionally beat blacks to death in their cells, to serve as an example to others who might think about challenging the community's racial codes.[32]

The determination of native whites to maintain segregation revealed itself most forcefully when Harry T. Moore and his wife were murdered in their home in Mims, Florida on Christmas night 1951. Moore, who was state president of the NAACP, had been a target of white militants for some time. A modest, low-key, and mild-mannered fellow, Moore was, nevertheless, extraordinarily courageous and persistent in his efforts to desegregate the state and to end racial injustice. In 1934, Harry Moore started the Brevard County NAACP and steadily built it into a formidable organization. In 1937, in conjunction with the all-black Florida State Teachers' Association, and backed by the NAACP attorney Thurgood Marshall in New York, Moore filed the first lawsuit in the Deep South to equalize black and white teacher salaries. Four years later, he organized the Florida State Conference of the NAACP and became its unpaid executive secretary. He began churning out letters, circulars, and broadsides protesting unequal salaries, segregated schools, and the disfranchisement of black voters.[33]

Following the NAACP victory in the landmark *Smith v. Allwright* case in 1944, in which the U.S. Supreme Court ruled that the "lily-white" Democratic Party primary was unconstitutional, Moore organized the Progressive Voters' League, and in the next six years he traveled the state, registering over 116,000 black voters in the Florida Democratic Party. This total represented 31 percent of all eligible black voters in the state. As a result of his activities, both Moore and his wife, Harriette, were fired from their teaching positions in 1946. Undaunted, Moore became a full-time, paid organizer for the Florida NAACP and built the Florida branch to over ten thousand members in sixty-three branches. On Christmas night, racial extremists—with the apparent assistance of sheriff's deputies in Brevard and Orange Counties—placed dynamite under the Moore's home. A huge explosion that evening killed both Harry and Harriette Moore as they slept in their bed.[34]

The state conducted a perfunctory inquiry at best, and no charges were ever filed. An FBI-led inquiry into the death of the Moores, however, uncovered a widespread conspiracy of local officials, police, and militants to murder them and to suppress evidence of those involved in their deaths. The investigation also found a far-reaching effort to suppress the rights of black citizens in central Florida. The FBI investigation did not come to light until the 1990s, however. It had been buried in the files because, at the time of the Moore murders, the federal government lacked the statutory authority to prosecute those involved in this local crime. Moreover, the close relationship between FBI agents and local law enforcement officials throughout the South and J. Edgar Hoover's opposition to civil rights reform acted as major impediments to equal justice for black citizens. The results of the Moore investigation were sealed in federal archives, and their murderers remained free to harass and intimidate other black citizens.[35]

But the brutality of the Moores' murders and the failure of law enforcement to arrest the perpetrators shocked and alienated many of the state's newcomers. They rejected the use of violence to control the black population and looked to the leaders of their new state to follow accepted legal practices. In the aftermath of the deaths of Harry and Harriette Moore, newcomers, new business leaders, and newspapers in south Florida became much more vocal in their criticism of racial violence and the state's racial customs.

The *Brown* Decision and Reapportionment

During the 1950s, as the issues of race and reapportionment became inextricably linked, native whites fought to maintain control of the state legislature. They recognized that those residing in south Florida lacked their commitment to preserving the state's racial traditions. As the struggle unfolded, rural legislators formed the "small-county coalition," or, as they were nicknamed by James Clendenin, editorial-page editor of the *Tampa Tribune*, the Pork Chop Gang. They took "a blood oath to stick together and did that on all legislation," especially those bills that sought to reapportion the legislature.[36] Opposing the Pork Chop forces and seeking a fair reapportionment of the legislature were Lamb Chops, residents of south Florida and their representatives, including governors, who were elected to office with voter support from the emerging population centers along the east and west coasts.

LeRoy Collins became the leading voice for reapportionment in 1955, when he won a special election with key support from southeast Florida to succeed Governor Dan McCarty, who died suddenly from heart complications. A tall, handsome, and urbane politician whom even his political enemies found charming, Collins governed Florida from 1955 to 1961 during one of the most traumatic periods in its history. Throughout the decade, the Florida Legislature remained among the worst-apportioned in the nation, with only 13.6 percent of the population electing more than half of the state senators and 18 percent choosing more than half the members of the House of Representatives. Collins promised south Floridians that he would reform the legislature to reflect the population growth of their region. He subsequently introduced reapportionment in every session of the legislature, only to see it stymied by the small-county coalition.

The reapportionment issue became immersed in racial politics when the U.S. Supreme Court announced its unanimous decision in *Brown v. Board of Education of Topeka* in May 1954. In one of the most dramatic pronouncements in the Court's history, the justices overturned segregation in public education in the South. But rather than ordering that desegregation be implemented immediately, the justices opted for "all deliberate speed," three words that became the bane of civil rights proponents.

Rural legislators in Florida immediately joined their counterparts in the region in rejecting the decision and calling for massive resistance to it. Representatives from urban south Florida also criticized the Court's pronouncement but urged the public to remain calm and refrain from challenging the Court's authority. While Lamb Chops focused on the reapportionment issue and worried that the Court's decision would derail that effort, they also feared the effects racial protest would have on Florida's development. Their concerns were realized when calls for a calm and reasoned response to *Brown* were rejected by Pork Choppers, who would have none of it. In the wake of the Supreme Court's decision and the relatively mild response from the Lamb Chop Gang, the Pork Chop delegation recognized how critical the reapportionment issue was to their efforts to preserve the state's racial customs. As with their position on race, so with reapportionment—they would brook no compromise.[37]

The 1950s witnessed a pitched battle between Democratic Governor Collins and Democratic Pork Chop leaders of the legislature over who would direct the state and the party following the *Brown* decision. This political battle would shatter the Democratic Party in the 1950s and 1960s and lay the stage for the emergence of the Republican Party.

Prior to the Court's decision, Collins championed the modernization of the state by encouraging additional migration into Florida, actively recruiting new businesses, and seeking ways to diversify the economy. He felt certain that legislative militancy over desegregation would destroy his efforts and set back the state. A native Floridian and married to Mary Call Darby—who was great-granddaughter of Richard K. Call, twice territorial governor of Florida—Collins had connections to Florida that extended deep into its past. Not unlike Lyndon Johnson, Collins believed that Florida had, at long last, the opportunity to cast off the vestiges of poverty and regionalism that had prevented it from modernizing and entering the national mainstream. Migration into the state continued to soar in the early 1950s, and there was every indication that well over 2 million people would relocate to Florida by the end of that decade. When combined with state growth in the 1940s, Florida stood to emerge on the national stage as the most dynamic state in the region and in the nation. It no longer had the smallest population in the South, no longer stood as the most rural, and, as some asserted, no longer epitomized the most backward state. Collins's challenge was to ensure somehow that the changes he proposed would continue to advance the state's national standing even when faced with legislative and public demands that Florida preserve segregation at all costs. In the end, his aspirations for his state proved unachievable amid the furor surrounding desegregation.

The Pork Chop delegation and their allies, much like those in other southern states, launched their counteroffensive in 1957 with a series of proposals designed to establish a constitutional amendment to close the public schools in the event of desegregation, fund a separate private school system with state funds, and establish a pupil-placement law that would allow local school officials to manipulate desegregation in their schools. Collins denounced the measures and promised, "I will never approve any plan to abolish any public school, anywhere."[38] But he fought mainly a rearguard action, working with moderate south Florida Democrats and using the legislative calendar and his veto to prevent passage of as many of these bills as possible. Moderates assisted Collins's strategy by forestalling legislative action until the end of the regular session. Since the legislature met only every two years, Collins's veto meant that the measures could not be reconsidered for another two years, during which he sought to repair the damage and to marshal his forces.

At the same time, the governor countered extremists with a series of modest segregationist proposals designed to ease public anxiety over racial change. Collins, for example, supported the efforts of Attorney General Richard Ervin to block Virgil Hawkins's effort to integrate the University of Florida and suspended bus service in Tallahassee to block the sit-in campaign being conducted by the NAACP to desegregate the bus lines. Northern critics accused Collins of being two-faced about desegregation and a fence-sitter, but the alternative approach, championed by the Pork Chop Gang and its allies, proposed closing the entire public school system to prevent desegregation and making it a felony to attend desegregated schools. If Collins had refused to act in the Hawkins case or in the Tallahassee bus boycott, the evidence suggests that the Pork Choppers would have challenged Collins's leadership directly and may have been successful in doing so. A state survey of eight thousand Floridians conducted by Professor Lewis Killian of Florida State University in 1954 revealed the difficult path confronting Collins as he tried to pursue a moderate racial agenda. Killian's poll found that most white Floridians opposed school desegregation, and a near majority of state legislators pledged to preserve segregation "by whatever means possible."[39]

Charley Johns, who was president of the state Senate and who briefly served as acting governor on the death of Dan McCarty, epitomized the Pork Chop alternative to Collins. Johns, a devout racist and a skillful backroom politician who looked like a backroom bookie, attended the Southern Governors' Conference prior to Collins assuming office in March 1955 and called on his fellow governors to join with him in blocking the Court's decision. A Johns gubernatorial administration would have led Florida down the road of massive resistance, joining its immediate neighbors Georgia and Alabama. Although Johns lost to Collins in the 1954 gubernatorial contest, he remained politically influential as Senate president, from which position he directed the segregationist fight against Collins.

With emotions boiling over and the Democratic Party sharply divided, Collins needed consummate political skill to govern in this political environment. The alternative was to have Florida thrown into a racial quagmire that engulfed the other former Confederate states and to take the easy path by surrendering to the extremists. Collins refused to consider doing so.

But the structure of the governor's office complicated his efforts to lead Florida out of this morass. The state constitution, adopted in 1885, limited the governor to one term in office and created six other executive officers, each of whom was elected separately and could be reelected indefinitely. Together with the governor, these officers served as the cabinet and were required to act collectively in many executive matters. Through custom and statute, the governor chaired the meetings, but he had no other special privileges. It was by any measure one of the weakest executive offices in the nation.[40]

In searching for allies to assist him in this battle, Collins turned to those who had flooded into south Florida after World War II and to business leaders who had founded or relocated companies to meet their needs. They became powerful allies for his moderate approach, and their backing gave him the moral and political support he needed to undercut many of the extremist legislative proposals that emerged in the 1957 and 1959 legislative sessions (the Florida Legislature met every other year up to 1970). Only in North Carolina, where Luther Hodges overlapped Collins as governor, did another southern state avoid the segregation cataclysm. Much like Collins, Hodges pursued a delicate balancing act—proposing some modest segregationist measures on the one hand while opposing more extreme ones on the other—in order to preserve the state's economic modernization. Both men have been criticized by some for not doing enough to desegregate their states. And while there is some merit to these arguments, it is hard to imagine a more difficult time to govern in the South and to persuade voters to abandon segregation laws and traditions that had infused their culture, social and educational institutions, and politics.[41]

Collins traveled frequently to urban areas in the state and to southeastern Florida, reminding civic and business leaders that racial discrimination and extremism would cripple the state's prosperity, his postwar modernization program, the state's population growth, and their business activities. In a speech in Miami in October 1957 to a Presbyterian men's convention, Collins told the audience, "You and I are under the pressure of a mob." He warned them that failure to respond would have devastating consequences for the state.[42] There was evidence that tourism and economic development slowed in Florida during the second half of the 1950s as southern resistance hardened, confirming the governor's warnings and alarming business officials. Moreover, the economic collapse in Arkansas, Alabama, Mississippi, and Georgia, where segregationists took control of state politics, convinced many in south Florida that moderate leadership was essential if the state economy was to remain robust.[43]

The developing situation in Arkansas especially caught the attention of many business leaders in Florida. Under the leadership of Governor Sid McMath and businessmen in Little Rock, Arkansas emerged as one of the fastest developing southern states in the 1950s, successfully recruiting major companies from the Midwest. But economic development ground to a halt when Governor Orval Faubus attempted to block the desegregation of Central High School in Little Rock and then closed Central High in 1958 in order to avoid federal court–ordered integration of the school. Many businesses that had relocated to Arkansas packed up and left when resistance continued and turned violent. These developments made a deep imprint on the minds of business leaders in Florida. Collins appealed directly to them to preserve racial harmony: "We must find responsible community leaders who can provide leadership for social adjustments which we must make."[44] Few business leaders wanted to get into the middle of this struggle. On the other hand, it became apparent that if they did not, their businesses, most of which depended on consumers in other parts of the country, would suffer significantly. This was particularly true of the state's booming tourist economy.

The mounting crisis in Little Rock became a backdrop for a speech Collins had agreed to deliver at the Southern Governors' Conference in Sea Island, Georgia, on September 23, 1957. Entitling his speech "Can a Southerner Be Elected President?" Collins told his colleagues that, in contrast to the message conveyed by Governor Faubus, the American public "believes that the decisions of the United States Supreme Court are the law of the land and insists that ours be a land of the law. It does not sanction violence, defiance and disorder."[45] Reiterating the message of moderation he had delivered to lawmakers and residents of Florida, Collins called on his fellow governors to resist wrapping themselves in a "Confederate blanket" and repudiating change. He assured them that if they did, they would miss the region's best opportunity for progress and bury the region politically and economically for decades.

On his return to Florida, Collins used his considerable personal skills to persuade members of the legislature of his moderate approach. Senator Mallory Horne, the only legislator in modern times to serve as Speaker of the House and president of the Senate, recalled that Collins's personal diplomacy was unmatched by any other politician he had known and that he "talked to everybody who would listen to him." Martin Dyckman, the author of the leading biography of Collins and former editorial writer for the *St. Petersburg Times*, noted, "The governor used even his limousine to advantage, inviting legislators to join him on long car trips" during which he would seek to persuade them of his position. Horne characterized these meetings as a series of sermons from which you could not escape.[46]

At the end of the 1957 session, the state legislature adopted, by a near-unanimous vote, the Interposition Resolution, modeled after the Kentucky and Virginia Resolutions written in the late eighteenth century by Thomas Jefferson and James Madison, respectively. The proposal called on the state to impose its will to block further federal court decisions that threatened Florida's racial traditions. While Collins could not veto the measure since it was only a resolution of the legislature, he nevertheless issued a blistering statement saying that the legislative resolution "stultifies our state." "It will do no good whatever," he added, "and those who say it can perpetuate a cruel hoax on the people." He subsequently vetoed a "last-resort" bill that would have closed all public schools rather than integrate them. In the 1959 session, Collins blocked thirty-three school segregation measures offered by his opponents. Many of the bills had been initially proposed in 1957 but had failed passage because of Collins's veto. A new bill, however, made it a criminal offense to teach in an integrated school, and Collins also blocked its passage.[47]

In mid-February 1959, Dade County school officials, after private meetings with Collins and his aides, agreed to integrate four black students into an all-white elementary school in Miami. This was the first school desegregation initiative in the state. Collins favored desegregation at the elementary school level since young children had not yet been contaminated by the racism of society. Moreover, such young children would not resort to violence as the high school students had done in Little Rock, Arkansas. Collins's rationale for pursuing desegregation at this level made good sense, but the selection of Orchard Villa Elementary school in Miami did not. Orchard drew from some of the poorest neighborhoods in the city. White parents saw themselves as victims of society, and the use of their children in a racial experiment angered them greatly.[48]

When the four black children arrived at school to begin classes on September 8, 1959, only eight white students showed up to register for school. As the week unfolded, fewer white students attended. By the end of the week, all white children had disappeared. Local school officials met with parents and sought to persuade them to return their children to school, but the meetings deteriorated into angry accusations by parents that their children were being made guinea pigs for a racial experiment. Within a short time, school officials gave up, and Orchard Elementary became an all-black elementary school on October 7, with 379 black students and an all-black administrative and teaching staff.[49] Although Collins called the attempt at desegregation in Miami a local decision, it was clear to most people that he had a hand in the effort. This defeat was a major blow to Collins's leadership and his reputation as a moderate spokesman for the region. He left office without having desegregated a single public school, and school desegregation would languish in Florida until 1967.

Frustrated at the failure to desegregate Orchard Villa Elementary and to establish a model that could work for the rest of the state, Collins decided that white Floridians failed to understand the significance of desegregation and opted to spend his final days in office educating them as to why it was right and proper. In a series of truly remarkable conversations for a southern leader during this era, he spoke frankly to Floridians about the values and ideals to which Americans had aspired but had never achieved: "We can never stop Americans from hoping and praying that someday this ideal that is embedded in our Declaration of Independence . . . that all men are created equal, that somehow will be a reality and not just an illusory goal." He reiterated his commitment to law and order. But, in what was an astonishing statement for a southern politician, he asserted, "it was unfair and morally wrong" for white store owners to encourage black patronage in some sections of the store but not in other sections. Legally, he added, they can do that, "But I still don't think [store owners] can square that right with moral, simple justice."[50] Later in the year, following racial clashes in Jacksonville, Collins used the occasion to continue his educational campaign. He noted that some contend that the violence was the result of actions by "colored trash and white trash," but all must share in the responsibility. "I am sure it must be observable to the people of Jacksonville," he asserted, "that conditions there are not what they should be in the Negro community."[51]

While Collins's leadership offered much to be admired, especially from the perspective of the 1950s, his actions angered and alienated perhaps the oldest constituency in the state Democratic Party in the 1950s and, in the process, put the political dominance of his party at risk for the first time in the twentieth century. Native and rural Floridians, Crackers, and Yellow Dog Democrats felt betrayed by Collins. Race and history had bound them to the Democratic Party for much of the nineteenth and twentieth centuries, but developments in the 1950s and 1960s persuaded many to consider abandoning the party. These so-called "Crackers" and "Yellow Dog Democrats" who, because of race and Reconstruction, had pledged their loyalty to the party initially tried to reassert their control of the party. But despite initial successes in electing Farris Bryant and Haydon Burns as successors to Collins, they could not halt the racial reforms pursued by the national Democratic Party and Presidents John Kennedy and Lyndon Johnson.

The transition away from the state Democratic Party by Crackers/Yellow Dog Democrats did not occur immediately, nor did it take place without some interesting twists and turns, but that transition began with the governorship of LeRoy Collins. And it was further influenced by the presidential election of 1960, when Vice President Richard Nixon was challenged by the young U.S. senator from Massachusetts, John F. Kennedy. Already troubled by Kennedy's Roman Catholicism, Florida's Crackers/Yellow Dog Democrats were further alienated when Kennedy called Mrs. Coretta King to express his concern about the sentencing of her husband, the civil rights leader Reverend Martin Luther King Jr., to the Georgia State Prison at Reidsville for four months. Reidsville was notorious as a hard prison where violence against prisoners was endemic. Coretta King and others feared for her husband's life. Kennedy had no answers for her but offered to assist her and her husband in any way he could and urged her to call him if he could be of help. Mrs. King immediately informed Dr. King's father, a loyal Republican, of Kennedy's call. Daddy King was so impressed that he told his daughter-in-law that he would cast his vote for Kennedy and urge his friends and parishioners at Mt. Carmel Baptist Church to support Kennedy.[52]

As the story of Kennedy's telephone call to Mrs. King spread throughout the country, the tide of the presidential contest took an intriguing turn. For every black vote that shifted into the Democratic column, a southern white vote went into Nixon's column. And Florida was no exception. Although Floridians had abandoned their Democratic roots to vote for Republican Dwight David Eisenhower in 1952 and 1956, so did most of the nation's voters, who had enormous respect for his role in directing the invasion of Europe and the defeat of Hitler's Germany. The 1960 election was a telltale election in many ways, for in it white Floridians, and especially those native Democrats in rural Florida, voted quite deliberately against the Democratic nominee, John Kennedy, because of his Catholicism, the civil rights agenda of the National Democratic Party, and Kennedy's expression of support for civil rights leader Martin Luther King Jr. Nixon carried Florida with nearly 795,500 votes and 51.5 percent of the vote, with significant majorities in north and southwest Florida, to Kennedy's 748,700 and 48.5 percent. Although Nixon lost the election to Kennedy and carried only Virginia and Florida in the South, he made sizable gains throughout the region and used this experience subsequently to launch his presidential campaign in 1968 with the aim of ending Democratic control of the South.[53]

Political and social developments in the 1960s would further divide the Democratic Party, and natives, Crackers, and Yellow Dog Democrats would commence a long-term courtship with the national and state Republican Party. Much as in other southern states, it would be a tumultuous courtship in Florida, fraught with disagreements and Democratic efforts to woo natives and Crackers back into the party. Gradually the courtship would evolve into something more permanent and, in the process, fundamentally alter the political landscape in Florida.

2

Racial Protest and the Emergence of Fault Lines in the Democratic Hegemony

Racial developments in the South took a dramatic turn on February 1, 1960, when four African-American students at North Carolina A&T College in Greensboro, North Carolina, sat down at a Woolworth's lunch counter and refused to leave; in doing so, they sparked the transformation of southern and Florida politics. Like so many places in the South, including Florida, lunch counters were reserved for "whites only." Black citizens typically approached the cash register near the counter to place a takeout order, but they were not welcomed at the counter, which was restricted to whites by both statute and custom. Ironically, blacks and whites occasionally engaged in friendly conversation while waiting for lunch, but they never sat together. The student sit-in in Greensboro was not accidental or fortuitous; all four young men had developed their plan in advance, understood the implications of what they were doing, and had a reasonably good idea of how local whites would respond. When they sat down at the lunch counter, however, they could not have imagined the full consequences of their decision.[1]

In fact, the sit-in protests and subsequent events came together in ways that no one foresaw. The advent of television as a national medium and its coverage of the sit-ins galvanized students throughout the region and around the nation behind the movement and brought the racial protests into the living rooms of Americans. The drama of the demonstrations, with its visual images of four young black men confronted by howling white mobs, could not have been scripted better for television. They entered Woolworth's just before noon on February 1 and sat quietly and respectfully at the counter, waiting patiently to be served. None of the store employees initially knew quite what was happening or how to respond. When asked to leave by the store owner, the college students quietly refused and then, after being ignored for more than an hour, left. When the students returned a second and then a third day, whites gathered in front of the store to jeer at them and then crowded around them at the lunch counter, threatening the students and screaming racial epithets at them. Other students from North Carolina A&T rallied to the side of their classmates and joined the protests. As the major networks focused their television coverage on the Greensboro sit-ins, the movement spread to many other communities in the South.[2]

Almost overnight the protests mushroomed into a substantial challenge to the region's segregation traditions. In Florida, ten students from Florida Agriculture and Mechanical University (FAMU) and the Tallahassee chapter of the Congress on Racial Equality (CORE) conducted a sit-in at a Woolworth's lunch counter on Saturday, February 13. Over the next three weeks, black students were joined by white students at Florida State University, and they expanded the Tallahassee sit-ins to include McCrory's lunch counter. Confounded by the demonstrations and especially by the engagement of white students, local officials ordered police into the stores to enforce the segregation codes and arrest the demonstrators.

On March 12, 1960, fourteen black and white students gathered at Woolworth's in Tallahassee and conducted a sit-in at the lunch counter at 9:30 a.m. The white students were initially waited on, but the manager closed the counter when he realized that they were all together. Mayor George Taff and police officers arrived shortly thereafter and told the students to line up to be arrested. One officer, "a small Barney Fife kind of guy," grabbed one of the white students and told him to "get over there with your nigger buddies."[3] When white militants from the city and surrounding areas threatened black and white students during sit-ins at Woolworth's and McCrory's with knives, baseball bats, and ax handles, police refrained from arresting or dispersing them, choosing instead to blame the student protestors for the rising level of violence. But student activists refused to be cowed by the threats of police and white militants, and over one thousand FAMU students marched from the campus into the city on February 15 to protest segregation and the actions of police and militants.

The sit-ins energized students, who exhibited little concern for their own physical well-being. Instead of being intimidated by the threats of police and white militants, they became more emboldened. Where once four black students entered a solitary drugstore, now thousands descended on hundreds of segregated facilities throughout the South. In Florida, student protests spread rapidly to DeLand, Sarasota, Miami, St. Petersburg, and Tampa, with high school students joining forces with older college students. Despite the efforts of white officials, police, and white militants, it quickly became apparent that the demonstrations could not be contained.

Serving in his last year as governor because the Florida Constitution forbade his reelection, LeRoy Collins expressed concern about the student-led protests. In his first statement about the sit-ins on March 3, 1960, Collins criticized the demonstrations to reporters, calling them unlawful and dangerous. "Demonstrations lead to disorder," he declared, "and, of course, disorder leads to danger to the general welfare." Collins noted that merchants had the law on their side. Much like President Kennedy, Collins worried that the demonstrations were undermining his efforts to improve race relations. But he also expressed sympathy with the students and concern about their well-being. Protesters wondered, however, whose welfare the governor was concerned about.[4]

Professor Lewis Killian, a leading religion scholar at Florida State University and a leading supporter of desegregation, independently approached the Woolworth's store manager about serving the students and thus sparing Tallahassee from the national limelight and national embarrassment. Store manager S. T. Davidson told Killian that his orders came from national headquarters and that he had been told to respect local customs. Davidson added, "I'll consider desegregating my lunch counter when you people at the university do more about desegregating it."[5] Killian walked away sheepishly, acknowledging to himself that state universities were no paragon of virtue when it came to segregation. By 1960, only one black student had been admitted to a state university in Florida, and he had only recently entered the University of Florida's College of Law.

As the sit-ins continued, Collins asked the president of FAMU to confine all the students to campus. But the genie was out of the bottle, and no college president or governor could contain the students. Collins subsequently joined President Robert Strozier of Florida State University in calling on city leaders to establish a biracial committee to air the student grievances and to seek ways to resolve the racial hostility. But city leaders were having none of it, emphatically rejecting his proposal, denouncing what they called the "gang action and mob rule" of the demonstrators, and calling on Collins to have the offending faculty, who had joined with their students in the protests, "properly dealt with."[6] The meaning was clear; they wanted the guilty faculty dismissed from the university.

Tempers frayed quickly as whites recognized the sit-ins as a direct challenge to the state's and region's racial traditions and were unwilling to compromise. The Chamber of Commerce joined city commissioners in rejecting the governor's call for a biracial committee. City Judge John Rudd rebuffed requests for moderation, sentencing student protesters to jail for sixty days and fining them three hundred dollars each. He angrily dismissed defense contentions of racial discrimination. But no official condemned the militants or arrested them for their physical violence against student demonstrators because these protests had become the battleground over racial traditions in Florida and the South.[7]

Democratic leaders in the legislature heatedly debated the sit-in crisis and the desegregation campaign, with Collins calling for a moderate approach, while others urged the dismissal of students and faculty. Reflecting the views of many in the Democratic Party and in the legislature, Speaker of the House Thomas Beasley called on Collins and the Board of Education to expel the demonstrators and threatened to have the legislature called into special session to deal with the crisis if the governor did not. Beasley and other Democrats accused faculty and students of being communist sympathizers, a view that many in north Florida shared because the sit-ins threatened the very fabric of southern society. A legislative investigation, led by Charley Johns, conducted a witch hunt at the same time to ferret out alleged communists and homosexuals from the state university system. Farris Bryant, an announced Democratic candidate for governor, told supporters and newspeople that he would have the student and faculty protesters arrested and removed from the university. The Republican Party, with little influence in the state legislature in 1960, refused to get involved in a crisis that threatened to tear the state and the Democratic Party apart. A few saw events as potentially advantageous to the party, but most were as divided as the Democrats about the proper course of action for the state and nation.

After listening to Beasley and many other Democrats and following the debate in Congress over a new civil rights bill, Collins, over the objections of most aides, decided to meet on March 15 with a small group of sit-in supporters, led by Professor Killian. During the course of the meeting, Killian told Collins that state leaders failed to appreciate both the moral and legal basis for the demonstrations. Collins listened closely to Killian, and a few days later, in a remarkable address at Florida Southern College in Lakeland, told his audience that communism had little to do with the crisis facing the state and the region. That was a red herring, he asserted. In his view, it was southern hostility to desegregation in any form and the region's unwillingness to debate the issue that furthered the communist cause. The region's uncompromising position on desegregation made the United States appear to be "incapable of dealing justly with one another in a spirit of mutual respect and brotherhood," he declared.[8] Two days later, during Lenten season, Collins raised the hackles of many whites when he told an audience at Florida State University that politicians who ignored racial problems—and here he was referring specifically to some of his fellow Democrats—reminded him of Pontius Pilate "attempting to wash his hands of responsibility for the execution of Jesus."[9] Few things would have been more likely to anger his opponents than being compared to Pontius Pilate. In north Florida and a good portion of central Florida, where Crackers and rural residents considered themselves devoutly religious, Collins's comments rankled them to the core. Their governor had not only sided with those attacking southern racial traditions, but he had placed their God on the side of the revolutionaries.

Moreover, Collins was not finished. Following these two speeches and amidst the continued pandemonium over the sit-ins, Collins told aides that he wanted to deliver a major television address about the protests and desegregation. The use of television by political leaders to address voters was still in its infancy—the presidential debates between Nixon and Kennedy were still months away. Not only was it quite unusual, but the use of this medium by a southern governor to deliver an address about civil rights was extraordinary. Only a few staffers knew what he planned to say, but others could guess after his previous two speeches. Some were concerned about what Collins's comments might mean for Doyle Carlton Jr., a moderate Democratic candidate for governor who was running to succeed Collins and who had the support of many on Collins's staff. Carlton faced two major opponents in Farris Bryant and Haydon Burns, mayor of Jacksonville, in the gubernatorial campaign—both of whom promised to preserve segregation.

With state and national attention focused on the sit-ins, all six major television markets in Florida agreed to carry Collins's address on March 20. The past six years in office had taken their toll on the governor's appearance. His hair was now fully gray and his face wrinkled where neither had been obvious when he entered office, but he was still a distinguished-looking man and the epitome of a southern gentleman. Speaking from the governor's office and seated behind a desk, he began by reminding Floridians that the governor represented "every man, woman, and child in this state . . . whether that person is black or white . . . rich or poor . . . influential or not influential." His recognition of both black and white citizens was in itself significant, and the positioning of black before white seemed deliberate and gave some indication of the direction he planned to take his speech. Referring to the comments Killian had made to him about the morality and legality of the civil rights protests, Collins stated that merchants had both a moral and a legal right in dealing with patrons, and then, in the most telling section of his address, he asserted: "I don't mind saying that I think that if a man has a department store and he invites the public generally to come into his department store and trade, I think then it is unfair and morally wrong to single out one department though and say he does not want or will not allow Negroes to patronize that one department. Now he has a legal right to do that, but I don't think that he can square that right with moral, simple justice."[10]

The journalist and biographer Martin Dyckman wrote that with this speech, "Collins became a spiritual ally of the civil rights movement, if not quite a comrade in arms."[11] Certainly Collins's reference to moral right and his reference to "a Christian point of view" resonated strongly with leaders of the Southern Christian Leadership Conference and the Congress on Racial Equality, almost all of whom were ministers. They embraced Collins's comments and his courage in making them. Understandably they were delighted to have a major, southern white politician finally recognize the legitimacy of the civil rights movement. The *Miami Daily News*, a leading black newspaper, praised the governor for having "courage and intelligence at a time when both of these human qualities are so badly needed to help solve this great moral issue."[12]

If Collins's previous comments had upset his opponents, this address—which reached most Floridians and was widely covered in the press, and in which he paired their position with anti-Christian values—was more than most could tolerate. In the eyes of segregationists, he had joined the enemy. Legislative leaders from north Florida immediately condemned Collins's remarks and accused him of setting back the cause of racial separation. Senate President Dewey Johnson spoke for many in the region when he called Collins "a strict integrationist" who "will sell his soul to prove it for the benefit of his national political ambitions." Johnson and others accused Collins of turning his back on the racial and cultural values of the state in order to gain appointment to a major position nationally.[13] They were convinced that his conversion to desegregation was contrived for personal gain. But with Collins ineligible for reelection as governor, he actually had very few options since neither U.S. Senate seat was up for election in 1960. The irony was that Collins's efforts to desegregate Florida would cripple his chances for election to higher office. Only a federal appointment or national office in the public or private sector was an option. Some of his enemies contended that he had betrayed the state in order to obtain such a position, but most knew the governor better after having fought him for five years over school desegregation. His actions were consistent with his beliefs, and they knew that no amount of political pressure could shake him from them.

Despite the hue and cry of his opponents, Collins also spoke for many new residents and new business leaders in central and south Florida who opposed the extremism of his legislative opponents. Although many were concerned about the sit-in protests, they were prepared to accept the elimination of Jim Crow and fair and reasonable opportunity for black citizens. They worried that the efforts of Collins's opponents threatened to take the state backward, and that was not why they had come to Florida. Although they were less vocal than the racial extremists, they represented the future of Florida, and the state's population growth meant their position would only grow stronger over time.

Political and Demographic Changes after Collins

Whatever the implications of Collins's speech for his postgubernatorial ambitions, his statements had an immediate effect on the gubernatorial campaign in Florida. With the Democratic primary scheduled for March, ten candidates had already entered the field, and Collins's statements on segregation became immediate grist for their campaigns. Farris Bryant, the front-runner, gave voice to those opposing Collins's leadership, informing supporters that Collins's views were not worthy of comment and that his own segregationist credentials had been firmly and "clearly established." Mayor Haydon Burns of Jacksonville joined Bryant in berating Collins's television address and said merchants owed blacks nothing more than "separate but equal" dining and restroom facilities. Significantly, Ted David, former Speaker of the House from Hollywood, Florida (just north of Miami), reflected the more moderate views of south Floridians and expressed support for Collins's position, promising to continue the governor's policies if elected.[14]

David's views, like Collins's, were a bit too progressive for many white Floridians. The instability created by the sit-ins and the protests occurring throughout the region pushed many whites into the conservative camp. While Collins's courageous leadership helped Florida continue its postwar emergence from its Confederate and Jim Crow past, he had also driven a wedge into Democratic politics by his statements about race relations. Native Floridians had embraced the Democratic Party for nearly one hundred years, principally because of its position on race. Now the party no longer spoke with one voice on this matter, and the head of the party, LeRoy Collins, had aligned himself with the forces of racial change—abandoning the party's core tenet. Where this would lead the Democratic Party and the state of Florida was not precisely clear in 1960. But the battle lines had been drawn. Racial developments in the 1960s would encourage the most devout Democrats, those Crackers and Yellow Dogs, to look for political alternatives and eventually to look beyond the Democratic Party.

Collins's statements and the continuing civil rights protests in Florida and around the region dominated the 1960 gubernatorial campaign and local campaigns. Candidates, especially north of Orlando, resorted to race-baiting; impugning an opponent's position on civil rights, whether accurate or not; and asserting their own commitment to segregation. In the Democratic primary runoff, Farris Bryant berated his opponent, Doyle Carlton Jr., as a puppet of LeRoy Collins, and most of his comments seemed as much directed at Collins as at Carlton. Bryant denounced the sit-ins, for example, in language that was precisely the opposite of Collins's. They had violated the rights of owners of private property, Bryant declared, and the "fundamental constitutional guarantee that no citizen's property shall be taken from him without due process of law."[15]

As the contest between Bryant and Carlton tightened, the two took turns accusing one another of being a "demagogue" and a "race baiter." Bryant called Carlton a "moderate integrationist" and a supporter of the *Brown* decision. The level of discourse reached an all-time low when Carlton alleged that he had witnesses who saw Bryant "eating dinner" with blacks in a Jacksonville restaurant.[16]

During the campaign, Carlton hesitated to seek Collins's endorsement because he feared Collins's statements on racial developments would hurt his candidacy. Near the end of the campaign, with his chances of victory diminishing by the day, he asked for Collins's support and got it, but by waiting so long Carlton lost whatever benefits Collins could have brought to his campaign in central and south Florida. When former Governor Millard Caldwell endorsed Bryant's candidacy, the Democratic Party seemed on the verge of imploding over racial developments. Bryant captured fifty-five of the state's sixty-seven counties, defeating Carlton by nearly one hundred thousand votes. But his votes were largely concentrated in north Florida—the section of the state north of Orlando and running into the Panhandle—where he received 70 percent of the vote. Carlton's support came from southeast Florida, Palm Beach to Dade Counties, and southwest Florida, where he took nearly two-thirds of the vote in Broward and Dade Counties and also captured majorities in Hillsborough and Pinellas Counties. But these results were not enough to offset Bryant's huge margins in north Florida.[17]

Below the political radar screen, southeast Florida was growing dramatically. This population growth assured that the Democratic Party's dominance would either decline or be redefined by it. The only question was how long it would take. Although Republicans ran an inexperienced and little-known figure in George Petersen against Bryant in the general election in 1960, and although Petersen had little money to mount a serious campaign, he captured 569,936 votes, nearly twice the number that Collins's opponent had attained in 1956, carried ten counties, and won 40 percent of the vote's cast in the November election. Most of his support came from south and central Florida, where moderates expressed their dissatisfaction with Bryant's political and racial views. While Bryant won easily, only one Democratic gubernatorial candidate in the twentieth century had come close to losing 40 percent of the vote, and that was in 1928, with Florida mired in the Great Depression. Collins, by contrast, had lost only 26 percent of the vote in 1956. Collins acknowledged that the election signaled the emergence of a viable two-party system in Florida.[18] Democrats in Florida were restless and frustrated by the turmoil over civil rights. What it meant for politics in Florida, where the Republican Party was still establishing itself, no one could be sure. But there had never been such division and such discontent within the state Democratic Party. Bryant's victory was also a major setback for Collins and a rejection of his moderate leadership. The New York Times called it "a rude political defeat" for the governor.[19]

Adding to the political and social instability in the state was the unexpected immigration of hundreds of thousands of Cubans fleeing communist Cuba in 1959 and 1960 and settling principally in Miami and surrounding Dade County. These new arrivals had little interest in or understanding of the civil rights debates, and they further magnified the growing regional differences within the state. Equally important, the arrival of these émigrés and the continued population boom highlighted the differences between Florida and its southern neighbors, suggesting that Florida might not march lockstep with the region in responding to the civil rights movement and racial reform.

As a result of immigration and population growth, Florida had become, in only two decades, more diverse than any southern state except Texas; had a larger senior population than any southern state; was in the process of becoming the most urban state in the region with a broad range of mid-sized cities; and had a wide array of religious denominations, including Catholics and Jews, making it much less Protestant and much less religiously unified than the rest of the South. The breadth of changes sweeping the state made no politician or political leader confident about the future and about campaigning in statewide races. Most felt more comfortable focusing on local issues and running for local office, where the concerns of residents were readily apparent.

Ironically, with the exception of Richard Nixon, the national Republican Party paid surprisingly little attention to events in the South and Florida in 1960, failing to appreciate the way events in the region and especially in Florida offered the party a legitimate future. That would change dramatically during the 1960s, as developments in Florida and in the South resulted in significant dissatisfaction among natives with the national and state Democratic Party as school integration began, as Vietnam and campus protests convulsed the nation, and as newcomers proved more receptive to Republican overtures.

Bryant and Burns and Democratic Failings

In Florida, Farris Bryant demonstrated that he lacked the political skills to hold the Democratic Party together and map a clear direction for the party's future. Bryant's career had been focused on getting and holding office, and becoming governor of the state. He was Harvard educated, a skillful politician, and a leading spokesman for interposition in the state legislature, but he lacked a political center and political wisdom, and he was unable to see that times were changing. Unlike Collins, Bryant had no firm position on race relations, other than opposing integration. He pledged in his 1960 inaugural address to "confine the activities of state government to the conduct of the state's business—not to the settlement of local issues best left in the hands of local officials."[20] He flip-flopped from support of the segregationists to a commitment to law and order, to ambitious goals for the state's economic development. At the same time that he denounced federal intrusion into state affairs at his inauguration, he declared that Florida had "its roots in the South, but its spirit fixed on Cape Canaveral."[21] This sounded well and good, but how Bryant thought Florida could reject federal interference in racial matters but gain federal support for its space ambitions was unclear, to say the least. About the best that could be said of Bryant was that he managed to steer Florida through these difficult years in the early 1960s without resorting to the demagoguery of Governor Ross Barnett in Mississippi, Orval Faubus in Arkansas, or Governor George Wallace in Alabama. To Bryant's credit as well, twenty school districts were desegregated during his four years in office, and he generally refrained from making inflammatory statements about race, despite pressure to do so by his political supporters.

When the Reverend Martin Luther King Jr. brought his nonviolent army to St. Augustine, Florida, in 1964, Bryant's indecisiveness on racial matters became transparent to voters. The governor refused to mobilize the state police to protect either the demonstrators or the press. His ill-timed public statements only made matters worse, as when he declared that he felt the same way about civil rights as he did about taxes: "I don't propose to collect taxes and I don't propose to enforce civil rights." Such comments only encouraged white militants. LeRoy Collins, who had been recently appointed by President Lyndon Johnson to head the newly established Community Relations Service, offered to help mediate the crisis in the city. But Bryant would countenance no interference from his former rival.[22]

The progression of events in St. Augustine had a particularly deleterious effect on the local economy. Businessmen in the state's Ancient City had developed plans to celebrate its four-hundredth anniversary in grand style in 1965. Although St. Augustine was known principally for its Spanish heritage, which the Chamber of Commerce widely celebrated in tourist brochures, the ten-story Exchange Bank dominated the town, rising well above the historic Spanish sites and the town square, suggesting to all that St. Augustine remained first and foremost a business community bent on profiting from its history, location, and tourist economy. Most business leaders in the community shared the prevailing racial views in Florida and preferred that such racial traditions be retained without disruption.[23] But local civil rights leaders and aides to the Reverend Martin Luther King Jr. refused to make life comfortable for businessmen and the community.

No one in St. Augustine, let alone the business community or Governor Bryant, was prepared for the national attention the city received and the way it would be portrayed in the media. Lacking experience in communicating with members of the press corps about civil rights disturbances, they became defensive when pressed about racism in the community and about King's contention that it was "the oldest segregated city" in the nation. The consequence produced an unflattering portrait of the community that circulated in the press nationally: white militants controlled events in St. Augustine; the community lacked any moderate voices; and police and city leaders actively collaborated with militants.[24]

As the protests continued into the summer months of 1964, plans for the community's four-hundredth anniversary in 1965 collapsed. Magazines and newspapers showed little interest in carrying promotional stories about the community's historic past and its anniversary celebration, focusing instead on the racial violence and civil rights protests. Tourism plummeted in 1964, with visitors proving averse to spending their vacation in the midst of the melee in the city, and business activity declined by over 50 percent. Hopes for a return to normalcy in 1965 gained little footing, but businessmen remained firm in their support of civic leaders and their refusal to negotiate with King and his aides. Much like Little Rock, Arkansas, where the economy and business activity came to a standstill because of the violence over the desegregation of Central High School in 1957, St. Augustine found itself isolated politically and economically by a nation that looked with increasing disdain upon segregation and racial violence against black citizens.[25]

Governor Bryant, who had made business and economic development a significant part of his election campaign and who actively sought to recruit northern businesses into the state, did not seem to understand the correlation between racial unrest and economic stagnation in the city and state. But the massive protests in St. Augustine and the extended media coverage persuaded the state's new business leaders, if not the governor, that instability caused by these events had to stop or it would affect the economy of the entire state.[26]

Haydon Burns, who succeeded Bryant as governor in 1965, received a quick education on the consequences of economic development for state racial traditions when he led efforts to recruit Walt Disney Productions to Orlando in that year. During the negotiations leading up to the public announcement in November 1965, Disney officials made it clear to Burns and others that they could not function successfully in an environment marked by racial unrest and social instability. Burns accepted Disney's terms and promised the state's "100 percent" cooperation with the company. In a major step, Burns appointed Clifton Dyson to the Board of Regents for Florida, the first black man to hold state office. Disney World, which opened its doors in 1971, and other major tourist industries that followed its lead would continue to urge political leaders to maintain social order and avoid racial extremism so that tourists would continue to come to Florida and ensure the financial success of their businesses. Racial turmoil persisted in Florida through the late 1960s as school integration and busing commenced, but despite this racial unrest, the state's political and business leaders had privately cast their lot with economic and tourist development and, by implication, desegregation.[27]

Race, the Democratic Party, and the Rise of Republicanism

Despite Collins's leadership and the state's commitment to economic growth, political leaders in Florida did not embrace racial reform. They may have allied themselves with the state's business leaders, but they also had to get elected. And even south Floridians hemmed and hawed about school desegregation. There was sufficient opposition throughout Florida to some or all aspects of public school integration that few legislators outside of Dade, Broward, and Palm Beach counties had the moral fortitude to campaign against segregation, let alone champion legislation eliminating it. In the end, it took the intervention of the federal government in the 1960s through the passage of the Civil Rights Act of 1964 and the Voting Rights Act of 1965 and the actions of a proactive federal judiciary to end segregation and voting discrimination. The national Democratic Party, led by President Lyndon Johnson, championed these federal reforms, which not only led to the integration of African Americans into American society but also resulted over time in the integration of Florida and the South into the nation.

The actions of the federal government and the federal courts deeply angered many white southerners, and they accused President Johnson of being a traitor to his southern heritage. In the 1964 presidential contest, Johnson won in a landslide, capturing 61.1 percent of the popular vote to only 38.5 percent for his Republican opponent, Barry Goldwater, but five southern states—Alabama, Louisiana, Georgia, South Carolina, and Mississippi—voted for Goldwater. In Florida, Johnson narrowly defeated Goldwater by capturing 51.1 percent of the vote to 48.9 percent for Goldwater. Johnson's victory came from supporters in central and southeast Florida. Despite the thrashing Goldwater received in the general election, his forces, in a significant step, took control of the Republican Party from the more liberal, pro–civil rights forces of the Midwest and the Northeast. In doing so, they embraced the new Sun Belt and overhauled the ideology of the party by soft-pedaling civil rights, opposing an activist central government, and embracing patriotism and anticommunism.[28]

The relative success of Goldwater's campaign in Florida reflected the continued political polarization taking place within the state's Democratic Party. As Johnson and Goldwater squared off in the presidential contest, state Democrats wrestled in 1964 with selecting a nominee for the gubernatorial contest. Despite the racial unrest that divided the state, Democrats seemed oblivious to the implications for the party as a field of six candidates announced for governor. The two leading candidates— Haydon Burns and Robert King High, mayor of Miami—represented opposite wings of the party. While Burns had moderated his racial views somewhat, he publicly opposed school integration, believing any other position would prevent his election. High had gained a statewide reputation as a liberal reformer and spokesman for a new Florida that was committed to racial equality and business development. It was a fierce and often ugly primary campaign that pitted north Florida against south Florida, aggravating old wounds between the two regional heartlands of the party. Ironically, their appearance highlighted the contrasts. High dressed nattily and came across as a smooth-talking, big-city politician, while Burns looked ill at ease, like a rumpled, small-town appliance salesman, which he had been. But Burns could give as good as he got, denouncing High as a "liberal" and an "integrationist" candidate. High berated Burns as an inept mayor with no vision for Florida. Enjoying greater name recognition and aided by public concern about what many perceived as the rapid pace of racial change, Burns defeated High handily in a runoff primary and turned his sights on Republican Charles Holley in the general election. Holley had less name recognition and much less political experience than Burns. That combined with a lethargic campaign ensured his defeat, even at a time when Democrats in Florida were vulnerable because of the mounting hostility toward the administration of President Johnson. Holley received only 41 percent of the vote, but many political professionals wondered what would have happened if Republicans had fielded a stronger candidate, or if High had been the party's candidate. Burns held on to the Democratic Party's base in north Florida and won the Democratic strongholds in southeast Florida. The evidence suggests that High would not have been able to do the same in north Florida.

Despite rising tensions within the Democratic Party, Democrats retained their dominance in state politics, holding all the cabinet positions, controlling all but one seat in the congressional delegation, 102 of the 112 seats in the state House, and 42 of the 44 seats in the state Senate. Resistance to an equitable apportionment meant that rural areas of the state retained disproportionate control of the legislature and of the Democratic Party in the legislature, which denied adequate representation to the dynamic cities and suburbs of south Florida. While the political environment suggested that Republicans had a mountain to climb, divisions within the state Democratic Party, public frustration with developments nationally, and the possibility of a genuine reapportionment that would recognize Republican growth in the cities and emerging suburbs of south Florida gave party members hope. That hope morphed into reality in 1966.

Continuing racial unrest in the state and throughout the South, together with the race riots in Detroit and Newark and growing opposition to the Vietnam War, angered Florida's voters and caused disillusionment with the policies of the national Democratic Party. President Johnson's civil rights reforms posed a serious obstacle for the party in the South, despite the fact that Johnson himself was from Texas. One of the most skilled politicians of the twentieth century, Johnson realized that his support for the Civil Rights Act of 1964 and the Voting Rights Act of 1965 threatened the future of the Democratic Party in the region. He told an aide as he prepared to sign the Voting Rights Act of 1965 that he feared he had doomed the party's future in the South and "delivered the South to the Republican Party for a long time to come."[29] The president's assessment may have been a bit premature in 1965, but his political instincts about the party's future proved to be dead-on.

When these developments combined with the enormous demographic changes, no state in the region seemed more disposed to political change than Florida. The state had grown by more than 3 million people since World War II, with the population increasing from 1.9 million to 4.95 million in 1960, and it would grow by nearly 2 million people during the 1960s. The addition of nearly two hundred thousand people per year for the decade was larger than the population of all but its biggest cities—Tampa and Miami. Demand for new housing, schools, roads, and infrastructure accelerated at a dramatic pace during this period. The state also continued to be a haven for retired Americans, with the senior population climbing to nearly 15 percent by 1970. Midwesterners, many of whom were registered Republican in their home states, began flocking into southwest Florida as well, nearly matching the numbers of northeasterners who had migrated into southeast Florida in the 1950s and 1960s.

The effects of the demographic changes and social unrest nationally became apparent in the gubernatorial election of 1966. Burns ran for reelection in that year after only two years in office as the result of a constitutional amendment that moved the state gubernatorial election to a nonpresidential year. Since Burns had served for only two years, much like Collins did upon the death of McCarty in the 1950s, he was eligible to run for reelection. Democrats wisely sponsored this constitutional change because many worried that mounting dissatisfaction with the national Democratic Party threatened the party's hold over the state and the election of Democratic gubernatorial candidates. Ironically, the timing of the amendment did not save Burns or the party.

The 1966 gubernatorial contest saw Burns once again facing Robert King High in the Democratic primary. In another bruising battle, the party's two regional strongholds contested for control of the state and the party. All of the issues that had surfaced in the 1964 primary emerged once again and then some, with the voters agitated about the mounting racial unrest, social protests against segregation, escalating public school integration, and the war in Vietnam. Understandably, Burns focused on state issues, claiming credit for the state's prosperity and attacking High once again as a "liberal" whose views were out of touch with those of Floridians. Accusations of corruption against Burns's administration, public opposition to his $300 million road bond issue that financially advantaged friends and supporters, and a general lack of confidence in his leadership undermined his public credibility, however.[30]

In contrast to the earlier race, High emphasized mainstream issues, steering voters away from his liberal position on social issues and highlighting instead his economic and political accomplishments in Miami and pledging to do the same at the state level. With the endorsement of Scott Kelly, state road commissioner, who had finished a strong third in the first primary, and the support of most state newspapers, which also questioned Burns's integrity and ability to govern the state, High could afford to be more positive. But this campaign, like its predecessor, went beyond the two candidates. It was a repeat battle between Democratic voters of north Florida, representing natives, Crackers, and racial conservatives, against those of south Florida, representing migrants from the Northeast, refugees from Cuba, and political moderates and liberals. High won by nearly one hundred thousand votes, but a half million Floridians, largely from north Florida, had cast ballots for Burns.[31] Would they now support High in the general election?

When few voters showed up at High's rallies in north Florida and when some of their spokesmen said they viewed High in much the same way they regarded John Kennedy, High's aides knew he was in trouble. High's identification with Presidents Kennedy and Lyndon Johnson, his endorsement by the NAACP, and his prior support for school integration made him anathema to voters in north Florida. The chasm between moderates and conservatives in the party could not have been more evident during the campaign when Burns refused to endorse High and many of his aides actively campaigned for his Republican opponent, Claude R. Kirk Jr. Although High may have been more progressive in his racial views than his political counterparts in south Florida, in most ways he reflected their values on diversity, modernization of the state, and economic development. Although Democrats still enjoyed a substantial 4 to 1 advantage over Republicans in registered voters, High faced an uphill challenge in the general election because of the active opposition of north Floridians. High, nevertheless, felt he could generate sufficient support from the population centers in the southeast to win the election.

Most northern Floridians, including Crackers/Yellow Dog Democrats, were in the process of morphing into Blue Dog Democrats. Put crudely, these dogs claimed they were being choked blue by the leash placed around their necks by the federal government and that they wouldn't necessarily "go home from the dance with the one who brung 'em." In other words, they may have gone to the polls as Democrats, but they were now likely to vote Republican, particularly in the aftermath of the Civil Rights Act of 1964 and Voting Rights Act of 1965. Would these Blue Dogs vote for a Republican governor? Kirk and his aides felt sure they would.

High's opponent, the dynamic and colorful but enigmatic Kirk, presented a serious challenge to Democratic hegemony in Florida. Kirk, who had led "Floridians for Nixon" in 1960 but who had been trounced by Democratic U.S. Senator Spessard Holland in a bid for his senatorial seat in 1964, privately cheered High's victory over Burns. Kirk felt Burns would be the more difficult opponent to attack because of his conservative views and the support he engendered from north Floridians. By Kirk's estimation, High's political views incensed most native, rural Democrats and offered him the chance to build a coalition between disaffected Democrats and Republicans.[32] The political scientists Donald Mathews and James Prothro observed at the time that a southerner's party identification no longer "tells us how he evaluates the parties." Party images, they contended, were "changing within the white electorate of the South—and changing toward a more favorable view of the GOP."[33] Such was the situation in Florida, where natives felt they had little in common with the politics of High.

Kirk kept High's campaign from gaining traction by labeling him repeatedly as an "ultraliberal."[34] The term had become synonymous in the minds of north Floridians with someone who favored integration, the federal civil rights acts, and an activist central government. Even for many Democrats in south Florida, the term *liberal* had lost much of its luster by 1966 because of national angst over the riots in the nation's cities, the Vietnam conflict, escalating black militancy, and a deteriorating economy. One seventy-year-old Florida woman who had never voted Republican reflected the views of other Democrats when she commented, "The name [Republican] offends my sensibilities but actually in some ways it is more like the old Democratic Party I once believed in."[35]

Joining natives in their dissatisfaction with national Democratic politics and with High's candidacy were increasing numbers of middle-class voters in urban and emerging suburban areas of Florida. They came to Florida searching for new opportunities and better jobs. They were not alienated southerners, but they were concerned about national Democratic policies that seemed to add to the social chaos in the nation's cities and favored certain racial and ethnic groups at their expense. While race factored into their disillusionment with the Democratic Party, they were more concerned about race-based policies that might limit their opportunities and job prospects. They also worried about the court-mandated integration of public schools throughout Florida. Although the full effects of these rulings would not be felt until 1967 and 1968, they viewed with concern the loss of neighborhood schools, which served their children well and which typically reflected their values. They were not against desegregation, but integrated schools with the prospect of large numbers of poor black children attending classes with their children worried them. In such neighborhoods as Pine Hills, a very large middle-class residential area to the west of downtown Orlando, and Avondale, a large and predominantly white middle-class neighborhood just to the southwest of downtown Jacksonville, whites anxiously followed these local and national trends and the implications they might have for their lives and those of their children. Emerging at the same time was the construction of new housing and neighborhoods in and around Florida's cities in the mid-

1960s and 1970s to meet the state's tremendous population growth. These developments coincided with and offered fertile ground for those seeking to resurrect the Republican Party in the state.[36]

Although the stars seemed to line up in Kirk's favor, he had a penchant for outlandish behavior and misstatements. The challenge for his aides was to keep his remarks under control and the focus on High. Kirk's aides highlighted his military experience with the Marine Corps in Korea, his conservative credentials, and his pro-business orientation. As the political scientists Mathews and Prothro suggested, political contests in the South during this period were less about the Republican candidate and more about mounting divisions within the Democratic Party. High's purported liberalism and north Florida's unwillingness to accept south Florida's leadership of the party, and therefore the state, determined the outcome of this election.

Kirk's campaign was particularly successful in equating High and his political views with those of the highly unpopular Lyndon Johnson and forcing High to defend such policies. During a campaign speech in De-Land, Kirk spotted a man in the crowd wearing a High campaign pin and asked if the man knew that his opponent supported Johnson's position on open housing. The man replied that he did not, whereupon Kirk called on High to explain his support for open housing. High had made no statement on open housing and carefully avoided doing so since it was such a politically explosive issue in Florida.[37] But High's smooth south Florida style and his demeanor did not help him with Blue Dogs, who viewed him as an outsider. As Kirk struggled to obtain support in north Florida, he kept up his blistering attacks and deceptions, effectively preventing High from gaining a political foothold in the region.

A shocked Democratic Party watched as Kirk overwhelmed High in the general election, capturing fifty-eight of the state's sixty-seven counties. High won only in Dade and Hillsborough Counties among the urban counties, losing Broward, Palm Beach, and Pinellas Counties. The results in Palm Beach especially caught many by surprise since it had been a Democratic stronghold since World War II. But there, as in Orlando and Tampa, middle-class voters were increasingly disillusioned with the policies of the Johnson administration and the social turmoil in the nation. High's outspoken liberal views and his position on racial change, together with national developments and his association with an unpopular president, made his candidacy an impossible sell to Floridians in the mid-1960s.[38] Kirk manipulated these issues to his advantage and finished ten percentage points above High, with 55 percent of the popular vote.

Despite Kirk's victory, he faced an enormous challenge in governing Florida because Democrats had huge majorities in both houses of the legislature when the U.S. Supreme Court ruled Florida's apportionment law unconstitutional. Although the Court had issued its "one man–one vote" order in the *Baker v. Carr* decision in 1962, rural Democrats in north Florida made only minor apportionment changes, persistently ignoring the principle of "one man–one vote," which promised to end their control of the legislature. In the case of *Swann v. Adams* (1967), the Court showed its frustration with the legislature's delaying tactics, declaring Florida's apportionment unconstitutional and appointing a three-member panel of federal judges in Miami to oversee the immediate redrawing of Senate and House districts.[39]

Alongside the election of Kirk, redistricting gave Republicans a unique historical and political opportunity as it shifted political power in Florida from the rural areas to the cities and suburbs, where the party's influence was growing. The party took full advantage of the ruling by fielding candidates, even though inexperienced and relatively unknown, in almost every legislative district in Florida in 1967. Running on platforms that incorporated many of Kirk's tactics against High and that denounced the policies of the national Democratic Party and labeled state Democrats as liberal, antibusiness, and generally out of touch with Floridians, Republicans made stunning gains in the Senate, capturing 20 of the 48 seats, and significant gains in the House, capturing 39 of the 119 seats. The results revealed that middle-class Floridians had serious reservations about national Democratic policies and were increasingly attracted to the Republican alternative. Ralph Turlington, Democratic incoming Speaker of the House, recalled that these developments, together with Kirk's election, made it appear "like the world was going to wipe out all the Democrats."[40]

1968

The gubernatorial and legislative victories provided an enormous boost to Republicans, and party leaders began to eye other state offices. The party got an unexpected boost when longtime Democratic senator George Smathers announced that he would not run for reelection in 1968. Smathers had been a popular but undistinguished three-term senator, who was best known for gallivanting around with John F. Kennedy when both were in the U.S. Senate and when Kennedy was president. Republican Edward J. Gurney, a three-term member of the House of Representatives from Winter Park who was well-liked in state Republican circles, quickly announced his candidacy. Also announcing as a Democratic candidate was the state's former governor, LeRoy Collins. Collins had not sought major political office since he stepped down as governor but had served as Lyndon Johnson's director of the recently formed Community Relations Service (CRS). As the foremost Democratic figure in Florida, Collins seemed to present a major obstacle to Republican ambitions. As the state's only two-term governor in its history and subsequently as president of the National Association of Broadcasters and director of CRS, Collins had the background and experience to suggest he would represent Florida well in the U.S. Senate. But he had been out of the state for much of the decade, and many Floridians had lost sight of him. Moreover, his support for desegregation and then his leadership of CRS in the Johnson administration posed a potential obstacle to his ambitions and, much like High's candidacy, threatened to splinter the northern and southern regions of the Democratic Party yet again.

While Republicans viewed Collins as a serious obstacle to their ambitions, Gurney and his supporters believed that Collins could be beaten, particularly because of his national prominence as a spokesman for civil rights reform. With significant financing from the national party, Gurney was well-positioned to defeat Collins, and he had the added benefit of modeling his campaign after Kirk's highly successful campaign against High.[41] Newspaper stories projecting candidates for the Senate seat aided Gurney by highlighting Collins's liberalism as both governor and director of the CRS. With mounting concern about race riots in the nation's cities, including seven such riots in Florida, protests against the war in Vietnam, and integration of public schools, middle-class Floridians lost their taste for liberalism, if they ever had it. Collins emphasized his moderate and conservative policies, correcting editors when they portrayed his gubernatorial administration as liberal. But his political opponents—State Attorney General Earl Faircloth in the Democratic primary and Gurney in the general election—would not allow such statements to go unchallenged.[42]

Collins and his advisers initially thought he would have no trouble beating Faircloth, his only serious opponent, in the Democratic primary. But Faircloth, who came out of the mold of former Governor Millard Caldwell, proved to be a tough and effective campaigner, and appealed to the conservative wing of the state party, which resented Collins's leadership on race relations. Faircloth ran a hard-hitting campaign with an emphasis on "law and order." A campaign poster literally shouted at voters: "STOP RIOTS—ELECT FAIRCLOTH—A CONSERVATIVE."[43] By 1968, concern about the urban riots and the looting and destruction in cities spread across the nation, angering white middle-class voters in particular and providing a platform for Republicans seeking to unseat Democrats. Accusing Collins of being "an aging ultra-liberal" and a "political chameleon," Faircloth ignored pleas by Pat Thomas, head of the Democratic Party in Florida, to cool the rhetoric for fear that a campaign of this nature would only serve to elect Republican Gurney. But Faircloth ignored his petitions. As the underdog in the campaign, he kept up a steady drumbeat of criticism of Collins and encouraged his supporters to display a national photograph taken in 1965 of Collins walking alongside Martin Luther King Jr. at the head of the Selma, Alabama, civil rights march. "Why is Collins afraid of a photograph?" Faircloth asked his listeners in various forums, and why, he asked, did the former governor turn "against the South when it was in deep trouble?"[44] As with many other politicians of this era, his repeated reference to himself as the "law and order" candidate became a euphemism for his opposition to civil rights reform and the policies of the Johnson administration. Highlighting his leadership as attorney general, Faircloth said he would continue to partner with the police to stop the urban violence, implying that Collins would not.

Collins attempted to counter the stream of invective by proposing an end to the war in Vietnam, a guarantee of justice for all Americans, fiscal restraint in government, fairness in taxation, and environmental protection. But with a campaign forced to take out advertisements to correct Faircloth's charges and rapidly running out of money, Collins had great difficulty in getting his full message before voters. It only got worse when Collins failed to defeat Faircloth in the first primary, enabling Faircloth to continue his political diatribe for another three weeks. The results of the second primary were extremely close, with Faircloth capturing much of north Florida, which was Collins's home turf. Although he lost the state-wide election to Collins by fewer than three thousand votes, Faircloth had severely damaged Collins's senatorial campaign and had given Gurney plenty of political ammunition to defeat Collins in the general election. The effectiveness of Faircloth's campaign also drained most of Collins's financial resources.

As the Senate race in Florida took shape in 1968, it was significantly influenced by the contest for the presidency that took one strange turn after another. Most Americans assumed Lyndon Johnson would be the candidate for reelection on the Democratic side, but mounting student protests against the war in Vietnam and public concerns about the economy, the direction of the war, and social unrest turned voters against the president. After narrowly defeating the relatively unknown U.S. Senator Eugene McCarthy (from Minnesota) in the New Hampshire primary, Johnson announced his decision not to seek reelection. In the wide-open race that followed for the Democratic nomination between Vice President Hubert Humphrey, Senator Robert Kennedy, and Senator Eugene McCarthy, Humphrey won the nomination but only after Kennedy was assassinated and the party went through a violent and angry bloodletting at the Democratic National Convention. As in Florida, where Republicans rallied behind Gurney, confident that they could defeat Collins, so at the national level Republicans united behind Richard Nixon, confident that he could capture the presidency over a badly splintered Democratic Party.[45]

The 1968 campaign was perhaps the most important presidential contest in the late twentieth century. During the course of this campaign, Republicans mapped out their strategy to secure the political majority in the nation. In doing so, they were aided by the presidential candidacy of Alabama Governor George Wallace, who ran as the third-party candidate of the American Independent Party. Unsure of the impact Wallace's candidacy would have on the presidential election, Republicans both welcomed and worried about his entry into the campaign. When his rhetoric demonized the Democratic Party and its policies, Republicans listened closely. Wallace's message appealed to white workers by castigating Democratic "Big Government" as dictatorial, guilty of reverse discrimination, and the enemy of workers through its tax and social policies. Wallace further asserted that liberal politicians and liberal bureaucrats, not working-class or middle-class Americans, were the real racial bigots, or, as Wallace referred to them, "pluperfect hypocrites" who hid out in their suburbs and placed their children in private schools.[46]

Nixon recognized that the political and social unraveling of the nation offered him a unique opportunity to capture the presidency as well as the chance to build a political coalition that would propel the Republican Party forward as the majority party. In order to do that, the historian Matthew Lassiter argues, Nixon's strategy rejected the populist extremism of Wallace as too polarizing and chose instead to reach out to a broad coalition of moderate, largely middle-class, white voters whom Nixon called the "silent majority." According to Lassiter, Nixon viewed a Wallace-like southern strategy as too narrow and one that would potentially alienate national voters. Instead he went after frustrated middle-class and suburban voters, who worried about the loss of their newly won economic gains to an increasingly intrusive federal government and a failed war in Vietnam. The historian Kevin Kruse also maintains that Nixon and fellow Republicans used issues of crime and law and order as subtexts to gain support among whites who were concerned about racial developments in the country.[47]

The 1968 presidential campaign and the political discourse about race devastated Collins's campaign for the Senate seat. Although Collins faced a marginally known politician in Gurney, with a notably weak record as congressman, the former governor found himself still on the defensive for his leadership of the Community Relations Service in the Johnson administration. Gurney and his Republican supporters followed the Democratic Senate primary closely as well as the presidential contest and launched their own series of negative advertisements, in which they highlighted Collins's civil rights record and his liberal politics. Referring to Collins as "Liberal LeRoy," Gurney mimicked Faircloth's strategy, showing the photograph of Collins parading alongside Martin Luther King at the front of the civil rights march to Selma. Although personalities and image played critical roles in this campaign, Gurney also hammered away at three issues of importance to Floridians: crime, law and order, and taxes.[48]

Collins tried mightily to draw attention away from his role at the Community Relations Service and focus it on Gurney's anemic congressional record and his many missed votes in Congress, but with very little success. Developments nationally and Collins's well-known record as a racial moderate simply overwhelmed Collins's campaign and his message, much as had happened to High two years earlier. One of Collins's oldest friends and campaign supporters, Eleanor Mizell McMullen, sent word that she and her husband, one of Collins's law partners, could not support him because of his racial views. Moreover, while Gurney had been ineffective in Washington, he was an attractive and reasonably articulate candidate, as the *Miami Herald* pointed out: "an elderly version of the all-American boy" and a "clean-cut, smooth talking, ex–war hero." In four public debates with Collins, he looked much younger than Collins and equally handsome. And he avoided any major misstatements that would have highlighted his limitations and inexperience. Collins, by contrast, fared poorly in the debates, often appearing tired and worn out by the primary and general election campaigns. To those who watched the debates, he looked like an old man.[49]

Of little help to Collins's campaign was the massive growth in south Florida, where many of the state's 1.5 million new residents had settled since 1960. Few knew Collins's record as governor and the leadership he had provided the state and region during the tumultuous 1950s. Since his last campaign in 1956, Florida had registered over 1 million new voters, a 72 percent increase. In many ways, Collins—with a public record that was little known to many voters but that could also be used selectively against him—became the first to experience the curse of being an experienced politician in Florida in the second half of the twentieth century. Ironically, Collins, whose Hollywood good looks and suave appearance had helped him with voters in the 1950s, now faced a man who was younger and equally attractive to voters. Such superficial factors came to play a major role in Florida politics in the last third of the twentieth century because the many new voters did not know the candidates or their records.[50]

What became known as the "Opie factor" also played an increasingly important role in the electoral process in Florida. Named after the child character once played by Hollywood director Ron Howard in the long-running television series *The Andy Griffith Show*, the term *Opie factor* referred to another Ron Howard, who ran for secretary of education in Florida in 1998 and nearly captured the Democratic nomination when many Floridians voted for him because they thought he was the actor. The candidate Ron Howard, in fact, had few credentials to serve as secretary of education but had run ahead of his much more experienced opponents in the primary. His major claim to fame as a Palm Beach County commissioner was his opposition to roadside vendors wearing string bikinis.[51] As the Opie factor demonstrated, state leaders, no matter how experienced and able, had to reintroduce themselves to voters at least every four years or risk the same fate as Collins. Both name recognition—such as that of a Ron Howard or, subsequently, a Jeb Bush—and being telegenic went a long way to helping a person get elected in ever-changing Florida.

Collins's campaign thus faced an array of developments that worked against his election. Much like High's campaign against Kirk in 1966, the senatorial election of 1968 had much to do with Collins, his record, and the record of the national Democratic Party. Faircloth's success in attacking Collins's record in the primary and in turning north Florida and middle-class voters against Collins was crucial to Gurney's victory. In this regard, Gurney benefited from Wallace's presidential candidacy. Wallace drew record crowds in north Florida, and his condemnation of the Democratic Party played right into the hands of Gurney's campaign. Without the support of rural Florida, Collins, like Robert King High in the 1966 gubernatorial election, could win only by turning out a supermajority in south Florida. And since many in that region of the state did not remember Collins well enough to provide that majority, many middle-class voters opted to support Gurney and Nixon. Gurney defeated Collins resoundingly by more than 200,000 votes, and like High before him, Collins captured only four of Florida's sixty-seven counties, even losing his home county of Leon. At the same time, Nixon carried Florida with 886,804 votes and 40.5 percent of the ballots cast. Wallace came in a close third, losing to Humphrey by less than 1.5 percent of the vote with 624,207 votes to Humphrey's 676,794. The breakdown of votes revealed that native and Cracker voters; middle-class voters, many of whom had voted Democrat in the past; and Republicans went for Gurney and Nixon. It was a dark day for the Democratic Party in Florida as well as in most of the South.[52]

With their victory over the most prominent figure in the state Democratic Party, state Republicans gloated about prospects for the future. The national Democratic Party appeared to be in free fall over Vietnam, the urban unrest, mounting taxes to pay for the war, and social welfare programs, and the state party was beginning to feel the effects of voter dissatisfaction with the national party. As Gurney noted, the Democrats were paying a heavy price for years of one-party rule and for the increasing differences between north and south Florida: "They gather around one man and they suffer this terrible schizophrenia between liberals and conservatives. As long as you've got that," he added, "the Republicans can come in and pick up the pieces."[53]

With reapportionment, the influx of midwestern Republicans into the state, the growing middle-class support for Republicans, and the shift of many natives/Crackers/Blue Dog Democrats to the Republican Party, Republicans felt their day in Florida had finally arrived. When one added in the dysfunctional nature of the Democratic Party, it appeared that Republicans had every reason to be optimistic about their political future.

Republican celebrations over the demise of the Democratic Party were premature, however, as events would soon reveal. Republicans had capitalized on the implosion of the national Democratic Party, the social and political turmoil nationally, and the concern among Floridians about the integration of society, public schools, and housing. But could Republicans build a future on the public's negative reaction to the policies of the Democrats, and could they find candidates to challenge Democrats for other statewide positions?

The answer to both questions was unclear in January 1968. Despite the losses suffered by High and Collins and the bloodletting that resulted within the Democratic Party during both campaigns, the party remained very strong at the local level, where it continued to field a vast array of very strong candidates for local and state office. State Republican leader and congressman William Cramer, a St. Petersburg resident who launched efforts to build a statewide party in the late 1940s, was convinced that Republicans needed an agenda that highlighted their differences with Democrats, an ideology that could appeal to disaffected Democrats, and strong candidates who could use this agenda and political ideology to challenge Democrats at all levels.

President Nixon and his political advisers built the party's new ideology on the foundation established by former Arizona Senator Barry Goldwater, embracing his proposals for a stronger military, smaller and more fiscally responsible government, lower taxes, individual freedom, and a commitment to strengthening capitalism and business development. Nixon broadened this appeal by reaching out to the so-called silent majority, middle-class and suburban voters who were frustrated by the social unrest and violence in the nation and who sought sensible policies that would end racial segregation and discrimination, gradually resolve the war in Vietnam, and restore law and order to combat rising crime and social unrest. Nixon's success, albeit limited in 1968, suggested that Republicans could finally wean the middle class away from the Democratic Party and construct a new Republican political majority.[54]

The Republican agenda may well have translated into Republican majorities at both the national and state levels in the 1970s were it not for dramatic leadership failures at both echelons. Paradoxically, although Kirk's victory signaled the passing of an era of Democratic dominance of the governor's office in Florida, it did not inaugurate an era of Republican leadership or even a period in which some equilibrium was achieved between the two parties. Kirk's shortcomings as a politician, of which voters got only a glimpse during the campaign, emerged full bore when he became governor. He proved ill-equipped by personality, maturity, political acumen, and leadership to govern the state effectively. In many ways, Kirk was a political maverick who sought the political limelight to promote himself and his ambitions. As a consequence, the Republican Party benefited little directly from his governorship and would, in the end, suffer a substantial setback because of his imprudent and sometimes boorish leadership.

Despite legislative gains through reapportionment, Kirk confronted a legislature in 1967 in which the Democrats still enjoyed majorities in both houses. Such an environment required a governor with diplomatic savvy, patience, and wisdom—in short, someone with substantial political skill. Kirk was not that person. Boisterous, flamboyant, even outrageous, Kirk made a mess of Republican direction of the state in fairly short order. His public courting of the glamorous and mysterious Madame X, who subsequently became Mrs. Erika Kirk, at fancy balls and parties may have played well in Key West and Miami Beach, but it wore thin with Floridians who expected more substance from their governor. Gradually, Kirk became the butt of many bad jokes and a source of public embarrassment. His political initiatives did not help his image.

Kirk made vice in Dade County a major issue in his campaign and launched what he called a "command post" to direct his fight against organized crime in Miami. But when he refused to divulge his specific plans to the press and then hired the Wackenhut Corporation, a private detective agency, to handle the investigation, instead of the State Bureau of

Investigation, the public recoiled. In April 1967, Secretary of State Tom Adams, a Democrat and critic of the governor, complained publicly that he was being followed by Kirk's agents, and shortly thereafter, the press reported that Kirk's "war on crime" was over $200,000 in debt. The governor appealed to voters to stay the course with him in his battle against national crime figures, and many in rural Florida were prepared to do so, but when he made the bizarre announcement that the underworld had placed a $50,000 price on his head, he lost all credibility and subsequently abandoned the campaign.[55]

It went from bad to worse when Kirk attempted to manipulate public concern over countywide school busing to further his national political ambitions. In 1970, U.S. District Court Judge Ben Krentzman ordered Manatee County school officials to begin busing students to achieve a ratio of 80 percent white to 20 percent black students in each school. Kirk interceded to block Krentzman's decision, suspending both the school board and the superintendent of schools and placing control of the schools directly under his office. Ironically, Kirk had established a reasonably moderate record on racial issues prior to the Manatee crisis. For reasons not altogether clear, he assumed that his resistance to Krentzman's order would bolster his reelection chances with middle-class voters in 1970 and enhance his prospects for the vice presidency in 1972. While few whites in the state favored countywide busing, most believed that Kirk's approach to the issue was shameful and only worsened a difficult situation. Krentzman immediately ordered the schools returned to county officials, and Governor Kirk to appear before him to explain his actions. Kirk refused, accused Krentzman of overstepping "his bounds," and suspended school officials again.[56] Democrats in the state legislature, who eyed Kirk cautiously following his victory over High, emerged from their passivity to denounce the governor's failings. Shouting matches were heard between Democratic leaders and Kirk in the governor's office, and cabinet meetings between Kirk and the Democratic cabinet members deteriorated into charges and countercharges of incompetence and malfeasance.[57]

Adding to the drama, Kirk stunned state and federal officials when he said that there might be the loss of life if they attempted to serve him with a subpoena. Although few things surprised Floridians any longer about their governor after three years of bizarre behavior, this statement left most amazed. Middle-class voters, offended by his boorish behavior, deserted Kirk, as did others, and few people rallied to his defense. When Krentzman cited Kirk for contempt of court and announced fines of $10,000 a day until he ended his interference in the Manatee schools, Kirk, sensing Floridians had had enough, bowed to the judge's demands the following day and directed school officials to comply with the judge's order. The crisis was over, but Floridians were left wondering out loud how and why they had elected Kirk as governor in the first place and whether he represented the best the state Republican Party had to offer.[58]

Although Kirk frequently disappointed, he offered rare moments of positive leadership, especially in environmental matters. He gained the respect of many voters and environmentalists for his decision to stop state support for the Cross-Florida Barge Canal, which cut through the heart of Florida, destroying water resources and pristine land. Subsequently he persuaded President Nixon to support the state's action by terminating federal funding for the project. Despite the merits of his environmental leadership, they were not sufficient to offset his other actions.[59]

Compounding Republican woes, charges of bribery, taking unlawful compensation, and three counts of lying to a grand jury while in office were filed against Senator Ed Gurney shortly after he took his Senate seat in 1971, raising further questions about the quality and integrity of Republican leadership in Florida. Gurney subsequently would be cleared of most of these charges—the jury deadlocked on two of them—but his reputation had been permanently tarnished in the process. Coincidentally, Judge Krentzman would preside at Gurney's trial.

The unraveling of the Watergate break-in and the involvement of President Nixon in the cover-up delivered the final coup de grace to the Republican Party in Florida. Nixon's denial of involvement in the Watergate break-in paralleled Gurney's repeated denials of lying to the grand jury, bribery, and so on. Although Gurney may not have been guilty, Nixon certainly was. The Watergate scandal unfolded over a twenty-six-month period from the break-in on June 17, 1972, until Nixon's resignation on August 8, 1974, during which time Nixon and his staff repeatedly denied any involvement in the break-in to the offices of the Democratic National Committee and refused to release evidence that suggested otherwise. The frequent lies, deceptions, and eventual resignation of Nixon, together with the questionable ethics and behavior of Kirk and Gurney, seriously eroded public support for the Republican Party in Florida. As with most Americans, middle-class Floridians shook their heads in disbelief following the Watergate debacle, and these events persuaded many to reconsider the Democratic Party.[60]

Although the Democratic Party still exhibited the same organizational problems that Gurney had identified in 1968 and that had plagued it for much of the twentieth century, it was about to introduce to voters a remarkable group of politicians, led by Reubin Askew, Lawton Chiles, and Bob Graham, all of whom had been inspired by LeRoy Collins's leadership. It was ironic that these new Democrats had been mentored by Collins, a political leader Republicans thought they had ousted and whose policies they thought had been repudiated by Floridians. But Republicans had underestimated Floridians, assuming that racial appeals on school integration and busing were sufficient to gain white voter support. While Askew and Chiles came from Cracker Florida, their politics, in fact, bore little resemblance to those of this region. Embracing LeRoy Collins's vision of a new Florida for all Floridians—black and white, Hispanic and Jew, rural and urban—these new Democratic leaders were about to offer the party a new lease on life and, in the process, bring middle-class voters back into the Democratic fold, provide the state with twenty years of strong and talented progressive leadership, and forestall the Republican ascendancy for another generation.

3

Reubin Askew, Lawton Chiles, and the Reinvention of the Democratic Party

Giddy over their dramatic victories in the 1966, 1967, and 1968 elections as well as Richard Nixon's victory in Florida in the 1968 presidential election, many Republicans predicted the party would seize political leadership of the state in the near future. Others, like William Cramer, who had toiled in the Republican trenches for nearly two decades, however, were not so naïve. Cramer recognized that opportunity beckoned, but it could be a fickle friend if Republicans were not attentive to the public interest. In many ways, Republican political successes in Florida came too quickly, before the party had sufficient time to recruit and develop able candidates and before it solidified its relationship with voters. Most importantly, the party's leading politicians of the 1960s failed supporters and the party badly: Nixon through political arrogance, Kirk through outlandish behavior, and Gurney through questionable ethics.

Their mistakes gave Democrats an unexpected second chance—the opportunity to reclaim the governorship in Florida and a U.S. Senate seat in 1970 and, in the process, political leadership of the state. Earl Faircloth, still fresh from narrowly losing the Democratic senatorial primary to Collins in 1968, announced his candidacy for governor. He was the clear statewide favorite in a field that included three regional candidates: Chuck Hall, mayor of Miami; Reubin Askew, state senator from Escambia County in the Panhandle; and John E. Mathews, state senator from Duval County, which encompassed Jacksonville. Seeing himself as the front-runner, Faircloth chose to ignore his lesser-known Democratic rivals, launching his campaign instead against Governor Kirk, whom he labeled incompetent and irresponsible.[1]

Faircloth and his challengers in the primary offered voters an interesting mix of alternatives. Hall of Miami provided great entertainment value in the campaign, flying around the state in his own DC-3 and being escorted between towns in a white Rolls Royce. A teetotaler and nonsmoker, Hall looked and sounded like a modern-day Billy Sunday, calling for the abolition of pornography, stiff penalties for drug possession and drug sales, and stricter codes of moral discipline on college campuses. But Floridians had tired of the pyrotechnics of the Kirk administration and yearned for more serious gubernatorial leadership. Moreover, Faircloth, like Hall, resided in Miami, and he had already mobilized most of the serious Dade County electorate behind his candidacy.[2]

The two other candidates were largely new to Floridians; both came from the same region of the state, which was rapidly being supplanted by south Florida. Faircloth's forces saw the two men as more serious rivals than Hall but were equally confident that Faircloth would defeat both and win the Democratic nomination in the first primary. Not surprisingly, both Mathews and Askew had the same goal—to deny Faircloth victory in the first primary and gain sufficient statewide recognition to defeat him in the runoff. Mathews's campaign, however, often mirrored Faircloth's, calling for responsible and fiscally sound government, conservative leadership, low taxes, and a business-oriented administration.

Askew was the great unknown in the contest. Widely respected among his peers in the state Senate for his leadership and integrity, Askew viewed Collins as his political mentor and had little use for Faircloth, whose personal attacks against Collins in the 1968 senatorial primary still angered Askew. Choosing to run an issue-oriented campaign instead of one that revolved around his personality, Askew called for greater environmental stewardship, racial justice, corporate responsibility, honesty and integrity in government, a stronger educational system for all Floridians, and more effective law enforcement. When asked why he had taken stances on such controversial issues, Askew told the press unequivocally, as was his wont, that he hoped to be governor, but "not so bad that I would spend four years of frustration with my hands tied." Askew finished ahead of Mathews and

Hall in the first primary and denied Faircloth outright victory, but he ran more than twenty thousand votes behind Faircloth and had less than one month before the second primary election occurred. (The first primary vote took place on September 8, 1970, and the second on September 29.) That both Hall and Mathews endorsed Faircloth for the party's nomination shortly after the first primary results were announced made Askew's task even more daunting.[3]

Although Askew had never run statewide, he revealed early on a knack for doing so. Tall, angular, with handsome, clean-cut features, Askew was an imposing figure in person, where his sermonlike addresses attracted a large following. But he was even more effective working a crowd and interacting with them individually, where his size, rugged good looks, and habit of looking each person directly in the eye made a deep impression on voters. Confident in himself and in his political values, most of which were rooted in his Christian faith, Askew's personal style and his religious values gained him strong backing among friends and neighbors in rural north Florida, who would normally have supported Faircloth because of his opposition to school busing and his advocacy of small government. Askew's campaign rhetoric also made an impression on other Democratic voters. One official seemed to capture the thinking of most Floridians when he said of Askew's campaign, "I'm just glad to see a candidate have the guts to say what he thinks."[4]

As the second primary unfolded and crowds increased at his political gatherings, Askew sensed that voters had warmed to his style and that he had the political momentum. He gave voters a foretaste of his personal philosophy, telling them he was "an apostle of hope, not a prophet of doom." And he began spending less energy attacking Faircloth and more time focusing on issues that he felt voters wanted to hear discussed. His denunciation of the politics of hate and his commitment to environmental reform, education, and honesty and integrity in government won a large following among newcomers to the state and middle-class voters, who had come to accept the legitimacy of integration. Askew captured the second primary in stunning fashion, defeating Faircloth by over 120,000 votes and gaining support among natives as well as middle-class urban and suburban voters in almost every section of the state.[5] The stage had been set for a lively, if predictable, general election campaign against Kirk.

Kirk, meanwhile, had faced a difficult primary himself against two opponents—Jack Eckerd, a drugstore tycoon and a leading supporter of the Republican Party, and Skip Bafalis, a West Palm Beach legislator. Republicans seldom fielded more than one candidate in a gubernatorial contest; the fact that two chose to run against the Republican incumbent suggested the degree to which Republicans were dissatisfied with Kirk's leadership of the party. Bafalis, a well-respected politician, accused Kirk of making Florida the laughingstock of the nation, while Eckerd, one of the party's major financial backers, called the governor's leadership an embarrassment to the party. Eckerd forced Kirk into a runoff and kept up a steady drumbeat of criticism of his governorship, but Eckerd, despite his backing by business leaders, lacked the political experience and personal appeal to win support among mainstream voters. Although Kirk won the second primary, he emerged badly scarred from the primary and financially strapped for the general election.[6]

In contrast to the disarray in the Republican Party, Democrats united around Askew's candidacy. Despite Faircloth's frustration at losing the party's nomination, he decided to endorse Askew, creating further difficulties for Kirk in the general election. Without the endorsement of a single prominent Democrat, Kirk faced an impossible task unless he could capture north Florida once again. But the Blue Dog Democrats in north Florida liked Askew. He was, after all, one of them, and his religious faith and military experience in Korea made it unlikely that Kirk could attract their support.

That, however, did not prevent Kirk from campaigning in his own colorful and inimitable way. Calling Askew antibusiness, pro-labor, supportive of pornography, a "mama's boy," and a "patsy powderpuff for polluters," Kirk remained entertaining if not terribly substantive. Askew did not shy away from Kirk's charges, highlighting his middle initials, "O'D." for O'Donovan, out of reverence for his mother. He later recalled attending a rally in South Miami Beach at which Congressman Dante Fascell introduced him: "I began my speech by saying, 'Well, today, Mr. Kirk called me a mama's boy. [I said,] I just wanted you to know that he is correct, because I love that mama of mine.' I looked out in the audience and I would say that probably the vast majority of that audience were Jewish mamas. Jewish people, like some other groups, have such strong family ties. They started clapping and gave me a standing ovation. I do not think I was able to say much. Every time I would start talking, they would start clapping. Finally

Dante Fascell shrugged and said, 'How can you top it?' It was actually one of the briefest speeches I have ever made."[7]

Kirk's contention that Askew was a "mama's boy" also hurt Kirk in rural Florida, where poverty divided many families. The fact that Askew and his five siblings had been raised by his mother, who worked backbreaking jobs to feed them after her husband abandoned them, resonated with the experience of others in this region. Still Kirk persisted, making every effort to win voter support by calling the legislature into special session to regulate insurance rates and to announce a new low-cost housing program for retirees. But such legislative efforts did not impress voters, who wondered why he had not proposed such measures during the regular session.

Askew drubbed Kirk, capturing 57 percent of the popular vote, defeating the former governor in every area of the state, and losing only Orange and Sarasota Counties among the urban counties in the state. Every segment of the voting population supported Askew, and he captured urban and suburban voters in such Republican strongholds as Hillsborough and Pinellas Counties. Askew also defeated Kirk in north Florida and rebuilt, at least temporarily, the north Florida–southeast Florida Democratic coalition. Askew's victory punctured Republican ambitions, although some would argue that it was Kirk's incompetence that derailed the Republican Party.[8]

The importance of Askew's election and the failure of Kirk's reelection cannot be overemphasized in the struggle between the two parties for political leadership in Florida. Republicans had every reason to believe that their electoral successes from 1966 to 1968 represented the shifting loyalties of Florida voters away from Democratic hegemony in statewide races. While Askew's victory gave the Democratic Party renewed confidence, political professionals wondered if he could draw Democrats back into the party's fold on a permanent basis, if he would be able to stymie Republican momentum, and if he could draw new state residents into the Democratic Party. His campaign offered considerable promise, but no one could be sure how effectively he would govern and if he could indeed resuscitate a party that had been deeply divided only two years earlier.

Aiding the party's revival was the emergence of a second important statewide Democratic figure, Lawton Chiles. A close friend and ally of Askew's in the state Senate, Chiles shared with Askew a commitment to the public trust and to reengaging native Floridians with the Democratic

Party through a serious discussion of the critical issues facing them and the state. Chiles campaigned for Spessard Holland's U.S. Senate seat in 1970 at the same time that Askew was running for governor. Like Askew, Chiles was unknown to many Floridians when he first announced, coming from the small city of Lakeland. Facing the much better-known former Governor Farris Bryant in the Democratic primary, Chiles launched his campaign by literally walking across Florida, over one thousand miles, to meet with voters. Nicknamed "Walkin' Lawton" as a consequence, his populist appeal to everyday Floridians along the way captured the interest of many who felt their government was losing touch with them. Floridians seemed to appreciate that, in an age of increasing mass media campaigns, Chiles was taking the time to introduce himself to voters as he walked from town to town. His campaign stroll also gained him considerable media attention, which spared him the cost of campaign advertisements and which was crucial in a state where so many lacked knowledge of state politicians and public issues. The fact that Chiles looked and spoke like a Cracker in north Florida and then transformed himself into a thoughtful political professional in south Florida added to his luster. His name quickly became a household phrase as local media covered his arrival in community after community. Although Bryant had been governor and had significant name recognition, he was unknown to newcomers and his campaign generated little interest or enthusiasm. The colorful Chiles vanquished Bryant in the primary.

The general election campaign, however, proved much more difficult as Chiles faced the well-respected William Cramer. In a very tight battle, Chiles defeated Cramer by a few thousand votes by reaching out to common folk in the state and by promising to use the U.S. Senate seat to address Florida's environmental, economic, and educational needs. But Cramer ran strongly in Republican strongholds in southwest Florida below Tampa and among Blue Dog Democrats, and middle-class urban and suburban voters. Embracing Nixon's southern strategy, Cramer appealed to "discerning Democrats . . . to join us in our fight to stop the cop killers, the bombers, the burners, the radical revolutionaries who would destroy America." Despite the victories of Askew and Chiles, Cramer's campaign revealed that the message of the Republican Party, when combined with a capable and thoughtful candidate, had broad appeal in Florida.[9]

The victories of Askew and Chiles also facilitated Democratic gains in legislative elections and together with the subsequent resignation of President Nixon temporarily derailed Republican aspirations in Florida. Republican legislative successes in 1967 as a result of court-ordered reapportionment faltered in the 1970 elections, when Republicans lost seven seats in the state Senate, leaving the party with only 15 of the 48 seats as opposed to 20 of the 48 seats in 1968. The party won a mere 38 seats in the House, down from 39 of the 120 seats in 1967.

Despite these setbacks, the state Republican Party remained optimistic about the future because of Cramer's close race. With many questions surrounding Askew and Chiles—both still relatively unknown to voters and lacking experience for the major positions they would shortly assume—Republicans could wait in the wings for the time being.

Askew's Governorship

Most of the attention and pressure to resurrect the party fell naturally on Askew, who, as governor, carried the burden of leadership in the state. Askew did not disappoint fellow Democrats or voters. Pulling together his advisers and Democratic leaders in the state Senate and House, Askew laid out his legislative agenda in a series of prelegislative meetings. As a legislative leader during the 1960s and now as a governor with an ambitious legislative agenda, Askew set about to rebuild relations between the governor's office and the legislature. "I tried to stay in contact with them," he remarked. "I would have legislators out to breakfast and for luncheons at the mansion. During the session I would usually stay throughout the whole day in the governor's office and invite them down for a sandwich, lunch."[10]

After four years of conflict with Governor Kirk in which few measures of significance passed the legislature, Senate and House members, especially Democrats but also several Republicans, welcomed Askew's decision to address the thorny problems facing Florida. Askew observed, however, that a governor had to exercise political discretion when working with legislators, who were quite mindful of their prerogatives. He knew well, for example, that "A governor never enters the chamber without an invitation. It is just an absolute taboo and not appreciated. So what I would do when there was a session and I really needed to talk to somebody, I would find out about all the receptions that were taking place when the session was over," he recalled. "Normally, three-fourths of the legislators go to these receptions and I would take a roll call and I would target not more than a half dozen people for the night." With the issue and their vote in his pocket, he would approach them at "these receptions and tap them on the shoulder and say, 'what in the world happened today?'"[11]

True to his campaign commitments, Askew pursued improved funding for education, environmental protection of the state, water and land preservation, a corporate income tax and severance tax on phosphates, better race relations, greater funding for public schools, and greater access to higher education. Shortly after taking office, he called for a new funding model to meet the needs of public schools, replacing the antiquated MFP (Minimum Foundation Program): "I appointed a governor's commission [Governor's Citizens' Committee on Education] to look into the matter and they proposed the FEFP [Florida Education Finance Program]," which allowed for "giving some programs more weight than others in terms of financial support."[12]

Few issues had greater importance to Floridians of all backgrounds than public schools and public school funding. Natives and newcomers felt Florida's schools were poorly funded and inadequate to meet their aspirations for their children; businessmen worried that the schools were so mediocre that they threatened their competitiveness; and politicians recognized that the tremendous growth of the state's population placed great pressure on the schools. Leaders of the state and local Chambers of Commerce commented that they had difficulty recruiting new companies to Florida because many felt the workforce in the state was not sufficiently well educated to provide enough skilled workers. Over a two-year period, the commission, which included education experts as well as legislators and business leaders, developed a funding formula based on the number of full-time equivalent student hours to address the needs of overcrowded urban school districts without jeopardizing support for smaller school districts. The funding formula also took into account program cost factors (recognizing that English classes for non-native speakers, for example, cost more than history classes), compensatory education supplements for physically and mentally disadvantaged children, district cost differentials, local tax effort (as an incentive for communities to provide greater support for schools), and local flexibility to help communities use these funds to meet their special needs. In June 1973, Askew signed the measure into law, noting: "This is a giant step. It completely rewrites the MFP and guarantees every school child an equal chance for a quality education."[13] While the Florida Education Finance Program significantly improved public education in Florida, it did not fully solve the education crisis in the state because of the continuing population boom and the immigration of children from the Caribbean and Latin America whose first language was not English. Nevertheless, Askew and the Democrats won high praise from the press, voters, and newcomers for addressing one of the most critical issues facing the state.

During his first address to the legislature, Askew also urged passage of his campaign pledge for what he termed a "fair share tax program." The proposal called for a corporate income tax, a severance tax on phosphates, and repeal of the intangible tax on cash in the bank.[14] In spite of a projected state budget deficit of $250 million and broad public support, the governor's tax proposals struggled to get legislative passage as Republicans and corporate leaders—led by Associated Industries, the leading business organization in Florida; Ed Ball, the steely head of the Florida East Coast Railroad and St. Joe Paper; the Davis Brothers, founders and top executives of Winn-Dixie groceries—vigorously fought Askew's tax measures. Amply funded by its membership, Associated Industries and Republicans resorted to fear tactics, alleging that this was Askew's initial step in a plan that would lead eventually to a proposal for a personal income tax and that the corporation and severance taxes would restrict business development in Florida. Their tactics worked, in part: the measure failed to obtain the necessary three-fourths vote in a special session of the legislature so that it could not be submitted to voters in the fall for approval.

Republican support for big business in this battle may have been initially successful, but it hampered party efforts to reach out to a larger voter constituency. Florida voters generally viewed Republicans as cronies of big business, and the party somehow had to get beyond this image if it hoped to compete effectively with state Democrats. Askew gave Republicans no quarter on this issue, reminding voters repeatedly of the fundamental differences between the two parties on his tax-reform proposals.[15]

During the period between the special session in January and the start of the regular session in March, Askew and his aides lobbied voters and legislators to allow the measure to go before voters in November 1971. The importance of this issue to the success of the Askew administration could not be overemphasized. If Askew lost this battle, his business opponents and their Republican allies would have crippled his administration and laid the foundation for defeating him in the gubernatorial election of 1974. Well aware that his ability to govern the state was at risk, Askew met with key legislators, denounced the business ties of his political opponents, and spoke to editorial boards and voters around the state. Few politicians have rivaled Askew in his knowledge of the issues, his almost mystical confidence in his position, and his persuasive abilities. Time after time he would take matters to voters and legislators, and very rarely did he suffer defeat. In seeking public support for the corporate and severance tax proposals, he emphasized the issue of fairness, noting that citizens paid taxes, and so why shouldn't the phosphate and corporate interests do so? Environmentalists rallied to the governor's side, too, fearing that the governor's defeat on the severance tax issue would dramatically set back the environmental campaign to clean up phosphate sites in the state.

On May 4, 1971, unable to defend themselves against the governor's withering criticism, legislators agreed to allow voters to decide the matter in November. In what would become an Askew trademark, he named a forty-two-member blue-ribbon committee to lead the battle for public ratification and appointed Ben Hill Griffin Jr., a Florida native and one of the state's most successful business leaders, to chair the group. Griffin and other members of the committee provided Askew with cover against those accusing him of being antibusiness and, most importantly, gave him the backing of key business leaders in the media campaign against such rivals as Associated Industries, Ed Ball, and the Davis Brothers.

But Askew never left an issue of this significance to a blue-ribbon committee, choosing instead to campaign alongside them to obtain voter approval. Emphasizing the reasonableness of the corporate and severance tax proposals, Askew explained to working-class and middle-class voters that "Florida imposed the fifth-highest level of taxes on small businessmen in the country, but large corporations were taxed at an average of 27 cents per $1,000 of income, whereas the national average was $6.51 per $1,000 of income." A state economist noted that only two other states lacked a corporate income tax—Ohio and Texas. Both states, however, required corporations to pay stiff franchise fees or net worth taxes. Florida, on the other hand, asked corporations to pay only a corporate stock tax, which amounted to only 0.5 percent of state revenues as compared with

6.7 percent for Ohio and 5.7 percent for Texas. While the arguments by the governor and his supporters seemed to make good sense, they did not energize voters, who had trouble following the argument about the rate of taxation per $1,000 of income and who found other aspects of the argument abstruse. He had greater success explaining to Floridians the severance tax proposal, noting that the phosphate industry had made millions from mining and had never paid one cent of tax or one cent toward the cleanup after they finished ravaging an area.[16]

In an interview years later about the corporate income tax, Askew recalled, "I was making speeches on [the] corporate income tax that I thought were fairly good, but I was not making any headway," when a legislator from Miami suggested he should compare the cost of shirts in Miami to those in Atlanta. One of Askew's campaign aides, Art Gray, went and bought an oxford cloth shirt at a Sears in Miami and another at a Sears in Atlanta, and Askew went on television with the two shirts. The governor told listeners that the shirt "cost more in Florida because we have a 4 percent sales tax and Georgia only has 3. But you know what Sears pays Georgia? Sears pays Georgia $500,000 to sell them shirts [because of Georgia's corporate tax], but do you know what they pay Florida? $2,000." Suddenly voters could visualize the argument and its implications for them and their state.[17] The populist aspect of the tax made it very difficult for Associated Industries to gain the essential backing of rural north Floridians and working-class residents, many of whom resented the fact that they contributed more to state coffers than wealthy corporations. The governor's tax proposals scored a resounding victory in November: 816,642 votes (70 percent) were cast for the referendum, and only 337,217 votes were cast against it. Republicans had played a bad hand and now found themselves confronting a governor with even greater statewide standing than when he had been initially elected. Moreover, their opposition to the referendum had cost Republicans dearly among working-class and middle-class voters, who enthusiastically endorsed the governor's proposals and resented the Republican alliance with big business at their expense.

During his fight for the corporate and severance tax reforms, Askew launched a broad-based call for environmental reform to preserve some of the state's remaining natural treasures from massive population growth and urban sprawl. He joined with many Floridians who feared that the state was in "great danger" of becoming a "paradise lost." In September

1971, he invited state and city leaders and environmentalists to a conference on water and land management at Bal Harbour, Florida, to discuss the major environmental issues facing the state and to assist him in addressing them. The use of such meetings to bring together experts was one of Askew's favorite devices. "My thesis in government generally has been that government rarely has the answers within and of itself," he observed. "It simply has the responsibility to bring together those who do, and out of it can come information that can create options for an executive to make public policy decisions."[18] Over two hundred political and environmental leaders attended, convinced that the governor's support and public interest were such that environmental reform had its best chance of success in the twentieth century. Polls showed that 74 percent of Floridians endorsed the need for greater environmental protection in south Florida, where population growth threatened both the water supply and the fragile environment.[19] Environmental reform was the one issue about which seniors supported a more activist state government and greater state funding. They had come to Florida because of its balmy weather and pristine beauty, and they did not want to lose their place in paradise to urban and suburban sprawl.

Proposals from the conference led to four important pieces of legislation in 1972. One was the Environmental Land and Water Management Act; a second was the Water Resources Act, which established water management districts in each region; the third was the Land Conservation Act, which created the borrowing program for environmentally endangered lands and recreation lands; and the fourth was a State Comprehensive Planning Act. In Askew's view, water was the crucial issue confronting the state and its future: "I believe that the availability of adequate water is the most important problem facing Florida environmentally and will continue to be for a good while, because of the uncertainty of the underwater aquifer," which was the principal source of drinking water in the state.[20] Despite his efforts to build political consensus around a water policy, he was ultimately unsuccessful, in part because heavy summer rains and occasional hurricanes led Floridians, especially those who had recently moved into the state, to believe that water was plentiful. It would take major droughts in the 1990s to persuade them otherwise.

Although Askew's environmental initiatives garnered support among many Floridians who worried about the state's future in light of its population growth, it also engendered opposition among some in the business community and particularly among developers. Residents of north Florida, meanwhile, were of two minds. Some wanted prosperity under any circumstances for the region, which had been largely bypassed by the development of south Florida. Others sought to preserve the area's environmental beauty and diversity. Askew was well aware that the Environmental Land and Water Management Act raised concerns that it would "inhibit growth."[21] And he and his administration had to wrestle with charges of being antibusiness throughout his eight years in office because of the adoption of the corporate income tax and legislation dealing with environmentally endangered lands.

The two central components of the Environmental Land and Water Management Act aimed at protecting areas of critical state concern and managing the developments of regional impact. Opposition from farm groups and developers almost derailed the proposals. Jim Williams, who was a state senator and then later became Askew's lieutenant governor in his second term, played a key role in working out a compromise with farmers that ensured passage. Askew noted: "We accepted a provision in that act that said we will not use the process . . . to declare an area of critical state concern unless or until funds are provided to assure availability of money for any type of inverse condemnation. Specifically it was tied to the Land Conservation Act that was going to allow us to borrow the money to purchase environmentally endangered lands." Farmers and homeowners were especially concerned that their land would be seized by the state without appropriate compensation. But voters ultimately sided with their governor, and in November 1972 they approved the allocation of such funds and the selling of bonds to acquire recreation space, which made possible the purchase of the Big Cypress Swamp and the acquisition of endangered lands, beach and greenbelt areas, and critical water properties. The benefits to the state's environment were considerable, but there remained an abiding concern among small-home owners that big government showed them little regard when using eminent domain to confiscate their property. Republicans eventually capitalized on this issue, portraying its use as a major example of the evils of big government.

Askew's environmental efforts won broad support among seniors and wealthy Floridians, who recognized the threat that massive growth posed to the natural beauty and fragility of the state. The governor did less well in convincing working and middle classes of their importance, principally because they were caught up in making a living and in meeting the needs of their families. They generally supported Askew because they trusted him to do the right thing for them and their state.

Askew, Race, and Busing

Although Askew's tax and environmental initiatives generated considerable controversy, they paled next to his decision to promote racial equality and opportunity. Taking office in the midst of the school busing crisis in Florida, Askew pledged in his inaugural, "Equal rights for all our people, rural as well as urban, black as well as white."[22] Askew and Lawton Chiles represented a new generation of New South politicians—including, most notably, several newly elected governors: Arkansas's Dale Bumpers, South Carolina's John West, and Georgia's Jimmy Carter, all of whom embraced racial justice.

According to the historian Randy Sanders, the election in 1970 of a group of moderate southern governors who defeated segregationist opponents marked a watershed in southern politics and "reflected the electorate's newfound attitude of racial moderation" as a result of the Voting Rights Act of 1965 and the subsequent registration of thousands of African-American voters.[23] This group of governors also shared many similar characteristics, which Sanders argues helped them succeed in their campaigns. Each hailed from a rural area, had modest beginnings, was active in his Protestant church, had a military background, and was well-versed in the politics of his state. At nearly the same time that Askew made his pledge to Florida's voters, Jimmy Carter declared at his inaugural in January 1971 that "the time for racial discrimination is over."[24] All championed the modernization of their states and regarded racial justice as a central component of this modernization process. They also recognized that busing to achieve racial balance in the public schools threatened their leadership, because so many white suburban voters resented it and Republicans manipulated the issue to their political advantage. Although all would have preferred to avoid the issue, they recognized early on in their administrations that busing and the opposition to it could not be avoided, and they would be best served by confronting the issue directly.

In August 1971, halfway through his first term in office, Askew received a petition with forty thousand signatures on it, asking that he urge the U.S. Congress to call a constitutional convention to prohibit busing as a means of achieving racial balance in the public schools. Several of the governor's close aides recommended that he ignore the petition because busing had so polarized Floridians. But they also knew Askew and recognized that he would not avoid a matter of this importance. Within a week, the governor told a summer graduating class at the University of Florida that busing was "an artificial and inadequate instrument of change. Nobody really wants it—not you, not me, not the people, not the school board, not even the courts." He reminded students, faculty, and parents, however, that it was necessary because the nation had failed to resolve the issue of discrimination and segregation. Pausing, the governor then added, "The law demands, and rightly so, that we put an end to segregation in our society," and busing in his view was one tool for achieving this goal.[25] Without some busing, Askew felt certain that schools in Florida would never be integrated because of housing patterns in the state, and that white and black students would not come to know one another on an equal footing.

Askew's address was made more remarkable by events elsewhere in Florida and in the South, where George Wallace, governor of Alabama, had launched his 1972 presidential campaign with a pledge to take the Democratic Party back from the "intellectual snobs who feel that big government should control the lives of American citizens from the cradle to the grave."[26] The fiery Alabama governor promised a large, boisterous crowd in Jacksonville that he would run for president if President Richard Nixon did not issue an executive order banning busing. At literally the same time, former Governor Kirk attempted to reactivate his political career by leading a more moderate Parents Against Forced Busing group in Pinellas County—he would later become national chairman of the organization. In contrast to Wallace and Kirk, Askew would have none of it, bluntly refusing to take the politically popular stance on busing. He would soon find himself alone among white political leaders in Florida.[27]

In February 1972, the Florida Legislature met in special session to take up the busing issue. In many cities throughout the nation from Charlotte to Boston, court-ordered busing had been met with protests and violence by whites. Northern residents, many of whom had condemned segregation policies in the South, fought the use of busing as vigorously as any southern community. No northern city struggled with busing more than Boston, where the use of busing to integrate the public schools of South Boston in the early and mid-1970s came to symbolize the nation's ongoing struggle with its racial heritage. The school busing crisis also gave added credence to complaints from poor whites that they had become the guinea pigs for this racial experiment by judges and decision makers who lived elsewhere and whose children would remain unaffected by their decision. The anger of poor whites spilled over into the streets, where they mimicked the actions of civil rights leaders, using the one resource they had at their disposal, their physical presence, to make their sentiments heard.[28]

In meetings with local voters, legislators in the state encountered opposition among working-class and middle-class whites to school busing. In cities like Orlando, Tampa, and Jacksonville, such groups feared the deterioration of their schools and the education of their children if busing was forced upon neighborhood schools. Middle-class whites and newcomers who had relocated to the suburbs in Orlando, Tampa, and Jacksonville were critical of busing, contending that it threatened to disrupt the education of their children and, by inference, their quality of life. Responding to voter anger, legislators endorsed a straw-vote measure on busing to be included on the presidential primary ballot on March 14. The measure asked Floridians if they supported a constitutional prohibition against forced busing.

After considerable deliberation with staff about what to do with this proposal, Askew concluded that legislators would override a gubernatorial veto, and that his only option was to seek an alternative to their proposed straw ballot. Askew told legislators that he would agree to place the measure on the ballot, but only if the legislature agreed to drop the adjective "forced" and accepted a companion referendum asking voters if they endorsed a quality education for all children and opposed a return to a dual system of public schools. Aides were understandably concerned that voters might decide to support the straw ballot and oppose the governor's companion referendum, handing him a double defeat and undermining his leadership and his legislative agenda.

In Askew's mind, however, there was no hesitation: "[There were many citizens and parents who were] not racially motivated, [and who] otherwise had been trying to improve the situation in terms of race in their communities. Because of their [genuine] concern for the disruption to their child, I did not want it to be assumed that [they and] every person who voted against busing was a racist. Bear in mind, there were enough people against it who were racist, but in my opinion, the vast majority of people who fought busing, really were not [necessarily] racially motivated." His aim was "to give them an opportunity of another vote, but I also wanted to challenge them to think about [the second vote] before they made up their mind on the first vote."[29]

Much like his political mentor and hero LeRoy Collins, Askew later remarked: "I felt my job was to help people overcome their fears and make sure that in no way was I going to do like a lot of political figures have done, and just exploit the fear. That was extremely important to me in my own conscience and heart, why I had to do what I did."[30] Askew also understood, however, that labeling all working- and middle-class whites as racists was grossly inaccurate and unwise, and that the national Democratic Party had gotten itself on the wrong side of this issue. Giving whites an opportunity to join with him in supporting a quality education for all children and opposing a return to a dual system of public schools would, he felt, help them and the state get beyond the issue of school integration and, perhaps, race—once and for all.

Much was at stake in this referendum, for both Askew and the state Democratic Party. Even more so than the battle over the corporate income tax, this issue threatened not only the governor's leadership but also the Democratic leadership of the state because of the extent of white concerns about busing. Askew recognized the issues at stake but was determined to convince voters that the state should not go backward and retreat from the racial progress that helped to modernize Florida. He looked to religious leaders to join him in supporting his companion referendum and convinced them to do so. He also raised $32,000 in private funds and launched his campaign at the state fair in Orlando, which was attended by many working- and middle-class whites. Drawing a distinction between the legislative referendum and his referendum, Askew reiterated his personal dislike of busing, but added that through "busing and other methods, we've made real progress in dismantling a dual system of public schools in Florida." He urged listeners not to take the state backward and jeopardize the progress Florida had made, saying, "It's time we told the rest of the nation that we aren't caught up in the mania to stop busing at any cost . . . , that we know the real issues when we see them, and that we no longer will be fooled, frightened, and divided against ourselves." Most importantly, he sought to counter the arguments of Alabama Governor George Wallace and to educate Floridians about the ways in which race had been used in the past and continued to be used to mask problems that affected both whites and blacks, noting that racial issues had long been used to obscure important "economic and environmental problems of the people, both black and white."[31]

Askew's appeal to "the better angels" of Florida voters and his missionary zeal had its effect. Floridians seemed to welcome the governor's efforts and his pledge to lead them out of the racist thicket that had ensnared the state and region for so long. Many Cracker elements also appreciated the governor's statement that he, too, did not favor busing and that he refrained from lecturing them about their past racist actions. The results of the straw ballots in March revealed that Floridians favored the referendum on equal opportunity for all children regardless of race, color, or creed by a margin of 4 to 1. They also approved the Wallace referendum on busing, however, by a margin of 3 to 1.[32] Askew and his aides chose to highlight the vote on equal opportunity for all children and praised its significance. Segregationists, not surprisingly, emphasized the vote against busing.

So what did the two votes mean? Wallace supporters in Florida argued that the vote on busing was the substantive and important one, and Wallace took it as evidence of support for his campaign against busing. A negative vote in Florida would likely have derailed his effort. Wallace told reporters he had the vote he needed and headed north to carry his battle to Congress and northern voters. Many scholars have argued, however, that the vote on busing was not just about race, that many white voters wanted to preserve neighborhood schools so that their children could walk to school and so that this geographic intimacy would allow them to be involved in their children's education. The scholarly argument had some merit, but Wallace had the media's attention and the enthusiasm of white voters who felt they and their children were being made victims of the campaign for racial integration. It was their children, they noted, who were being bused to integrated schools, not the children of the well-to-do or even of the middle class. The anger over busing and the way in which busing was being implemented would find fertile soil among working-class whites in many parts of the nation.[33]

While the results represented only a partial victory for Askew, he adroitly emphasized the results of the straw ballot on equal opportunity for children and praised Floridians for their commitment to a quality education for all children. By emphasizing this vote, Askew was also making a statement to voters and the nation about where Florida stood in the 1970s. No longer was it just another southern state dedicated to preserving the racial values of the past. Florida had changed, and, Askew contended, Floridians had put race behind them. The state was now free to pursue a future that would benefit all Floridians, Askew argued, and that would allow the state to take up its political, economic, and social ambitions no longer encumbered by racism and segregation. The governor had overstated his case, but it made for great public relations, and his masterful leadership inspired black citizens and offered them the promise of a better day.

Askew did not hesitate to deliver on his promise to them. Shortly after taking office, the governor had his aides conduct an employee survey. Among other things, the survey revealed that the overwhelming number of black employees in state government held subordinate positions, and that more than 89 percent received salaries from the state that were below the poverty level. To demonstrate to Floridians that he was serious about the future he envisioned for all residents, he issued an executive order establishing an affirmative action plan to correct the underrepresentation of black employees in state government and ordered annual reports to indicate the record of progress by the state in diversifying employment. Askew then appointed Justice Joseph Woodrow Hatchett to the state Supreme Court, the first African American to hold this position in the twentieth century; James Gardener, the first African American to sit on the state Board of Regents, which oversaw higher education in Florida; and Athaelie Range as secretary of community affairs. The first state progress report published in 1972 disclosed that the number of black employees had doubled, that salaries had improved significantly, and that black citizens had begun serving in prominent state positions. Askew explained to black leaders and reporters his purpose in appointing black citizens to higher office: "I want to, in some specific ways, give some hope to young black people that the establishment is not inherently hypocritical."[34]

Why had Askew become such a strong advocate for an integrated society and, along with Governor Jimmy Carter of Georgia, the leading spokesman for a New South? At first glance, Askew's background suggested he should exhibit many of the same racial biases as others from his region.

Although born and initially reared in Oklahoma, he had grown up in a poor white household in Pensacola at the western end of Florida's Panhandle, where many people from Alabama had settled and where racial biases ran strong. Many of the leading spokesmen for the Pork Chop delegation in the state legislature came from this region. Moreover, Askew's family was quite poor, and many such families embraced racial stereotypes as a way to compensate for their own lowly standing in society. But Askew's mother instilled in her children a fundamental belief in the inherent value of all people, no matter their station in life. His mother never complained about her lot in life, nor did she seek to blame others or resort to racial epithets to describe fellow workers or black residents of the community. Her spirit and his family's economic situation combined with strong religious values that Askew acquired in the Presbyterian Church, much like those Jimmy Carter developed in the Baptist Church, convinced him that people should be judged on the content of their character, not on the basis of skin color or religion.

As Askew grew up in Pensacola, his closest friends were two Jewish brothers, David and Fred Levin. It did not matter to him that he was Irish Presbyterian and they were Jewish. His subsequent military experience in a desegregated army and air force and his education at Florida State University and the University of Florida only further cemented his racial values. As student body president at FSU, he initiated meetings with black student leaders at FAMU and pursued efforts to open FSU to greater student diversity. No less important were his first two years in the Florida House of Representatives as he watched, listened, and supported Collins's efforts to persuade Floridians that racial discrimination and racial violence were fundamentally wrong. Collins's courage reminded Askew of his mother's struggle against very difficult odds and of the persistence of both, even when it would have been easier to give in to racism. Askew remained dedicated to the memory of his mother and of LeRoy Collins when it came to addressing school integration, busing, and discrimination against black Floridians.

Askew's commitment to the public trust persuaded him to sponsor a constitutional amendment requiring full financial disclosure for all public officials. In part because of his own family background but also because of his political experience, Askew felt that government belonged to the people and that this relationship was jeopardized by special interests. For much of the previous decade, the state's developers and leading business-men had heavily influenced the governorships of Bryant, Burns, and Kirk and many in the legislature. Moreover, the cost of campaigning for pub-lic office in Florida had escalated to such a degree that it threatened the integrity of the political process and the ability of the average citizen to shape the political dialogue, in Askew's view. He contended that there was no such thing as shining too much light on government and that the press served as an important counterbalance to shady legislative efforts to reward major supporters. Askew recalled, "I would sometimes when Claude Kirk was governor go down on a Tuesday morning while the leg-islature was in session, to the old Ramada Inn, and Associated Industries would have breakfast for everybody [the legislators], and the cabinet used to literally go down there for breakfast every Tuesday morning and decide everything they were going to do that day."[35] It was during the course of his campaign for a financial disclosure amendment that opponents began re-ferring to him derisively as "Reubin the Good." But voters liked what they saw in their governor, and the good government and populist aspects of his proposed amendment garnered widespread support in Florida. When several legislators tried to sabotage the amendment, Askew and his allies expanded it to place all legislative meetings as well as legislative donations in the "sunshine."[36]

The proposal for full financial disclosure spoke to a strong streak of antigovernmentalism in Florida. Many new residents to the state brought with them a basic dissatisfaction with government spending and govern-ment intrusion from their home states, and they joined ranks with small-town and rural conservatives who complained about government interfer-ence in their lives and the increased taxes they were required to pay. The populist nature of Askew's political leadership and his commitment to transparent government appealed to their skepticism about government.

Philosophically, Askew differed with those who questioned the es-sential value of government. He believed, for example, that government had an obligation to protect the poor and ensure fairness in the political and economic sectors as well as to foster the health and well-being of the poor. Askew thus allowed state workers, many of whom came from mod-est backgrounds and had low salaries, to organize so that their interests could be represented to the legislature and state administrators. He also expanded and enhanced public services to the poor and to children.[37]

Askew's sense of injustice emerged from his roots, and it fueled his determination to make government the instrument of the people. Askew never doubted the special nature of American society, where a child could rise from humble beginnings and, as in his case, obtain a college degree and become governor of the state. And he was determined to preserve these opportunities and freedoms for other children. Opponents might belittle Askew's commitment to good government, but what they failed to see or understand was his determination to preserve what was fundamentally important to the success of the nation—and that being an open, free, democratic process enabled Floridians to make measured decisions about the state's future.

Askew's political philosophy infused all aspects of state government including the entire area of state taxation, which he felt was inherently unfair to the poor and middle class. Askew did not split hairs about his dislike of the state's reliance on a sales tax and the way in which it spared the rich and burdened the poor. In addition to championing the corporate tax, he reached out to seniors by supporting an increase in the homeowners' homestead exemption from $5,000 to $10,000 for the elderly and the disabled, repealed consumer taxes on household utilities and apartment rentals, which had hurt the poor profoundly, and rolled back school taxes by two mills. The latter, while understandable, probably had a deleterious effect because of the tremendous increase in school-age children throughout the 1970s and the pressure for additional schools and teachers. Even rural voters and poor urban voters, who had resented his support of racial reform, appreciated his commitment to fairness, openness, and integrity in government. Askew's political foes acknowledged the governor's extraordinary standing with the people. As one commented, "He has established a kind of morality in office that causes people to have faith."[38]

The governor's broad-based appeal facilitated the Democratic Party's resurgence among working-class and middle-class voters in statewide elections in Florida. Although much of Askew's appeal was personal, he strengthened the party in the process by attracting new candidates to political office and by placing the party behind government reform and integrity in office. Republican gains in Florida came to a standstill during Askew's governorship, as state office after office went to Democratic candidates. And Democratic representation in the legislature, in fact, grew during his tenure, so that by the middle of his second term in office Democrats had once again obtained large majorities in both houses: the Senate had thirty Democrats and only nine Republicans, and the House had ninety-two Democrats and twenty-eight Republicans. Black and white voters stood together in support of Askew and his party, and this coalition impeded Republican ambitions.

By 1974 and his campaign for reelection, Askew had become a nationally prominent figure. Together with Georgia's Jimmy Carter and Arkansas's Dale Bumpers, Askew became a favorite of the national press for his leadership of a South that embraced racial reform, modernization, and integrity in government. Askew, in particular, became the subject of much political speculation because of the increasing importance of Florida nationally and its prominence as both a southern and Sun Belt state. His decision to seek reelection and his growing national reputation were significant advantages to the state Democratic Party. During an era in which Republican President Richard Nixon resigned in disgrace as did his vice president, Spiro Agnew, and in which many other politicians were under public scrutiny for accepting gifts from special interests, "Reubin the Good" looked mighty good to Floridians.

Adding to Askew's reputation as a people's governor was his decision to limit contributions to his reelection campaign to $100. As he himself noted, he could not have done this and won the gubernatorial election of 1970 when he was a virtual unknown. But in 1974, his state and national standing made him an overwhelming favorite to be reelected, and he enjoyed enormous name recognition in the state. When Askew told his aides that he wanted to limit campaign contributions, they asked what the limit would be. At this point, Floridians could contribute $3,000 per person or corporation. "They said, 'do you want to limit it to $1,000?' I said, 'No.' '$500?' 'No, I want to limit it to $100.' And I tell you what, they were upset. They thought I was putting them in a position where they were going to have to work a lot harder. But then, all of a sudden, you could almost see a light come on, with the whole group. I think Fred Levin was the first one to think about it. . . . Then he said, 'You know, maybe it is not such a bad idea.'"[39]

Despite Askew's standing within the party, he faced two intriguing challengers in the 1974 gubernatorial primary. His former lieutenant governor, Tom Adams, who had been privately censured by Askew for his failure to level with him about his debts, announced his candidacy. Adams would have been a formidable opponent for Askew in 1970, but by 1974 his image problems and Askew's popularity made Adams unelectable. Also seeking the nomination was Ben Hill Griffin Jr., who had been Askew's principal spokesperson in the campaign for corporate tax reform. Griffin wanted to be governor, and despite his close relationship with Askew, he did not want to wait another four years. Although Griffin was an extraordinarily successful entrepreneur in Florida, he was fairly naïve about state politics, as was evident by his selection of his wife to be his lieutenant governor. Despite their opposition and his $100 limit on campaign contributions, Askew won easily in the first primary with nearly 69 percent of the vote.[40]

Republicans selected Jerry Thomas, who had been a Democrat until quite recently and had served as Democratic Senate president, to oppose Askew. Thomas's candidacy reflected a persistent weakness of the Republican Party during this period as it remained heavily dependent on Democrats who shifted party affiliation, like Thomas, for major state offices. There were Democrats, of course, who had always preferred the conservative values of the Republican Party but had seen it as a nonstarter to winning political office in Florida (and in the South generally) until the mid-1960s. Thomas had been one of those. During the course of his campaign, Thomas claimed he had abandoned the Democratic Party because of the liberal leadership of Reubin Askew. Accusing Askew of being pro-busing, antibusiness, and a radical environmentalist, Thomas said the governor did not represent the values of Floridians. Thomas's indictment of Askew as a liberal reflected a common theme that ran through Republican campaigns during this era.

The use of the term *liberal* by Republicans to attack Democratic opponents had grown increasingly common and was meant to connote the role Democratic liberalism played in the establishment of excessive and intrusive government and in the moral decay of the 1960s. Charges of being liberal or by implication out of touch with civil behavior and appropriate American values placed Democrats on the defensive in Florida and elsewhere. In state and national elections in the 1970s and beyond, Democrats had to defend themselves repeatedly against charges that they were liberal and that their programs fostered policies inimical to the nation's political traditions.[41]

Thomas's accusations that Askew was a liberal Democrat, however, boomeranged on him. The governor's personal popularity and support for his programs transcended Thomas's accusation. In fact, only Askew's record on race relations and on transparent government could be labeled liberal, and the public overwhelmingly supported the latter. Askew chose to run on his record and generally ignored Thomas. The governor also published his financial and income tax records and then chided Thomas when he refused to release his. Although television was still in its early stages as a campaign medium in state races, the governor opted to use it to get his message out to voters. Even Askew guffawed about the unsophisticated nature of his campaign advertisements: "It helped me enormously, but bear in mind, Arthur Gray just set me behind the camera and I talked. You will see that almost all my commercials are just me speaking."[42] Askew defeated Thomas in a landslide, garnering 61 percent of the vote, and he won support among all ethnic and racial groups as well as among working-class, middle- and upper-class whites.

Askew completed his eight years as governor in 1979 and left office as the most popular governor in Florida history. Many voters assumed he would continue to play a major role in state politics for a long time to come, and Askew subsequently served as U.S. trade ambassador under President Jimmy Carter; ran a half-hearted and ineffective campaign for president in 1980; and launched an abortive U.S. senatorial campaign in 1984 before withdrawing from the race and then from the political spotlight altogether. His decision about the 1984 senatorial campaign stunned supporters and opponents alike, but Askew detested asking "special interests" for money to run his campaign and abhorred the fact that such campaigns had gotten so expensive. Rather than accept the system as it was, he turned away from it completely. Although his political career had effectively ended in 1978, no prominent candidate would run for the governorship in the next two decades without referring to Askew's legacy. Moreover, all subsequent Democrats through 2000 were influenced by his leadership style and his programs, and many pursued political office because they had been motivated to do so by his example.

As Askew prepared to step down as governor, the Democratic Party sought to capitalize on his popularity with voters and his success in attracting middle-class voters, but Republicans had not been sitting idly by as they had in the past. The nucleus of the party, while still located in southwest Florida in the rapidly expanding cities and suburbs of Hillsborough and Pinellas Counties, was steadily expanding along the I-4 corridor from Tampa to Orlando and along the southwest coast from Sarasota to Naples—some of the fastest-growing areas in the state. In such places, midwestern Republicans were joined politically by northerners who had relocated for job and business opportunities. Concern about stagflation and the slumping economy of the 1970s and rising crime rates helped the Republican Party strengthen its relationship with these voters.

Race was a minor factor at best in the Republican advances in Florida. The typical Republican voter in 1970 was not an alienated southerner, but a transplanted Ohioan, Michigander, or Minnesotan who found in Florida the freedom to register as a Republican or whose family had been Republican for several generations. Most of these newcomers were not motivated by school integration and busing. They moved to the suburbs or certain areas of cities because of land values; the price and quality of housing; the quality of schools, if they had children; and the lower crime rate. Tradition, taxes, and crime were often the most important issues in their decision to become Republicans.

State Republicans pursued these issues with some success. Their difficulty was that on most of these issues they were virtually indistinguishable from the state Democratic Party. Statewide elections typically came down to the quality and personality of candidates, and in the immediate wake of the Askew administration, most voters sided with the Democrats. But Florida voters—like Democrats throughout the region and in the Sun Belt—were uneasy with the national Democratic Party. Key elements within the national party did not reflect their stance on women's rights, abortion, taxes, crime, and the role and scope of government. So while most middle-class whites and Florida's retirees were content with the state party, they experienced dyspepsia when thinking about or discussing the national party. That anxiety had not led them to abandon the state Democratic Party just yet, but it remained a constant threat to the party's future. For the time being, Askew and his fellow Democrats retained their following with voters, but would the party continue to do so in the 1980s?

4

An Era of Political Transition

Askew's legacy to the Democratic Party had been vital, but he hedged when it came to establishing a much-needed party structure for the future. As with his predecessors, Askew recognized the party needed a stronger organizational base, but he hesitated to be the one to establish it because the process would have led to intense political infighting among those who feared that tighter party control over the nomination process would limit their political ambitions. Don Pride, Askew's press secretary, observed that it was very difficult, if not impossible, to impose order on a primary process that had historically been based on a candidate "running his own campaign" and constructing "his own [political organization] outside the party structure." Such divisive campaigns also opened up opportunities for the Republican Party, because, as Pride recognized, they often turned some segment of the party's constituency against the eventual nominee.[1]

While Democrats refrained from organizing, Republicans remained much better organized and more disciplined, with party regulars acknowledging that it was the only way to compete effectively for political office against such a dominant Democratic Party. Similarly, the Republican ideology was also more consistent with candidates embracing its emphasis on low taxes, limited government, economic development, social stability, patriotism, and traditional cultural values.

By contrast, the Democratic Party often divided ideologically with progressive forces, like many who supported Askew, endorsing an activist government to protect the environment, improve the quality of life for Floridians, address critical areas of need, and foster economic development. Most conservative Democrats opposed busing and advocated limited government, low taxes, and traditional cultural values. The ideological differences were magnified in party primaries when strong candidates from separate regions of the state contested for the governorship. These divisive primaries repeatedly undermined party unity, heightened internal ideological differences, divided constituents, and created opportunities for the Republican Party.

Campaign of 1978

In 1978, the Democratic primary once again became a free-for-all contest with seven candidates, including four major figures in the party, seeking the gubernatorial nomination. They included Lt. Governor Jim Williams, Attorney General Robert Shevin, State Senator Bob Graham from Dade County, and State Senator Betty Castor from Hillsborough County. As long as prominent figures like Williams, Shevin, Graham, and Castor felt that victory in the Democratic primary ensured victory in the general election, multiple candidates would continue to enter the primary, undercutting support for a strong party structure. By contrast, Republicans fielded only two candidates for their party's gubernatorial nomination—Jack Eckerd, a wealthy drugstore magnate, and Lou Frey Jr., Republican congressman from central Florida.

Most experts predicted that Williams and Shevin would finish one-two in the first Democratic primary and face one another in the runoff. But Williams, who was from Ocala, was not well known in the state despite having served as Askew's lieutenant governor for the previous four years. With the party's strength concentrated in the populated southeastern section of the state, Williams was not guaranteed a place in the runoff. When he ran an uninspiring, low-key campaign that some said reflected his personality, he had minimal success in mobilizing Askew's supporters. Bob Graham, the young state senator from Miami, took a page from Askew's campaign book in 1970, with a goal of mobilizing enough support to finish second in the primary and then building on the first primary to capture the runoff. Graham hired a relatively unknown national political consultant, Bob Squier, as his media adviser. (Squier subsequently became a leading consultant for the national Democratic Party.) It was Squier who helped Graham develop the most effective media campaign Florida had seen in the twentieth century.

Prior to the gubernatorial campaign, Graham had gained a reputation in the legislature for being progressive and thoughtful on a host of educational, environmental, and social issues. Certainly by comparison with most Democrats and Republicans in Florida, Graham was to the left of center. The fact that he was a Harvard graduate and half-brother to Phil Graham, the publisher of the *Washington Post* who had died in the early 1960s, also contributed to his political reputation. While his father had been a well-regarded state senator and still owned a cattle ranch in northern Dade County, Bob Graham was much less well known than Bob Shevin in southeast Florida. The challenge facing Graham's campaign was to elevate his name recognition statewide in a short period of time. Squier encouraged Graham to feature his "Workdays" program, which Graham had started in 1974 as a way to introduce himself to voters statewide. Through that program, Graham took on a variety of jobs that ranged from teaching in a public school classroom to unloading ships to working in a sawmill. The related political advertisements helped enormously in connecting him with working-class and middle-class Floridians. At the outset of the campaign, Jim Apthorp, Askew's press secretary, who had seen an early tape of Graham's ads, told Askew, "Bob Graham is going to be the next governor." "Is that right?" Askew responded; he recalled that Apthorp said, "Yes, I have just seen his commercials and they just blow you away, they are so good." As Askew noted: "Beating Bob Shevin was no small task. Bob Shevin already had tremendous support throughout the state, but Graham just ran an unbelievable campaign." It was "the most effective media campaign I have ever seen," recalled Askew.[2]

The Workdays media campaign could well have backfired on Graham if it had been a political gimmick, but those who worked alongside Graham praised his grit and his character and told reporters they would vote for him. Shevin's campaign aides tried to focus voters on his approach to the critical issues facing the state, where they felt Shevin was much the superior candidate. But Florida had become such a large state and was growing so dramatically that personality repeatedly trumped issues in political campaigns. By throwing the media spotlight on Graham as a regular, down-to-earth fellow who valued working-class Floridians, the Workdays program introduced him to voters around the state who would not have known him otherwise. Shevin, a politician of considerable ability and accomplishment, ran a hard-hitting campaign against Graham, but his efforts struck many as mean-spirited. The scowl on Shevin's face over the turn of events in the campaign did not help his appeal to voters and stood in sharp contrast to the confident, baby-faced good looks of Graham. Together with his Workdays program, Graham's pledge to increase state support for public schools, to strengthen economic development, and to protect the environment resonated with Democratic voters and helped him secure their support.[3]

If voters in the northern reaches of the state had been asked about their preference prior to the campaign, few would have selected Graham. Television proved critical to the outcome, and the sophistication of Graham's campaign ads set a new standard. What was also significant, however, was the way in which Graham replicated Askew's campaign. Like Askew, Graham had to defeat Williams to get into a runoff against the heavily favored Shevin. He also had to establish a relationship with Democratic voters in the first primary to have a chance in the second one. Moreover, like Askew, he had to use momentum from the first primary and television to overtake Shevin in the runoff. But Graham had a substantial hole to climb out of—he trailed Shevin by more than one hundred thousand votes as they entered the second primary. By contrast, Askew had trailed Faircloth by forty thousand votes as they headed into the second primary. Television made it possible for Graham to overtake Shevin. Askew himself observed that "when Graham ran, it [television] really had come of age," and Graham had taken it to a new level in political campaigning. Indeed, it is very unlikely that Graham would have defeated Shevin without the benefit of television. In the largest political turnaround in modern Florida political history, Graham defeated Shevin with 482,535 votes to 418,636.[4]

The general election in 1978 pitted Graham against pharmaceutical magnate Jack Eckerd. Republicans had fielded a strong candidate in Eckerd, who had been long prominent in state and national Republican circles. Although Eckerd lacked political experience, he made up for it in name recognition and in the acknowledged success of his business. He also ran a very effective campaign, highlighting the fundamental differences between himself and Graham on taxes, economic development, and the role of state government. But Graham's media campaign had created a political juggernaut, and with the endorsement of his Democratic opponents, Graham came into the general election campaign with enormous momentum from the Democratic primaries. Although he was not a particularly effective public speaker, Graham could work a crowd: he liked to meet and greet people after he spoke, was very focused in listening to people who talked to him, and had an extraordinary memory for names. Eckerd failed to fragment the Democratic coalition that Askew had reconstructed and attract support in north Florida, where voters saw him as little more than a highly successful corporate executive. Graham's Workdays sold Floridians on his candidacy, and he captured almost every county in north Florida and combined that with strong voter support in southeast Florida. Eckerd captured over 1 million votes, but he still lost to Graham by nearly three hundred thousand votes.[5]

Graham's victory following on the heels of Askew's governorship conveyed the strength of the Democratic Party in Florida. With the likes of LeRoy Collins, Askew, Chiles, and now Graham, the party continued to attract both talented people and new voters and won a large following among independents for the quality and integrity of their leadership. The reputation of the party's leadership carried over to the cabinet and the legislative branch, where there was great depth, with high-quality people running for and holding state office.

The Strengthening of the State Republican Party

Despite the strengths of the Democratic Party and the quality of its leadership, state Republicans, with considerable assistance from the National Republican Party, had started recruiting their own array of talented young politicians. The national party regarded Florida and the South generally as fertile ground for its expansion. While the likes of Eckerd and Cramer laid the foundation for the party's future and were in turn joined by Democrats who had flipped to the Republican Party, the future rested with young people, many of whom came to the party through Republican clubs on college and university campuses.

Despite a third consecutive loss to Democrats in the governor's race in 1978, Florida Republicans began drawing on the talents of these young people and fielding stronger and more competitive candidates at the local and state level in the late 1970s. Republicans picked up two seats in the state Senate and three seats in the Florida House in 1978, and while it remained in the distinct minority in both houses, the party held 11 of the 40 seats in the Senate and 31 of the 120 seats in the House. In 1980, it would pick up 2 more seats in the Senate and 8 more in the House, with most of the gains occurring in the growing regions of central and southwest Florida. Much of this was occurring below the political radar screen, but Democrats were well aware of the gains made by Republicans at the grassroots level, and they no longer casually dismissed or ignored the party or its candidates.[6]

Aiding the Republican Party's growth were three key developments: the gradual shift of natives/Crackers to the Republican Party; the rapid population growth of the central and southwestern regions of Florida; and the shift of Cuban voters to the Republican Party. Only a long heritage of loyalty to the Democratic Party built on racial traditions kept natives/Crackers from north Florida in the party, but those historic ties were steadily eroding in the post–civil rights era. That relationship deteriorated further as a result of the massive social unrest of the late 1960s and a declining economy. Only the failings of the Nixon and Kirk administrations and the leadership of Askew kept this native/Cracker constituency from bolting the Democratic Party permanently. But ideologically they shared more in common with state Republicans than with Democrats, and it appeared only a matter of time before they acknowledged this and switched parties.

Increasing crime, deteriorating schools, and rising property taxes in Florida's cities in the 1970s and 1980s drove more and more middle-class white residents into the suburbs, where they looked increasingly to the Republican Party to address these problems. As newcomers arrived in growing numbers in the last three decades of the twentieth century, real estate agents advised them to locate in certain sections of the cities or in suburbs where there were good schools and less crime. By the 1980s and 1990s, newcomers were increasingly inclined to live in Florida's suburbs and exurban areas, where they could acquire more property for their money than in exclusive communities in cities; where commuting was initially easy and cheap; and where schools were newer and better than those in most cities. By 1990, approximately half of Floridians lived in unincorporated areas of the state. In Orlando, for example, in the 1970s black residents moved steadily into Pine Hills, and by the late 1970s whites began leaving because of increased crime and the community's growing reputation as "Crime Hills." In Jacksonville, whites struggled to preserve neighborhoods such as Avondale, but school busing made it difficult, and the growth of suburban neighborhoods, even with unified government

Party Affiliation in the Florida Legislature

	House of Representatives			Senate		
Year	D	I	R	D	I	R
1945	95		0	38		0
1947	94		1	38		0
1949	94		1	38		0
1951	94		1	38		0
1953	94		1	37		1
1955	89		6	37		1
1957	89		6	37		1
1959	89		6	37		1
1961	88		7	37		1
1963	109		16	43		2
1965	102		10	42		2
1967	80		39	28		20
1969	77		42	32		16
1971	81		38	33		15
1973	77	1	43	25		14
1975	86	1	34	30		9
1977	92	1	28	30		9
1979	89		31	29		11
1981	81		39	27		13
1983	84		36	32		8
1985	76		44	31		9
1987	75		45	31		9
1989	73		47	23		17
1991	73/74*		47/46*	20		20
1993	71		49	20		20
1995	63		57	18		22
1997	59		61	17		23
1999	47		73	15		25
2001	43		77	15		25
2003	39		81	14		26
2005	43		86	14		26
2007	41		78	14		26

Source: *The Florida Handbook* for the relevant years and the Online Florida House and Senate Web sites.
*Member changed party.

in Duval County, offered middle-class whites the opportunity to escape deteriorating integrated schools and urban social pathologies.

The writers Thomas and Mary Edsall contend that these middle-class voters gradually lost faith in the Democratic Party because of its failure to resolve their concerns about crime, schools, and taxes, and thus were prepared to listen to overtures from the Republican Party.[7] Moreover, few newcomers to Florida were prepared psychologically for trouble in paradise. One woman told a *New York Times* reporter, "There's this sense that we've moved to this place where we can have our boat and our sunshine and ludicrously low taxes. . . . Nothing bad is supposed to happen to you in Florida. It's where the Magic Kingdom is and where you wish upon a star."[8] Nixon's appeal to this group that he termed the "silent majority" by calling for "law and order," a more limited role for the federal government, and opposition to busing to desegregate the suburbs attracted more and more middle-class suburban voters. In Florida, Republican policy on these issues and its support of low taxes played especially well among most newcomers who strongly resisted the high property taxes and income taxes they experienced in their native states.[9]

Third, the influx of Cubans throughout the 1960s and into the 1970s and the massive migration of midwesterners into the Sunshine State during this period also bolstered Republican aspirations. The party's strong anticommunist position resonated with Cuban émigrés, who believed it offered the greatest promise for toppling the Castro regime. Many midwesterners who located principally in the southwestern section of Florida and along the I-4 corridor had been registered Republicans in their native states, and they joined the Republican Party in Florida, with a particular passion for keeping taxes low.

Other smaller but no less significant developments in the state also favored the Republican Party. In the Panhandle, the large number of military personnel and increasing number of military retirees were drawn to the Republican Party's commitment to a strong military defense. Bob Graham observed that during the late 1970s and 1980s the number of military retirees in this area grew by one hundred per day.[10] In central and southwest Florida, many of the new residents were well-to-do retirees who generally favored the conservative economic and fiscal policies of the Republican Party. Ronald Reagan, a fellow senior, soothed their concerns about Republican fiscal policies by pledging his commitment to Social Security. Thus, despite the political achievements of Askew, Chiles, and Graham, social and demographic changes in the state advantaged the Republican Party, even as the Democratic Party continued to dominate state races. If Republicans could find the right leadership at both the federal and state levels, they posed a substantial threat to Democratic hegemony.

Graham's Governorship

The ability of the state Democratic Party to retain power was conditioned on its ability to control the governor's office, to continue to recruit new leaders, and to keep its distance from the national Democratic Party. With their control of all major statewide offices as well as the state legislature, they appeared well positioned to retain political leadership for the near future. Although Bob Graham did not inspire Floridians in the fashion of Reubin Askew, he governed the state well and remained very popular throughout his eight years in office. Most importantly, the economy stayed reasonably strong throughout his governorship, even when the nation and state suffered through a short but severe recession in the early 1980s. Growth drove the population and the economy, ensuring continued economic expansion in the state, even as it wrestled with the sharp decline in 1982–83.

Graham's popularity relied heavily on the state of the economy and his public relations, especially the continuation of his Workdays program throughout his governorship. He spent one day a month working alongside common folk in Florida. Providing Graham a chance to serve as firefighter, day laborer, pea picker, longshoremen, and so on, the Workdays "gave him the ability to talk to regular people and not just people from Harvard Law," according to his biographer, S. V. Date.[11]

But Graham struggled during his first four years to establish a leadership style and an identity that were distinct from those of Askew. His political enemies, led by Dempsey Barron, Democratic power broker in the Senate, compared him unfavorably to Askew and characterized him in his first years as "Governor Jell-O."[12] Much of the criticism resulted from Graham's struggle in his first term to cope with the massive influx of approximately 125,000 Cubans into the state in 1980, when Castro emptied his prisons and mental hospitals and sent a Cuban flotilla, referred to as the "Mariel Boatlift," to Miami. Florida found itself confronted with an enormous fiscal and social challenge, and neither Presidents Carter nor Reagan showed much interest in providing federal assistance to the state because of mounting federal deficits and rampant inflation. The state struggled financially to meet the challenges of these immigrants, and its social services as well as police and prison personnel were strained to the limit. Eventually the federal government appropriated $100 million to help the state, but Graham noted that state costs were four times that.[13]

After a rough beginning that placed his governorship on the defensive, Graham laid out his popularly known "E's Agenda"—economic development, education, and the environment.[14] As governor, Graham traveled widely to the Far East, Europe, and South America to recruit high-tech manufacturing, tourist investment, and new markets for Florida's agricultural goods. He sought to continue the modernization of Florida through such booster efforts and to keep Republicans from seizing these issues as their own. During his administration, the unemployment rate in Florida remained well below the national average, more than 1 million new jobs were created, and the state's business climate ranked first in the nation from 1981 through 1983.[15]

At the same time, Florida's educational system remained a huge challenge as business leaders and the state's Chamber of Commerce continued to express frustration at efforts to obtain employees who possessed the skills they required. Businesses that relocated from other sections of the nation frequently were told to bring their employees because not enough skilled workers were available in Florida, and the public school system was too weak to provide them. Graham pledged to move Florida schools into the top tier nationally. With the help of the Democrat-controlled legislature, he pumped several million additional dollars into public schools, lengthened the school day, reduced class sizes, and provided additional funding to strengthen the university system. Per-pupil spending rose from twenty-first to thirteenth in the nation in four years, a figure more consistent with the state's rapid growth and its rise to the fourth most populated state in the nation. Charlie Reed, one of Graham's chief aides and subsequently chancellor of the state university system, asserted that the governor "made the state believe in itself again."[16] In many ways, Graham's leadership continued Florida's modernization, offered natives and newcomers a promising future, and retained the confidence of state voters in its Democratic leadership. But the massive growth of the state and the escalating diversity of its population jeopardized educational reform and advancement at every turn.

Graham also committed his administration to protecting and strengthening Florida's fragile environment and, in doing so, gained a national reputation for his environmental stewardship. He launched a series of initiatives that included the Save Our Coasts, Save Our Rivers, and Save Our Everglades programs in 1981, 1982, and 1983. The legislature added the Water Quality Assurance Act in 1983 and the Warren S. Henderson Wetlands Protection Act in 1984. During Graham's two terms as governor, Florida brought more environmentally endangered lands into public ownership than any other state in the nation. This included acquisition of sensitive lands surrounding rivers, beaches, and barrier islands. The Save Our Everglades program, launched in 1983, was designed to restore the Everglades—what Marjory Stoneman Douglas had called America's "River of Grass"—and protect Florida's wetlands and its endangered species and their habitats. Graham also increased the state acquisition of property to preserve endangered lands and coastal sites and led the effort to block offshore oil drilling along Florida's coastline. Although Graham received regional recognition for his efforts to strengthen public education, it was his campaign to protect and enhance Florida's environment that established his national reputation and won him and the party the support of environmentalists in the state and of many senior voters who remained anxious about the state's environment in the face of Florida's massive population growth.[17]

In many ways, Graham was one of the ablest students of government to serve in the governor's office in Florida. He read widely in both the popular and academic literature, and he kept extensive notes on his activities as a legislator and governor. It was his habit of writing detailed notes to himself about daily activities that led critics to deride him as an "egghead" politician and, unfairly, as a governor and subsequently as a U.S. senator who understood the issues but could not make a decision. The following from his calendar was frequently cited as an example of Graham's compulsive behavior and his inability to see the big picture:

8:25 Awake at MLTH, dress in red golf shirt, khaki pants
8:50–9:15 kitchen—brew coffee—eat breakfast (Raisin Bran cereal)
. . .
9:45–10 sign mail, collect materials
Adele gives President Clinton Coke can . . .
10:45–10:55 Carriage cleaners—pick up Adele's dry cleaning
Food Spot to buy Herald, NYT . . .

11:15–11:20: MLTH kitchen—give Adele dry cleaning—
newspapers—
collect Coca Cola . . .
12:30–1:15: grill—eat lunch (cheeseburger)
1:15–1:20: walk, cart to 1st tee
1:20–6:10: play golf with President Clinton, Hugh Rodham, Aaron
Podhurst
(1:22—4:47:07:69) Start of the round and duration, to hundredth of
a second . . .
11:20–11:50 MLTH bedroom, bathroom
dress for sleep
watch XFL Chicago at LA[18]

In his defense, Graham observed that he began this practice of taking daily notes after watching his father do so at his cattle ranch when he was monitoring the feeding of cattle and their health. Graham claimed it helped him as a politician keep track of events and where he was when they occurred, and it also helped him remember whom he had met. "It's been a valuable part of my effort to be disciplined," he observed, "and to be responsive to the people by assuring that I have it written down, what they expect, and that I can check off that that request was responded to."[19] Although opponents belittled Graham's obsessiveness, their efforts had little effect on his political reputation and his standing among voters.

Few politicians were as keenly attuned to the needs of Floridians as Graham, and no single group interested him more than the growing numbers of retirees in the state. Observing their increasing numbers and prominence as voters, Graham sought them out in an effort to align them politically with the Democratic Party. In addition to his environmental programs, he expanded Community Care for the Elderly, a service program that enabled frail or infirm older citizens to remain in their homes. Many seniors and their families had expressed concern to him about fellow retirees being forced out of their homes as they aged and their health deteriorated. The loss of their natural surroundings, family members and professionals argued, often led to their rapid decline and death. Graham's program helped ensure self-sufficiency and independence for older Floridians and resulted in less than 2 percent of Florida's elderly residing in nursing homes, versus 5 percent nationally. Seniors never forgot Graham's efforts in this regard and in other ways, remaining politically loyal to him throughout his career.[20]

However one measures Graham's achievements in office, he proved to be a superb politician, one of the ablest Florida had ever seen. In 1984, he defeated Republican Skip Bafalis for reelection by an overwhelming margin of two to one. Bafalis captured only one large county in the state, Sarasota County, and lost all the others by decisive margins. The Republicans had yet to find a candidate in the post-Kirk era who could challenge his Democratic opponent, rally the Republican base, and mobilize natives, Blue Dogs, and independents. By the end of his second term in office, even the iconoclast Dempsey Barron observed of Graham's eight years in office, "He was a strong and decisive governor, sometimes almost hard-headed but he always did his homework."[21]

In the absence of a strong party organization, Graham developed his own organization through small groups of supporters in every city and town in Florida. He used these groups to keep informed about local issues, to supplement his Workdays program, and to strengthen his relationship with constituents. These groups also kept him informed about people in the community that he should know and developments in their lives, to which he might respond by telephone or letter. The governor never went anyplace in the state without being briefed on who would be present and whose names to recall. He and his wife also entertained frequently at the executive mansion in Tallahassee, and included on the guest list were Floridians from various backgrounds, not just legislators and lobbyists. Although Graham often struggled as a public speaker when communicating with a large audience, he more than made up for it by his attention to constituents and his genuine interest in the needs of individual Floridians. In a state where change seemed constant and where few people knew their neighbors, let alone their political representatives, Graham's attention to the names of voters, their anniversaries, the birth of a child or grandchild, and other significant events in their lives gave him a personal standing that none of his state counterparts enjoyed. Graham understood that, in a state like Florida, the ability to personalize politics had greater significance than the latest and best policy proposal.[22]

Republicans, Reagan, and Floridians' Search for Community

When Graham stepped down as governor in 1986, the Democratic Party began to falter almost immediately. It was ironic, indeed, that the state Democratic Party should begin to stumble at a time when it looked on the surface as strong as it had at any point in the twentieth century. The number of Republicans in the state Senate had actually declined from a high of 13 seats in 1980 to just 9 seats in 1986, although Republicans had made slight gains in the House, increasing their numbers from 39 in 1980 to 45 in 1986 out of 120 members. Democrats, however, held all major statewide offices, with the exception of one U.S. Senate seat held by Paula Hawkins, and she would be defeated by Graham in her reelection bid. If there was a groundswell for the Republican Party in Florida, state and local election results yielded few clues.

Askew and Graham had also drawn more talented people into the party than at any previous period in the party's history. Additionally, Senator Lawton Chiles served as a leading figure in the U.S. Senate and brought many young Democrats to Capitol Hill to work with him and his office staff. But the party faltered for many reasons. Although many new politicians entered the Democratic ranks because of the influence of Askew and Graham, the party offered them little in the way of support, structure, or political guidance. Most Democrats, because of personal ambitions, refused to recognize that a strong party could well ensure the party's dominance for the future. The cult of personality, the absence of party organization, and internal ideological differences threatened the party's future in the absence of powerful politicians like Askew and Graham. Indeed, Democrats were about to find out how quickly events and demographic developments could change the political equation and overturn their political control of the state. It may well have been that Democrats, even if they had been better organized, could not have stymied the national and state momentum that swung toward the Republican Party in the 1980s.

With the state continuing to grow by more than three hundred thousand people per year in the 1980s, and with a diverse mix of people arriving from the Northeast, Midwest, and the Caribbean and Latin America, Florida politics was anything but stable, despite the dominance of the Democratic Party. Because newcomers came seeking political freedom, a healthy retirement, an opportunity to start over, or a better life and better job, the political party that was best positioned to facilitate their aspirations had the best chance of securing office. Republicans, led by President

Ronald Reagan, spoke most effectively to these aspirations during the 1980s, and Reagan's leadership and rhetoric proved critically important in persuading these voters to become Republican.

Floridians, like most Americans, embraced President Reagan on a personal level, even when they disagreed with him on one or more of his political initiatives. After the 1970s, a decade of so much uncertainty and self-doubt surrounding the direction of the nation, the economy, and the nation's foreign policy, Americans and Floridians generally applauded Reagan's confidence, optimism, and decisiveness. His skill before the television camera matched former President John Kennedy's, and Reagan persuaded viewers and voters that he understood their concerns and desires. As governor of California, which had much in common with Florida, he seemed to understand the particular aspirations and needs of those who were drawn to Florida. His commitment to smaller government, his call for the decentralization of power to the states, lower taxes, strong military defense, anticommunism, and traditional American values together with his bold reaffirmation of the principles of democracy, political freedom, and capitalism had a profound influence on voters. Most Floridians also shared his views on such cultural issues as marriage, heterosexuality, the right to life, and equal rights but not special rights. They liked him, they affirmed his values as their own, and they welcomed his decisiveness and seeming transparency following an era of doom and gloom.[23]

In the 1980 general election, Reagan overwhelmed Carter in Florida with 55.5 percent of the vote to Carter's 38.5 percent. Only four years earlier, Florida had helped elect Carter as only the second southern president since World War II. Moreover, by bringing together Blue Dogs, Cubans, military retirees, suburban middle-class residents with traditional state Republicans, Reagan constructed a coalition that suggested the future of state politics. In the 1984 presidential election, Reagan defeated Walter Mondale by a larger margin, capturing 2.73 million votes out of the nearly 4.2 million votes cast in Florida. Solidifying the coalition of Florida voters who supported him in 1980, Reagan also placed state and local Republicans on a firm political footing in the state.[24]

But Reagan's popularity and support for his political message was just one of several drivers that reshaped Florida politics. The ongoing massive migration, increasing immigration, and the rise of middle-class suburbs continued to transform the state throughout this period, opening avenues of opportunity for Florida's GOP. Because so many people were new to the state, the party was able to reinvent and reassert itself. When Democrats reminded voters of the past failings of Kirk, Gurney, and other Republicans, those who had moved to Florida after 1980 knew little of these events and had little interest in them. Embracing their popular president and Reagan's political philosophy, state Republicans launched a party makeover that was rooted in the politics of Goldwater and Nixon but presented with Reagan's more appealing language and charm. Gone were references to race and busing. In their place were arguments about the failure of liberalism and its commitment to a secularist society. State Republicans joined with Reagan in pledging to restore the nation's core principles, including its religious values.[25]

5

Migration of the Middle Class, the Search for Community, and the Emerging Hispanic Presence

Aiding the Republican Party's efforts to reinvent itself was another critically important demographic development in this period. Often lost in a discussion of the retirees and immigrants who came to Florida were the vast number of mostly middle-class families who moved to the state in search of better jobs and new beginnings. In relocating to Florida, these new arrivals left their extended families behind and joined the throngs of migrants in new communities, new neighborhoods, new workplaces, and new schools. The absence of social and familial anchors made their adjustment to life in Florida very trying, indeed disorienting, for most. The massive wave of newcomers increased the sense of isolation in Florida. While the Peninsula may have seemed like paradise at first glance, it did not feel that way for many who actually made the move. Although most lived near the ocean and enjoyed the gentle sea breezes and the sunshine, they did not know their neighbors, their children's teachers, the paperboy, the postman, the neighborhood store manager, or their colleagues. Few new residents knew anyone! Moreover, they did not have their extended family nearby to help with the children. Once they cut through the facade of paradise, they did not find contentment but experienced instead a deep sense of isolation. Such loneliness was particularly widespread in many of the fastest-growing communities in the state and throughout the Sun

Belt. Religion professor David Hackett observed, "One thing that is new, and you can't underscore enough here, is the desire for intimacy, the desire for connectedness, the desire for bondedness, that is so characteristic of contemporary society."[1]

Religion and Community

Individuals and families searched for ways to counteract the isolation and loneliness at work and in their leisure activities, but few found the intimacy they were looking for. Although the workplace offered opportunities to meet colleagues and develop friendships, these relationships seldom continued outside work because few lived in the same neighborhoods and distances were magnified by the burgeoning traffic problems. Similarly, labor unions, which organized workers in factories and also offered a social network and social activities for employees and families, functioned in few areas of Florida because it was "a right to work" state. Few workers found the social networks that unions had provided back home. Rarely were there company barbecues, baseball games, labor rallies, or outings where employees and their families could gather, begin to develop family friendships, and establish a social network—the sort of activities that unions had been instrumental in providing workers elsewhere. Even social clubs such as the Lions or the Elks Clubs were not as prevalent in the new towns and cities of Florida as they had been back home.

By contrast, businessmen had a much greater range of opportunities than did blue-collar workers. Rotary Clubs and Chambers of Commerce welcomed new white-collar businessmen and offered contacts and social outlets to them. But even for businessmen, these organizations typically met but once a month, making it difficult for social bonds to broaden to include one's family members.

New people kept coming and coming. But many also drifted away. Indeed, moving vans seemed everywhere. People one met at work or in the neighborhood and with whom one might have developed a friendship were often gone within months. An estimated 1,000 arrived per day in the 1970s, and approximately 300 left. This trend continued into subsequent decades, with *Florida Trend* magazine estimating that 1,800 arrived daily and 600 left in the first decade of the twenty-first century.[2]

Cynics commented that Florida had become an oxymoron for "community." Others described Florida as four regions in search of a state.[3] Because of its rapid growth, Florida shared more in common with the Sun Belt states of Texas and California than it did with its southern neighbors. But unlike Texas and California, Florida had no historic or mythic identity. The poet Campbell McGrath said: "Florida ought to be more like Texas, but it isn't. Texas has the Alamo; we have Alamo rental cars. While it has none of the burdens of history, Florida has no mythic identity, no sense of place or self."[4]

Despite the marketing of the state, it was not a place that comforted newcomers. Many could not deal with the isolation and loneliness, and they joined others in returning home within the first year, desperate for family and friends. A good job, warm sunshine, and a beautiful environment proved insufficient for many who relocated to Florida. And who could blame them? Others who could afford to do so because of wealth or retirement opted to live in Florida for only half the year or some smaller portion of the year, and then returned home where they had family and lifelong friends. But the vast majority of those relocating to Florida were not well-to-do or retirees. Workers could not afford to live in Florida part-time. Others, as Bob Graham observed, chose to remain Cincinnatians, New Yorkers, or Chicagoans even in their new Florida location by getting the newspaper from their former hometowns, calling family and friends daily or weekly, and going home for Christmas and lengthy summer vacations.[5]

Seniors had the benefit of living mainly in residential complexes, such as those constructed by developer Irwin Levy and others, and these developments typically provided breakfast, lunch, and dinner in common rooms where people congregated, ate together, and got to know one another on a more intimate basis. Here they established the social bonds that facilitated genuine friendships and developed a social network. These facilities also offered social events and activities for retirees where the social awkwardness experienced by newcomers was soon eased.

Ethnic communities as well provided many of the same opportunities for those from their homelands who had only recently migrated to Florida. In such communities, fellow refugees greeted them, introduced them to others from their homeland village or city, and directed them to religious and social events at churches and social clubs, where they could meet and develop social ties and friendships. In the Cuban community of Miami, for example, it was not uncommon for a Cuban family to take in a new immigrant family from Cuba until the new family could get on their feet financially.[6] Many of these activities depended on the size of the immigrant community, but the Miami of the post-1960 period became one of the largest immigration reception centers in the United States, and large ethnic conclaves emerged from almost every Latin American and Caribbean nation. The Cuban population became so large in Miami that it developed its own newspaper, *Cuba Libre*, to keep Cuban residents informed about events in the community and about events back home. Ethnic groups also celebrated their heritage with events like Fiesta Calle Ocho, a large street fair of Latin American music, which later expanded into Carnaval Miami and became a ten-day event, drew 1.5 million people, and provided Latinos with a sense of place in Florida.[7] Other festivals, surrounding special religious holidays and historical events, brought together ethnic groups and their families and helped provide the community that many Cubans, Haitians, and Vietnamese lost when they fled their native countries. One of the great ironies in Florida was that immigrants typically found a social network more readily than those who migrated from other sections of the United States.

Still, many immigrants and in-migrants sought out a church to help combat the isolation that resulted from the loss of family and friends. Of the Jewish experience, the historian Gary Mormino wrote, "Jews brought to Florida a heritage of and a commitment to voluntary associations and institution building."[8] These associations proved critical in the development of a strong and vibrant Jewish community in southeast Florida and included the Greater Miami Jewish Federation, the *Jewish Floridian*, a substantial number of synagogues, and Mount Sinai Hospital. While Jews constructed a strong community and built social relations in their houses of worship, few non-Jews initially found the same bonds in the traditional Protestant and Catholic churches. Those who turned to such churches were not as homogeneous as Jews, and as a consequence, they did not have a shared ethnic or religious heritage. While their churches back home offered family suppers and an occasional social gathering of one sort or another, many did not attend church because they felt socially isolated. By and large, they went to church in their home communities for the religious service and the traditions of the church that were important to them and their families. Frequently that constituted the extent of their contact, because their extended family, including grandparents, mothers and fathers, aunts and uncles, brothers, sisters, and children typically lived nearby and provided the social milieu that enriched their lives. In circumstances where family did not offer such a social context, labor unions, veterans associations, and social clubs provided a worthy substitute. But when these people arrived in Florida and encountered the social and spatial isolation from friends, family, and neighbors, they sought some alternative and began looking to houses of worship to fulfill this role.[9]

Many came away disappointed with traditional churches, which offered a familiar liturgy but little else. They failed to find the social networks and social activities that they were looking for. Toward the end of the 1970s, new religious congregations took root in the state and across the Sun Belt, many of which were independent churches established by dynamic leaders who preached a fundamental, charismatic, and evangelical Protestant doctrine based on Bible study and religious community and who reached out aggressively to newcomers. Some of these churches were loosely connected to one another like the Calvary Chapels; still others, such as those known as the Rock, operated quite independently from one another.

Many nondenominational churches espoused a similar doctrine that had no liturgy or body of rites to guide people in religious worship at Sunday and weekday services but focused exclusively on the teachings of the Bible. This religious movement took hold in many communities in Florida with amazing rapidity, connecting with a significant need that existed among newcomers, and it exhibited many of the earmarks of a religious Great Awakening. The movement made itself felt throughout the fastest-growing states of the South and the Sun Belt, particularly in communities that were undergoing rapid change as a result of the massive in-migration and immigration of people from other sections of the country and other nations. All of the four states with the most megachurches are in the Sun Belt: California (178), Texas (157), Florida (85), and Georgia (73).[10] Over time, the evangelical movement infused the traditional churches as well, including such Protestant faiths as the Episcopal, Methodist, Baptist, and Presbyterian churches, as well as the Roman Catholic Church.

During the 1980s, many of these churches reached extraordinary size, with some claiming as many as five thousand to seven thousand members. Over the next decade, a few grew to as many as thirty thousand members, but most large churches had two thousand or so members in regular attendance.[11] The size of these churches made them small communities in their own right, and that is what, in fact, appealed to so many residents. These churches brought together people en masse who longed for a shared sense of community. Because of their sheer size, such churches were able to offer a rich variety of programs to congregations. Programs ranged from religious assembly, to child care, church school, day school, family programs, singles programs, outreach activities, publishing houses, missionary movements, and radio and television networks.

In these ways, churches provided activities that enabled families and individuals to build social bonds with others who had no other way of meeting in the new, dynamic cities of the South and the Sun Belt. One person commented that the church "is the family that I never had." The religious scholar Donald Miller writes, "these individuals do what extended families have done for centuries: they share each other's burdens, comfort one another, rejoice in each other's victories, and acknowledge their dependency by reaching out to grasp one another."[12] Much like the Jewish synagogues that took root in Greater Miami, these congregations provided much more than a chance to come together in religious observance once a week; they provided a chance to meet your neighbor, to become a neighbor, to develop a community, and to connect with people who had been little more than strangers previously. Such churches touched a deep-seated religious and social need among new residents and among those whose communities had changed dramatically as a result of the in-migration. Miller adds, "Indeed, members of the new-paradigm churches are struggling to rediscover the meaning of authority and accountability as they try to rebuild families, community, and an ethic of personal responsibility."[13] The dramatic size of these churches, the range of their programs, and the number of such churches throughout the region testified to the religious, psychological, familial, and community need of this movement.

In Florida, the traditional Protestant church faced stiff competition from "the non-denominational SuperSized Church" in the suburbs. As of 1980, the state had but two such megachurches; by 2005, there were eighty-five. One of the largest examples of the new megachurches is Calvary Chapel in Fort Lauderdale, where everything is "supersized": a 75-acre church campus, complete with a sanctuary that seats 3,800; a 1,180-student K-12 school; a gymnasium; three restaurants; a $40 million annual budget; 550 employees; and average total attendance of 18,000 adults and children at four services. Pastor Bob Coy, an attractive youthful-appearing man with neatly trimmed mustache and beard, heads Calvary Chapel. Dynamic and charismatic but also self-effacing and humorous, he dresses casually and preaches to the congregation over a big-screened television, which in turn is broadcast on radio and television. Coy and his assistants offer a substantial array of programs that address the individual and collective needs of members, including those active in sports, seniors, parents, those seeking family and financial counseling, HIV/AIDS sufferers, and quilters. The reporter Mike Vogel observed, "A focused approach to community-building shows in an emphasis on small groups." The church also helped arrange meetings at homes for Bible study, prayer meetings, and family gatherings. Although many megachurches are criticized for being bastions of white conservatism, Calvary Chapel in Fort Lauderdale and many others in Florida are quite diverse, with 10 percent of the congregation being African American and 20 percent Hispanic on any given Sunday.[14] Calvary Chapel and similar congregations also offer trips and cruises for members who are interested in traveling and spending leisure time together.

A church and religious movement as substantial and interwoven as this one, especially in those states that have been transformed by in-migration, could not help but have political consequences over time. One such development saw the emergence of the Roman Catholic Church as a political force after being the object of virulent nativism and anticlericalism for much of the period prior to World War II. In 1916, for example, Sidney J. Catts captured the governorship by pledging to defrock Catholic monks and nuns. Twelve years later, Florida's Yellow Dogs broke ranks and voted against Democrat Al Smith for the presidency because he was Irish-Catholic. By 1960, however, the massive influx of Catholics from the north and from Cuba led to politicians actively seeking support from the state's largest religious sect. And, ironically, conservatives who had hurled epithets at Catholics now reached out to them on such issues as abortion, homosexuality, and the right to life.[15]

Equally significant, every president since Jimmy Carter, excepting George Herbert Walker Bush, has identified himself as a born-again Christian, and all came from the Sun Belt region of the United States (although the elder Bush was raised in New England, he claimed Texas as his residence during his political career). The fact that Carter, Reagan, Clinton, and George W. Bush—Democrats as well as Republicans—highlighted their connections to this religious movement attests to its significance as a political force.

Despite efforts by Democrats, religious leaders of this movement aligned themselves with Ronald Reagan and the Republican Party because of their stance on such issues as family values, abortion, women's rights, and gay rights. If there was one issue around which the various elements of this religious movement—from these megachurches to the Roman Catholic Church—united, it was their opposition to abortion. A fetus in their eyes was a creature of God. Some compared abortion to the Holocaust, while others denounced abortion as inconsistent with the teaching of Jesus and the Bible. In any case, the issue presented a mammoth problem for the Democratic Party because of its leadership in women's rights and a woman's right to choose whether or not to have an abortion.

Religious leaders of the megachurches denounced the party's position and called for judicial and legislative action to overturn *Roe v. Wade* and to ban abortion. The issue sharply divided various elements within the Florida community and gave Republicans a unique opportunity to capture this large, expanding, and important religious constituency in the state. While most women, Jewish voters, and retirees supported *Roe v. Wade* and remained supportive of the Democratic Party, other Floridians, especially many post-1980 newcomers, turned to the Republican Party, and the doctrinal beliefs of the megachurches facilitated such political considerations. While churches like Calvary Chapel resisted letting politicians use their pulpit in order to preserve their tax-exempt status, they held voting registration drives and distributed to all members candidate-position guides from the Christian Coalition of Florida. Vogel concluded, "Both major political party chiefs in Broward view Calvary Church, like most megachurches, as Red State country."[16]

How all this would influence state politics in the 1970s and 1980s was not immediately obvious. Some analysts dismissed this religious movement and its opposition to a woman's right to choose as a phenomenon that would pass in time, arguing that its influence prevailed only among members of the lower middle and lower classes, many of whom did not participate in the political process. These observers failed to appreciate, however, the capacity this movement had to mobilize members to participate politically. And because they shared a common viewpoint, it did not take much direction by clergy to mobilize parishioners politically. Many political professionals, especially within Democratic circles, also had little or no background working with those who embraced this religious awakening and, consequently, overlooked its potential influence initially. When a few extreme elements in the movement turned to bombing abortion clinics and murdering physicians who provided abortions, most Democratic leaders dismissed them as a bunch of fanatics and kooks. But the "kooks" were the exception; others involved in this religious movement would breathe new life into the state Republican Party.

Electing a Republican Governor

Following the end of Bob Graham's eight years in office in 1986, Democrats remained confident that they could hold on to the governorship, despite the support Floridians had given Reagan's election in 1980 and reelection in 1984. Five candidates announced for the Democratic nomination for governor, with three considered serious candidates: state Senator Harry Johnston from West Palm Beach, former Attorney General Jim Smith from Tallahassee, and State Representative Steve Pajcic from Jacksonville, although only Smith had statewide standing. Smith served as attorney general from 1979 to 1987 and as chief of staff for Graham in 1987. Many regarded him as a talented administrator, but few cabinet officers had become governors in the twentieth century. And questions persisted about Smith's campaigning abilities. His serious and somewhat reserved personality did not hold up well to public scrutiny. Johnston had been a popular member of the state Senate from 1974 to 1986 and president of the Senate from 1984 to 1986, but he was not well known outside of the legislature. Pajcic served as a leader in the Florida House from 1974 to 1985 and was even less well known to Floridians.

All three men were well respected in Democratic circles, and Johnston and Pajcic had championed many of Graham's initiatives in the Senate and House. Although Johnston had been a very able state senator and had the strongest political base of the candidates, his campaign languished from the outset. His media spots were notably ineffective and unsuccessful in mobilizing Democrats on his home turf in southeast Florida. Smith, who had a reputation for not suffering fools quietly, came across as distant and prickly at times during the campaign, much like Shevin had in the 1980 campaign. By contrast, Pajcic, the least known of the major candidates, conducted a very effective media blitz that portrayed a bright, energetic, personable, and engaging young lawyer who supported strong environmental and educational initiatives and seemed a worthy successor to Graham. Pajcic and Smith emerged from the first primary with Pajcic surprisingly in the lead. Smith still faced a realistic possibility of overtaking Pajcic, who had tallied only 40 percent of the vote in the primary. Leading in the first primary had, in fact, been a distinct liability in the 1970 and 1978 gubernatorial races, when Askew and Graham came from behind to defeat their more experienced and better-known opponents. Could Smith do the same?[17]

He ran a much more aggressive campaign against Pajcic in the party's second primary, appealing to conservative Democrats by portraying Pajcic as a political liberal who was out of touch with Floridians. In an age when personality mattered more than substance, however, Pajcic ultimately proved the more likable and appealing to Democratic voters. Debates between Smith and Pajcic also favored Pajcic, who was very effective and polished on his feet. Pajcic won by only nine thousand votes in a contest that polarized Democrats, much like in 1966, and left the door open for the Republican candidate.[18]

The lack of unity in the Democratic primary and the bloodletting between Pajcic and Smith in the runoff gave Republicans confidence about the general election. But the party's primary and general election had been almost as divisive as those of the Democrats. The party fielded three major candidates for the gubernatorial nomination: Congressman Lou Frey Jr., who was running once again for governor; Tom Gallagher, a young, up-and-coming Republican whose blond good looks attracted many voters; and Bob Martinez, mayor of Tampa, who had only recently switched to the Republican Party in 1983, but who had built a strong following in the Tampa Bay area. With Republican strength still concentrated in the greater Tampa Bay area and to its south, Martinez raised substantial campaign funds among business leaders in the region and statewide and ran a very effective media campaign, winning the primary with nearly 44 percent of the vote. Frey narrowly defeated the well-regarded but not well-known Gallagher for the second spot. The runoff was a disaster for Frey, with Gallagher endorsing Martinez and with his candidacy unable to gain any traction with Republican voters because of limited campaign funds.

Martinez captured two-thirds of the vote in defeating Frey and set the stage for an intriguing gubernatorial contest.

A product of West Tampa's Cuban community, Martinez had majored in labor relations at the University of Illinois and at one time headed Hillsborough teachers' union, leading it in the controversial teachers' strike in 1968. A former Democrat, he was elected mayor of Tampa as a Republican on a fiscally conservative platform. In his campaign, Martinez capitalized heavily on the popularity of President Reagan in Florida, the president's public endorsement of his candidacy, and on a political platform that mirrored that of the national party. He also benefited significantly from divisions within the Democratic Party and the stunning announcement by Smith that he was endorsing Martinez and would become the Republican nominee for secretary of state. Politically Smith, like Martinez, had more in common ideologically with state Republicans and their commitment to smaller government and fiscal conservatism than he did with the political values of the national Democratic Party and its support of big government. Smith, however, was also angry about his rejection by Democrats and their selection of someone he regarded as too inexperienced to be governor.[19]

With state Democrats sharply divided over his candidacy, Pajcic faced a difficult road to the Governor's Mansion. Martinez appealed to conservative Democrats in a split advertisement that showed "where I stood and where he stood" on such issues as taxes, crime, and big government.[20] Two debates between the candidates failed to help Pajcic, and Martinez, who was not a very effective public speaker, refused a third debate when polls showed him well in the lead. During the rest of the campaign, Martinez highlighted Pajcic's opposition to the death penalty, his liberalism, and his affinity for bow ties. Having spent most of his campaign funds defeating Smith, Pajcic was ill-equipped to counter these accusations.[21]

With Smith and his supporters in his corner, most of whom were north Florida Democrats, Martinez defeated Pajcic decisively, capturing 54.6 percent of the vote and nearly 1.85 million votes to Pajcic's 1,538,620. More importantly, Martinez dismantled the Democratic coalition in southeast and northern Florida, capturing many of the traditional Democratic counties in north Florida by appealing to their desire for limited government, economic development, and strong families; rallying the party's base in southwest Florida; and capturing Miami-Dade County, where a substantial Hispanic turnout helped him capture the normally Democratic county. A closer examination reveals that much of the Cracker/Blue Dog Democrat vote extending from the Panhandle through central Florida went to Martinez, as it had for Ronald Reagan. It was this coalition of voters from Crackers to Cubans that began to define the future of the Republican Party in the state. It was a coalition that would have been unheard of in the 1960s. The party had much to cheer about in 1986. In addition to Martinez's victory, Republicans made inroads into the Democratic majority in the state House, increasing their numbers to 45 of the 120 seats, up from 28 seats in just ten years.[22]

Democrats could still take some satisfaction from this election: Graham won the U.S. Senate seat decisively against Republican Paula Hawkins with literally the same percentage vote as Bob Martinez, and the party maintained its large majority in the state Senate, holding a 31 to 9 majority. The massive changes in Florida's population, however, posed a serious challenge to both parties. Neither could predict the future or interpret the recent election results too confidently. The party that was best organized, most effective in communicating its message to voters—the party that built a substantive relationship with the various voting constituencies—stood the strongest chance of becoming the majority party. Republicans felt confident with their gains among Hispanics and native Floridians and with the popularity of President Ronald Reagan in the state, but Florida was still up for grabs. The question also remained: Could Republicans, having captured the coveted governorship, now demonstrate that they could govern?

The Growing Hispanic Presence and Their Political Influence

Martinez's election benefited particularly from the increasing diversity of the state's population as a result of immigration from the Caribbean and Latin America. Most of those fleeing the Castro Revolution in Cuba settled in Greater Miami and gradually transformed the community politically from a bastion of Democratic liberalism to one of political conservatism. They also restyled its culture from one that embraced the social and cultural expressions of a largely white and Jewish population to one that reflected the energy and color of a Hispanic community. Initially, the Cuban population played a relatively minor role in state politics, in large measure because they were not initially eligible to vote and because they viewed themselves as exiles from Cuba with the goal of returning home in the near future. By late 1965 it became increasingly clear that the Castro regime would not soon fall from power. Moreover, to prevent internal unrest, Castro started the Freedom Flights that September, which brought approximately three hundred thousand additional Cubans to the States, with most eventually finding their way to Miami. Those exiles joined with friends and family who had arrived in 1960 in denouncing communism and in calling on the United States to overthrow Castro. One writer quipped that Miami is the only city in the United States with a foreign policy.[23] Certainly the prominence of the Cuban population in Miami-Dade made its influence unique. But Jewish residents in Miami had long lobbied the federal government on behalf of Israel and hosted many fund-raisers for Israeli leaders. Cubans were no different in this regard.

Initially and briefly, Cubans supported the Democratic Party because of President John Kennedy's assistance to those fleeing communist Cuba, his support of the Bay of Pigs invasion to overthrow Fidel Castro, and his Catholic faith. Cuba and Cubans became pawns in the Cold War strug-gle between the United States and the Soviet Union. In contrast to most immigrant groups, including other Hispanics—and despite the general wealth, education, and skills of this first generation of Cuban émigrés —Cubans received considerable financial and other kinds of support from the federal government. The Kennedy administration was anxious to impress upon people in developing nations that Cubans, with access to greater freedom and economic opportunity provided by the United States, had achieved much greater success than other Cubans were experiencing under the communist regime in Cuba. Despite their initial support of the Democratic Party, Cuban exiles developed stronger ties to the Republican Party because of its strong stance against communism and its support of traditional values. When President Kennedy refused to call in air strikes during the Bay of Pigs invasion, and when President Jimmy Carter proved more reluctant than either Presidents Nixon or Reagan to support a block-ade isolating Castro's Cuba from the rest of the world, Cubans in Florida cast their lot with the Republican Party. The irony of the Cuban position was that they sent hundreds of millions of dollars each year to relatives in Cuba to help them withstand the economic hardships that resulted from the U.S. blockade of Cuba and its boycott of Cuban goods.

Beginning in the mid-1970s, Cuban émigrés began to play an increasingly important role in Miami politics, and their prominence grew steadily statewide as they sent fellow Cuban Americans to the state legislature in Tallahassee and to the U.S. Congress. Their political significance was inescapable when they turned out en masse to vote for Bob Martinez in 1986. By the 1990s, Miami had become one of the major immigration receiving stations in the United States, alongside New York, Los Angeles, and Houston, as a result of the Cuban cultural influence on the city and its resulting appeal to other Latin Americans. The cultural transformation of south Florida also attracted younger Americans, who found the rich culture and diverse lifestyle appealing. The process, however, led to the out-migration of Jews who had settled in Miami and Dade County in the post–World War II period and who had heavily influenced the Miami scene for much of the period from 1950 to 1980. By 1980, however, many Jews and other aging seniors, most of whom were Democrats, moved north to Broward and Palm Beach Counties, where the politics, culture, traffic, and lifestyle were more to their liking.[24]

It seemed ironic to some that the place Ponce de Leon named La Florida and that served as an outpost of New Spain in the sixteenth century, only to subsequently fall to the British and then the United States, should become by the turn of the twenty-first century a hub for Hispanic and Latino life. As Cubans transformed Miami into a cultural center for Latin America, the leading banking center in Latin America, and a place of freedom and opportunity for immigrants from Latin America, others followed. The economic and political stability of the United States as well as the educational possibilities for their children appealed to many from the Caribbean and Latin America. From 1980 to 2000, immigration produced a steady stream of people from the Caribbean and Central and South America, so that by 2000, Cubans constituted slightly less than 50 percent of the Hispanic population in Miami-Dade County, leading some elsewhere in Florida to contend that Miami was not a city in south Florida, "it was a foreign country."[25]

Unlike Cubans, who live the life of exiles, most first-generation Hispanics are "birds of passage" who move back and forth between Miami and their countries of origin. The experience of these Hispanics differs markedly not only from that of Cubans but also from that of previous immigrant groups because of the proximity of their homeland and the pervasiveness of the Hispanic language and culture in Miami. Hispanics have consequently retained their cultural identity for longer periods than those who emigrated from Europe and Asia. Even among Hispanics who were second- and third-generation residents, the pull of their homeland has often proven stronger than that of the United States. The result has been that few of these Hispanics have taken part in the political process, and they certainly have not voted to the degree that Cubans have. They thus have had a much more limited influence on local and state politics. For now, the story out of Miami continues to be about Cubans, who dominate local events and local politics. In time, as subsequent generations of Hispanics are educated in the United States and as they begin to view the States as their homeland, this situation may well change. Moreover, should communism collapse in Cuba, some Cuban émigrés will return to their homeland, and that will affect their influence on the Miami scene.

Martinez's Administration and the Service-Tax Proposal

Martinez's election as governor enabled Republicans to develop a strong political relationship with Cuban and Hispanic voters, even as many other Floridians wondered how effective the new governor would be given his limited political experience. Largely unknown outside of Tampa and lacking the magnetism of an Askew and the public relations skills of a Graham, Martinez had much to do to convince legislators and Floridians that he was the right choice for governor. He quickly demonstrated, however, that while he was an honest and dedicated public servant who aspired to improve the well-being of Floridians and to protect the state's environment, he was not a strong or a decisive leader and he lacked a political vision.

As governor, he aggressively expanded upon the environmental protection initiatives of Reubin Askew and Bob Graham and created additional protections for Florida's surface waters, including Lake Okeechobee, Tampa Bay, Lake Jackson, and the Kissimmee River. In 1990, Martinez established a blue-ribbon commission to evaluate the state of Florida's environment. After completing its review, the commission warned that about 3 million acres of wetlands and forests would be converted to other uses by the year 2020 at the 1990 rate of development. The commission concluded that the single most effective way to accomplish large-scale gains in Florida's environmental well-being was to increase the level of funding for the state's land-acquisition programs.

In response to the report, Martinez proposed Preservation 2000, a $3 billion land-preservation fund to acquire endangered lands over the following ten years. It was a bold initiative; not all Republicans shared Martinez's commitment to the environment, and not all believed that the state's resources should be used in this manner. But a coalition of Republican and Democratic legislators supported the governor, and in 1990 they provided annual funding for $300 million in general obligation bonds backed by the state's documentary stamp, or real estate transfer, tax. The ten-year program conserved over 380,000 acres of land to protect water resources and over 350,000 acres of land to conserve Florida's natural environment. By 2000, Preservation 2000 was responsible for the acquisition and protection of a total of 1.25 million acres of land in Florida. Through his environmental stewardship, Martinez reestablished the party's standing with the environmental community, which had largely disappeared following Kirk's administration, and in the process Martinez strengthened the party's relationship with many seniors who were committed to protecting the environment.[26]

At the same time, Martinez aggressively strengthened the party's close ties with the state's business and corporate interests by personally heading several international trade missions to recruit new companies into the state. Martinez proved particularly adept at developing strong ties with Latin American business and banking interests. During his four years in office, Martinez facilitated the dramatic growth of Miami as a center for hemispheric banking, trade, culture, and music. Martinez was not solely responsible for these developments as Miami's large Cuban population and expanding Latin American population attracted the attention of businesses and corporations in the hemisphere, but as a Hispanic governor, he was particularly effective in promoting Florida's prominence in the hemisphere.

Martinez also won praise for launching a major statewide anticrime, antidrug campaign. The state's swelling crime statistics, much of which were drug-related, caused widespread public concern and threatened the state's reputation as a safe place for family vacations. Much like Republican governors in other states, Martinez used the fight against crime and drugs to enhance the Republican Party's reputation among working-class and middle-class voters who were concerned about the decline of law and order in their communities and neighborhoods.

Although Martinez's gubernatorial term was marked by a series of solid accomplishments, his record was overwhelmed by a singular event: the proposed service tax. The state depended heavily on general and selective sales taxes that were consumption-driven for three-quarters of its revenue, but most experts agreed these taxes did not generate sufficient funds to meet state needs in such areas as roads, family and children's services, crime prevention, education, and the environment. Moreover, sales-tax revenues were particularly sluggish in the late 1980s and early 1990s as tourism and the national economy slowed, raising serious questions about whether Florida could meet its financial needs as its population continued to expand throughout this period at the rate of three hundred thousand people per year.[27]

In the face of these developments, the legislature had approved a tax on services in 1986, and a bipartisan commission had been appointed to implement the legislative action when Martinez was inaugurated as governor. Legislative leaders had examined alternatives to the sales tax to help address Florida's near-term and long-term financial needs, and they had focused on a service tax as a more reliable source of revenue for Florida than an additional sales tax. Following his election, Martinez appointed two members to serve on the commission and indicated his support of the service tax proposal. During their deliberations, commission members recommended that a service tax be placed on professional services and that it be based on a percentage of gross receipts. The enormous growth of the service sector convinced commission members that services ought to be taxed and that a service tax would generate added revenue as the population and services continued to expand, unlike the sales tax base, which grew only marginally for each penny of sales tax. The report also noted that while tax revenues had been shrinking, the costs of state programs were skyrocketing—Medicaid costs were up dramatically and projected to increase even more substantially because of the number of seniors residing in the state; prison and crime-related costs were also up significantly because of a dramatic rise in crime in Florida due, in part, to a much larger population and a slowing economy; and education costs had escalated because of the continued flow of families into Florida. The tax on services mimicked a similar tax in Europe that had proven effective in helping its nations modernize and was less punitive on the poor and working classes.[28]

But Martinez and his staff should have been wary of this proposal because no other state in the United States had adopted a service tax, and Floridians had repeatedly resisted any new forms of taxation, subscribing to the old adage: "Don't tax you, don't tax me, tax the man behind the tree."[29] The man behind the tree was the tourist. And Floridians convinced themselves that tourists, as consumers, contributed the largest percentage of sales-tax revenue to the state. The myth had gained so much standing over time that even spokespeople for the lower middle class and the poor ignored the regressive nature of the sales tax. The proposed service tax had three basic components: a tax on services generally consumed by individuals; a tax on certain services consumed by business; and a use tax on business services.

With the commission's recommendations in hand, Martinez hemmed and hawed before deciding to throw the weight of his office behind the proposal without first convincing Floridians of its merits and despite grumbling from many in his party who had embraced an antitax message. Martinez's decision revealed his inexperience and indecisiveness; neither Askew nor Graham, for example, would have allowed themselves to be forced into supporting such a controversial proposal.

As the news media, lawyers, and other businessmen examined the particulars of the tax, they realized that it would have a far-reaching impact on their businesses. The proposal, for example, promised to tax advertising revenue from all mediums—billboards, magazines, newspapers, radio, and television. It was this feature of the tax that generated a firestorm of protest from national advertising groups, some of whom said they would pull their advertisements from media outlets in Florida. While the complaints of advertisers gained the most attention, it was not the only problem brought to light by the tax. The measure seemed to underscore all that was wrong with taxing something as generic as services. One major concern was the tax's pyramiding effect. For example, an architect "purchasing" consultant services was required to pay a tax on those services. However, the consultant services were taxed again when the client was presented with the fee for the entire project. The double tax, or pyramiding effect, was later remedied in a legislative "glitch bill," but opponents were not satisfied.

Opposition to the tax escalated dramatically. Leading the call for reconsideration and revocation of the tax were the state newspapers, radio and television stations, lawyers, and developers. They were joined by virtually all segments of the business community in Florida. Martinez recalled, "You could not compete with the incredible numbers of ads on television, columns, editorials, and new articles" against the tax.[30] The governor found himself caught in a public and political maelstrom, and he froze like a "deer in the headlights of an oncoming car." The situation deteriorated further when members of his own party bypassed him and called for revocation of the tax.

Within a month of the enactment of the tax, opponents had taken out advertisements in the state newspapers, purchased advertisements on television, and begun drafting a petition calling for a constitutional ban on service taxes. Polls disclosed that Floridians had been persuaded by the onslaught of press and television advertisements that the service tax was excessive, punitive, and should be revoked. Newspaper publishers and television owners failed to note their personal stake in leading the effort to annul the service tax, but opposition had become so widespread that mea culpas would have had little effect. It was ironic, however, that the press, which had insisted that politicians reveal any conflict of interest in their dealings, failed to note their own conflict in the battle to repeal the service tax.[31]

Few governors in Florida history have been faced with a political crisis of this magnitude, especially one that was partially of their own creation. The only similar incident in the twentieth century occurred when Governor Doyle Carlton recommended in 1929 and 1931 that legislators raise gasoline taxes to offset a $2.5 million state deficit during the Great Depression.[32] LeRoy Collins faced a more intense and longer-lasting battle over racial desegregation in the 1950s, but that had not been of his choosing. Significantly, neither of these men was ever elected to another office in Florida.

Despite opposition from the leading businessmen and from members of his own party, Martinez held firm initially. His dilemma was that he was doomed if he reversed himself on the tax and doomed if he did not.

When legislative leaders demanded a special session of the legislature to reconsider the service tax, Martinez relented. In a dramatic announcement, he told Floridians in September 1987 that he had erred in proposing the tax and would endorse its repeal. In a second special session of the legislature in December, the service tax was repealed after being in effect for four short months. The fate of the tax would, in fact, doom Martinez's administration and his political future. He became known as "Governor Floppo" for changing his mind on the service tax.[33]

Martinez had also violated one of the central tenets of the Republican Party in Florida and nationally, namely, its commitment to lower taxes. Much like President George Herbert Walker Bush, who had pledged his administration to "no new taxes" in his 1988 election campaign and then had reneged on this pledge in order to deal with mounting federal deficits, Martinez discovered that party loyalists were fundamentally opposed to taxes under any circumstance, even if, as Bush and Martinez believed, it was in the best interests of the nation or the state.

Martinez tried to regroup in the wake of this political disaster, but nothing seemed to work and the measure plagued the governor and everyone involved in it. Republicans and Democrats, almost without political distinction, felt the wrath of voters and were overwhelmingly defeated for reelection. The service-tax imbroglio also stalled Republican political ambitions in Florida. Between 1986 and 1992, the party's gains in the state legislature remained between nine and seventeen seats in the Senate and between forty-five and forty-seven seats in the House.[34]

Despite the devastating political effects of the service-tax crisis, it did not tarnish the Republican Party to the degree that Claude Kirk's governorship had. Even political experts and reporters acknowledged that Martinez faced a major fiscal crisis and that some tax reform seemed essential. More importantly, the Republican Party had built such a solid base of candidates and voter support in Florida by 1990 that it would take more than the governor's service-tax measure to devastate the party. That was certainly not the case during the Kirk years, when the party was in its infancy. By 1990, Republicans had many candidates running successfully for state and local office, many of whom had developed broad support at the local level. It was, in fact, that support which had broadened to include military retirees, Cubans, natives and Blue Dog Democrats, and a large group of well-to-do retirees that made the state Republican Party formidable competition for the Democratic Party. Republicans had thus positioned themselves reasonably well to challenge Democrats for political supremacy in the 1990s, despite the service-tax fiasco.

As Martinez prepared to leave office, the GOP recognized that for the second time in history it had failed to reelect a Republican governor. For all the hype and praise about the party's achievements, the plain facts were that Kirk and Martinez had not solidified Republican political gains. Moreover, both administrations had ignored the party's core values in the process. Future Republican governors and gubernatorial candidates would not make that mistake again.

6

Holding Back the Republican Tide, but for How Long?

With the service-tax proposal still weighing heavily on voter attitudes, Republicans were not sanguine about retaining the governorship in 1990. They privately hoped several Democrats would seek the governorship, leading to another intraparty bloodbath and a weakened candidate, as had occurred with Steve Pajcic in 1986. But these hopes turned to consternation when rumors circulated that Lawton Chiles, one of the lions of the Democratic Party, had expressed an interest in returning to politics and was being courted by party leaders. Chiles retired from the U.S. Senate in 1989 after serving for three terms and earning the respect of both parties for his political prowess and his efforts to reduce the nation's budget deficit. Near the end of his third term, Chiles developed clinical depression and was treated with Prozac, at the time a quite controversial drug. He struggled with depression, what he called the "blacks," while teaching political science at the University of Florida, and it was unclear whether he was healthy enough to run for political office, let alone serve as governor. However, as he began to recover his health, several supporters convinced him that the party needed his leadership to recapture the governorship. With the well-respected Buddy MacKay, who had been narrowly defeated by Republican Connie Mack in the 1986 Senate race, agreeing to serve as his lieutenant governor, Chiles's health became of less concern to Democrats. Throwing his name into the campaign ring in April, Chiles pledged

to reinvent government by making government less costly and more responsive to citizens and by limiting campaign contributions to $100, a
tactic Askew had employed in his reelection campaign in 1974. Chiles and
MacKay constituted a formidable team, but it also looked like an aging
ticket in an aging party, designed to enable Democrats to recapture power
for at least another four years.[1]

The Reemergence of Lawton Chiles

While Chiles's political reputation was without peer in the state—he had
never lost a campaign—questions abounded about his health, persuading
the ambitious Democratic congressman Bill Nelson to run against Chiles
in the primary. Nelson had been in the House of Representatives for eleven
years, and although he had not gained much state or national attention
for his legislative service, he was well known for having flown aboard the
Columbia space shuttle in January 1986. Nelson was a relatively young,
attractive candidate, but he gave many voters the impression that he was
little more than a pretty face more interested in gaining and holding office than in serving the people well. Nelson attempted to make an issue
of Chiles's age and health, contending that the governorship required a
person with great energy. But Nelson's strategy angered Democrats and
backfired in a state where a large retiree population was personally offended by his efforts to impugn Chiles's age, his health, and, therefore, his
ability to serve.[2]

As he had in his senatorial campaigns, Chiles appealed to middle- and
working-class voters by pledging to make government more responsive
to the citizens of the state. Much of Chiles's thinking about government
had been shaped by his years in Florida politics and in the U.S. Senate
and by his involvement in the Democratic Leadership Conference (DLC),
a group of mainstream Democrats that included Bill Clinton. The DLC
sought a new vision for the party in the mid-1980s, aimed particularly
at recapturing middle-class voters by offering moderate social and economic programs and fiscally responsible leadership that would provide a
constructive alternative to the rights, responsibilities, and values agenda
of the Reagan administration.[3] At heart, Chiles was essentially a populist
who embraced the values of the common folk, whether they were seniors,
immigrants, workers, or Crackers. But Chiles had also been persuaded by

David Osborne's book, *Reinventing Government*, that governors could accomplish more with less by stressing outcomes and accountability and by
privatizing some government programs. Chiles's pledge to make government responsive to the people and his limit on campaign contributions
gained a broad following among middle- and working-class voters following the service-tax imbroglio and reports of widespread insider influence by lobbyists in the state capital. Chiles had no difficulty in defeating
Nelson in the party primary, capturing nearly 70 percent of the popular
vote.[4] More importantly, the campaign did not wreak havoc within the
Democratic Party as Chiles entered the general election with the endorsement of Nelson and the backing of all leading Democrats in the state.

Republicans, however, faced a major quandary as they wrestled to decide who would represent the party in the gubernatorial contest. Martinez
carried such baggage into the election that few political experts thought
he could win. But the party had few alternatives since no other political
figure enjoyed a sufficient statewide reputation to challenge either Martinez in the primary or Chiles in the gubernatorial election. Four candidates
ran against Martinez in the Republican primary, reflecting the divisions
within the party over Martinez's leadership, but not one was known outside his or her district, and even in their districts they were not terribly
well known. Martinez won the primary contest with surprising ease, capturing 69 percent of the vote in the first primary, but he faced an enormous uphill challenge in trying to defeat Chiles. While both candidates
defeated their opponents with 69 to 70 percent of the vote, Chiles received
a total of nearly 750,000 votes to Martinez's 460,000 votes, and, although
Martinez won easily, he came away badly bruised by primary opponents
who berated his support for the service tax.[5]

Defeating a political legend was challenging enough, but for Martinez
the campaign was a disaster in other ways. Much as he tried to focus voters on the state's future, he was constantly hounded by questions about
the service tax and why he had supported it in the first place. It was not
so for Chiles, who largely ignored the service-tax issue and concentrated
his campaign on reestablishing his populist reputation with Florida's voters. Chiles was not a much more effective speaker than Martinez but was
skilled at working an audience and in communicating a message that resonated with voters. Few politicians in state history have been as well regarded by common folk in Florida. While Bob Graham worked alongside

them, it was Chiles whose persona resonated with the poor and working classes. Republicans feared Chiles as an opponent because of his effectiveness on the campaign trail and because his links with the working and middle class impeded the party's efforts to capture these important constituencies. Chiles seemed reenergized during the campaign, and many commented that he looked better and seemed stronger than he had in several years.[6]

With the endorsement of every major newspaper in the state, Chiles defeated Martinez with 2 million votes and 56.5 percent of the popular vote. Martinez lost by over fifty thousand votes in his home county of Hillsborough and by nearly one hundred thousand votes in Miami-Dade County. It was the type of shellacking that Republicans had experienced during the Askew and Graham years and seemed to suggest that the party had once again been relegated to the political garbage heap in Florida.

But had it? The evidence indicated that this election was about the service tax and little else. When asked several years later if the service-tax issue led to his defeat, Martinez replied, "No question about it."[7] He added that reporters would not let him discuss any other issue in the campaign. Despite Martinez's defeat, however, Republicans added two seats in the state House of Representatives and three seats in the state Senate, where they now shared power with Democrats for the first time in state history, with twenty seats on each side of the aisle. The legislative results revealed the party's growing stature at the grassroots level, where its message of low taxes, limited government, economic development, educational reform, law and order, and traditional values resonated well with many natives and newcomers.

As in Atlanta and Charlotte, Republicans captured white middle-class support in Florida's suburbs by appealing to the self-interest of these voters with a broad array of initiatives.[8] Most new residents had moved to Florida in search of economic opportunity, and they looked to state government to keep the economy strong. It was one of the major reasons why all governors in the post–World War II era traveled widely on trade missions and to recruit new business. The Republican agenda also spoke deftly to the desire of these suburban residents to protect their quality of life by highlighting the need for strong law enforcement, stiff prison sentences for criminals, better schools, educational reform, and traditional family values. Change was such an everyday characteristic of living in

Florida that middle-class voters could not help but be concerned about preserving their quality of life. And frequent headline stories of violent crimes by residents or itinerants who were passing through were sufficient for many to embrace the stability that Republicans promised.

Also driving the Republican's hard-line ideology was the sharp decline in voting in Florida. Many newcomers were so absorbed in the everyday necessities of life that they did not bother to vote or paid little attention to the campaigns. Many young voters also stayed away from the polls because of indifference or alienation. Republicans recognized this trend better than Democrats and concentrated on getting supporters out to the polls by accentuating their agenda and Democratic failings.

Republican successes in the predominantly white suburbs of Florida, however, were not uniform. In traditional Democratic counties like Palm Beach, Broward, and Miami-Dade, the party continued to receive support from middle-class voters who relocated to the suburbs. In these counties, the party's commitment to a strong and healthy environment, public education, racial justice and equality, and good government helped it retain voter approval. Suburban whites also voted Democratic in Miami-Dade because of concern about the extent of the Cuban and Latin American immigration and its growing influence on the city's culture and politics. Also aiding the Democratic Party in these counties and in Orange County was the migration of the black middle-class into the suburbs, where they continued to support the party. So while the migration of whites to the suburbs in Florida generally strengthened the Republican Party, as it did in other southern states, the results were not uniform.

Reapportionment and the Republican Challenge

Despite Chiles's victory and the continuation of Democratic control of the state legislature, the developments mentioned above as well as the reapportionment of the legislature and the rise of Jeb Bush boosted Republican fortunes dramatically in just a few years in the early 1990s. No development had a bigger impact on Republican legislative fortunes than reapportionment. The redrawing of district maps takes place every ten years, following the federal census, and is one of the most partisan and quarrelsome of legislative tasks because of its implications for both parties. The state

Democratic Party had controlled this process throughout the twentieth century as the dominant party and used it to maintain their control and to assist their incumbents. Although Democrats had the legislative numbers to control the map-drawing of legislative districts that took place following the 1990 census, Republicans—led by Lee Atwater and Benjamin Ginsberg at the national level and state Senator Tom Slade of Jacksonville at the state level—began building alliances with African-American leaders to ensure a favorable outcome for Republicans and African Americans.

The aim of Atwater, Ginsberg, and Slade was to confine most black Democratic voters to certain legislative districts and thereby enhance Republican opportunities in the remaining districts. By packing these Democratic loyalists into relatively few carefully drawn districts, Republicans significantly reduced their influence in most other districts. Slade, who chaired the Florida Republican Party from 1993 to 1999, described the deal in the following manner: "The redistricting plan drew odd-shaped districts to capture all blacks in a geographic area to maximize the number of elected black lawmakers." One federal judge described Florida's third congressional district as having "the appearance of something lifted from a Rorschach test."[9]

Democrats tried to dissuade their African-American colleagues from accepting this deal. But when they offered only one additional congressional seat, Darryl Reaves, an African-American legislator from Miami, condemned his white colleagues and derided his black colleagues who sided with white leaders as "having a leash around their necks." In the end, black leaders sided with Republicans.[10] The apportionment deal literally assured black leaders that the number of black state legislators would increase from fourteen to nineteen and that the number of black members in Congress would increase from zero to three. That compromise gained black Democrats legislative members but cost them influence over public policy. That development was repeated by Atwater and Ginsberg in seven other states in the South.

By increasing the percentage of whites in the remaining districts, Republicans enhanced their chances of wresting legislative control from the Democrats. A pleased Slade observed: "The creation of every black Democratic district creates two Republican districts. Now, as far as the eye can see, Republicans will control both houses in Florida." By 1994, Republicans had taken control of the Senate by four seats and narrowed the Democratic margin in the House to six seats. Two years later Republicans took control of both houses for the first time since Reconstruction, as Tom Slade had predicted. By the turn of the century, as a result of the redistricting plan of 1992, one could literally predict the outcome of races and the number of Republicans and Democrats who would claim seats in the state Senate and House. In fact, Allan Lichtman, professor of history at American University in Washington, D.C., did just that, coming within one seat of predicting the final election results in Florida. Based on the districts drawn by Republicans, Lichtman predicted that they would win eighty-two state House seats (they won eighty-one), twenty-six state Senate seats (they won twenty-six), and eighteen U.S. House seats (they won eighteen). The Democrats not only fell into the minority, but their representatives became decidedly ethnic and racial as well—of the thirty-nine Democrats in the state House in 2003, only fifteen were not black or Jewish. Of the fourteen Democrats in the state Senate, only two senators—Rod Smith and Walter "Skip" Campbell—were neither African-American nor Jewish. And of the seven Democrats in the U.S. House, only two—Jim Davis and Allen Boyd—were white and Protestant.[11]

Despite the effects of reapportionment on local races, Florida remained a competitive state in national and statewide campaigns, as demonstrated by the presidential election of 2000; the U.S. Senate race of 2000, won narrowly by Democrat Bill Nelson; and the Senate race of 2004, won narrowly by Republican Mel Martinez. Slade agreed that in statewide races, "The state is basically a very competitive two-party state."[12] While more Floridians continued to be registered as Democrats than as Republicans, by a margin of 350,000 voters, many registered Democrats were Blue Dog Democrats, whose loyalty to the party often faltered in national elections and increasingly in local and state elections.

The second important development for the Republican Party in this decade was the selection of Tom Slade as chairman of the state Republican Party in 1993 and the emergence of Jeb Bush as a gubernatorial candidate. A blunt-spoken, no-nonsense Republican from Jacksonville, Slade served in the state Senate and had been instrumental in forging the redistricting deal with black Democrats. Even with the success of reapportionment, Slade felt the party had to continue to identify and develop candidates for political office, to promote greater diversity among those running for office as Republicans, and to develop a clear-cut message that remained consistent over time. Slade wanted the party to reflect the diversity of the citizens of the state so that it could broaden its appeal. He recognized that having a group of prominent, conservative white businessmen heading the party in a state that was diversifying rapidly would not ensure its long-term success. Additionally, he regarded the decision by Governor Martinez on the service tax as a vivid example of where the party had lost its focus and pursued an initiative inconsistent with its political philosophy.[13]

Over the next six years, Slade presided over a party that exercised discipline, outreach, and ingenuity in ways that had not been seen in Republican circles previously. Some in the party compared Slade's leadership to that of the urban political bosses of the late nineteenth century: "His word was the only word. And when it came to many issues, his was the only vote that was counted."[14] It was true, too, that Slade not only directed the campaigns of Republican candidates, but he also orchestrated legislative policy and raised money. Slade was a thoughtful and innovative, if demanding, party leader as well. By 2004, the Republican Party, not the state Democratic Party, had more talented women campaigning for and holding office and more Hispanic candidates and officeholders, and had taken significant steps to recruit candidates from the retirement community and the African-American community in Florida. The transition in party leadership and the discipline of the party during the 1990s were remarkable, especially when compared with the party's past performance.

Slade and the party also benefited significantly from the emergence of Jeb Bush. In a state where one's name had greater impact than one's experience because so many Floridians were new to Florida and unfamiliar with its politics, Bush figured prominently in the party's future and gave the party a much needed star quality. He served briefly as secretary of state under Martinez in 1987 and 1988, before resigning to work on his father's presidential campaign. The latter experience sparked his decision to pursue a political career in Florida. Slade and Bush would provide the party with the leadership, direction, energy, and strength that it needed to become the majority party. It is difficult to imagine any other combination that could have transformed Florida politics so effectively in the decade from 1993 to 2003. And they began to do so while the Democratic Party held the governorship with one of its most popular and successful figures in the twentieth century.

The Chiles Administration, Jeb Bush, and the Election of 1994

Chiles entered office with a promise to address the state's economic, educational, environmental, and social challenges. But, unlike Reubin Askew and Bob Graham, Chiles did not have the luxury of political majorities in both houses. Indeed, Chiles became the first Democrat in the Governor's Mansion to grapple with a Republican-led legislature.

At Chiles's inauguration, heady discussions circulated about a return to Camelot and to the Askew years. Looking back on these early years of his governorship, even some of his closest aides and friends acknowledged that expectations had been too high and that they had underestimated their political opposition. "We were not realistic when we came in and neither were many of the people around us," said Doug Cook, the head of the Agency for Health Care Administration.[15]

Adding to the challenges, Chiles faced one crisis after another. First came a recession, forcing spending cuts of $2 billion during his first eighteen months in office. In August 1992, Hurricane Andrew, one of the most powerful storms of the twentieth century, slammed into south Florida just below Miami, leaving little but devastation in its wake. Homestead and nearby communities were leveled. Indeed, the destruction was so extensive that federal and state officials initially seemed paralyzed by it, and the mayor of Dade County was nowhere to be seen. Chiles filled the leadership void, spending weeks in Miami comforting victims and negotiating federal and state aid packages to cope with the nation's most costly natural disaster up to that time. One year later, in 1993, a string of tourist murders, including that of one British couple, triggered another crisis of international proportions as Chiles struggled to reassure tourists that it was safe to come to Florida. Between the crises, he launched his reinvention revolution, outsourcing the state's foster care system that many felt was a disaster, privatizing some state prisons, and endorsing a proposal to create charter schools financed with state dollars. Beyond these reforms, he could claim only a few accomplishments of note, including new limits on campaign contributions; a new Department of Elder Affairs; a Governor's Commission for a Sustainable South Florida, which brought together sugar barons and environmentalists to safeguard the major source of freshwater for south Florida and preserve the Everglades; and the creation of health care–purchasing alliances to insure more than one hundred thousand employees in 1994 whose companies otherwise could not afford to offer coverage.

Chiles got nowhere, however, with his two major initiatives—a $2.5 billion tax-reform measure and broader health-care coverage based on federal and state Medicaid savings. He would later claim that he pursued tax reform to fulfill a campaign pledge to working-class and middle-class Floridians and that bad timing killed his health-care reforms. Taking up tax reform was unquestionably a political blunder, which a younger Chiles almost certainly would not have made. Legislators, including many of his fellow Democrats, and Floridians were in no mood to consider tax reform after the debacle over the service tax. In recommending tax reform, Chiles fell into a defensive position in his relationship with legislators in his first year in office and struggled to reestablish a more constructive and effective dialogue thereafter.[16] Perhaps more importantly, Chiles returned the tax issue, and with it many middle-class voters, to the Republican Party. It was a huge political error and, alongside the reapportionment of the state legislature, greatly aided the Republican Party in realizing its political ambitions in the 1990s.[17]

In 1994, Chiles ran for reelection against a relatively unknown Republican candidate with a politically famous last name—Jeb Bush. That campaign pitted the aging lion of the Democratic Party and what some regarded as an aging Democratic Party against a youthful, brash, and ideological Republican candidate and an energized Republican Party. The outcome would say a great deal about the direction of state politics in the late twentieth and early twenty-first centuries.

Although Jeb was unknown to most Floridians, the Bush name gave him tremendous standing with Florida voters. His father had captured Florida in the 1992 presidential contest, narrowly defeating opponents Bill Clinton, who would win the national election, and businessman and independent H. Ross Perot. Jeb had worked hard on his father's campaign in Florida and helped him secure the votes of Blue Dog Democrats in the central and northern sections of the state, and of Cubans in Miami-Dade. This experience prepared Jeb well for his 1994 gubernatorial contest. In the Republican primary, Jeb showed surprising statewide strength, decisively defeating six other candidates, including the more experienced Jim Smith and Tom Gallagher. Bush ran so far ahead of his six opponents in the party primary, winning 45.7 percent of the vote compared to 18.4 percent for Smith and 13 percent for Gallagher, that Smith opted to withdraw from the race rather than force a runoff. Smith's decision allowed Bush to avoid the expense of a runoff election and the divisions it would create within the party. In exchange for his decision, Smith became the party's nominee for state secretary of agriculture. Chiles had a single, relatively unknown opponent, Jack Gargan, in the primary and defeated him handily.[18]

Chiles was initially the overwhelming favorite to be reelected, and yet he faced some serious obstacles in this campaign. First, negating to some degree his experience and reputation was the fact that, according to the 1990 census, nearly two-thirds of state voters were not native-born Floridians and were thus largely unfamiliar with Chiles. The political scientist Susan MacManus observed, "You've got a whole bunch of voters that really are pretty unfamiliar with his past record as a senator and not terribly familiar with his record as governor."[19] Second, a self-confident Bush came out of the starting gate attacking Chiles's record and, with tongue-in-cheek, claimed that Chiles would impose an "excuse-me-for-living tax" if he were reelected. The immodest Bush promised to dismantle much of the government structure created by Chiles and his Democratic predecessors. "I'm not kidding when I say that government's power needs to be controlled," he told an audience, "so we have to dismantle the welfare state." He proposed to begin by dismantling the State Department of Education.[20] Bush's passionate conservatism surprised many in Florida, who thought the younger Bush would be a more moderate Republican, much like his father. But as would become apparent, Jeb Bush was not his father's Republican. Much like his brother George in Texas, Jeb embraced the conservative values of Ronald Reagan and viewed "big government" as an albatross around the neck of the nation.[21]

Bush's negative campaign and the attention he received because of his famous father angered the normally placid Chiles. He had invested much of his life and his entire political career in making government work for Floridians and was offended that someone as inexperienced as Jeb Bush could denounce government so brazenly without having any experience or firsthand knowledge of it. Bush's pledge to eliminate the Florida Department of Education particularly struck the governor as sheer nonsense. While acknowledging that the agency needed reform, Chiles pointed out to voters that a modern state could not just eliminate the state's Department of Education and serve its citizens responsibly. But Bush's strategy had placed Chiles on the defensive, and early polls revealed that Bush's campaign tactics were working.[22]

Although his aides were concerned about Bush's rise in the polls, Chiles never doubted that he would win the contest. Much depended, however, on his ability to hold on to voters in Blue Dog country in northern and central Florida and to generate a large turnout, especially among seniors and traditional Democrats, along the southeast coast. Ultimately the election would turn on these voters.[23]

The candidates agreed to three debates, during which Chiles portrayed himself as a man of the people, a populist who cared deeply about his state and especially about its poor and working-class citizens, while Bush highlighted his neoconservative credentials and his commitment to religious and cultural values. Neither candidate was terribly comfortable on television or effective in the debates, but by the final debate, Bush was more polished in his speech and demeanor, looked more like a governor, and even took time to speak to the Tampa audience in Spanish. The hunched and rumpled Chiles, by contrast, kept to the homespun image and to his populist rhetoric. After Bush finished speaking to the television audience in Spanish, Chiles concluded his remarks with the line, "The old he-coon walks just before the light of day." Most people in attendance at the debate, including his opponent, looked befuddled at his statement, and few Floridians understood what he was talking about—only the state's Crackers grasped his point. The governor was telling them that, like the old he-coon who depends on his resourcefulness to go about his business and survive another day, the common folk in Florida could rely on him to defend their interests against political predators and he was counting on their support to do so.[24]

In the last days of the campaign, Bush revealed his hard-nosed political instincts when he aired a controversial campaign advertisement accusing Chiles of being soft on crime and the death penalty. The ad portrayed the anguish of a Florida woman whose daughter had been kidnapped and murdered while on her way to school. The perpetrator had subsequently been convicted and sentenced to death but had not yet been executed because his case was on appeal. The Bush ad accused Chiles of being reluctant to execute the man. The ad reminded many of the Willie Horton advertisement that Jeb's father had used to defeat Michael Dukakis for the presidency in 1988. Chiles denounced the ad, pointed out that the case was still in the courts, and he had no jurisdiction over it as a consequence. Judges and prosecutors substantiated Chiles's claims. The Governor saw the Bush ad as a great opportunity in a close campaign, and he publicly denounced Bush for knowing "it was false."[25]

Some analysts have attributed the advertisement and the final debate as decisive in turning the election in Chiles's favor. But others, including many in the Bush camp, felt that calls made by Chiles's supporters to Florida's retirees during the last weekend of the campaign that warned seniors that a Bush election would result in a reduction of their Medicare benefits turned the tide of the election. After vigorously denying this charge, Chiles subsequently acknowledged months after the campaign that his staff had made thousands of misleading telephone calls to elderly voters.[26]

In retrospect, it does appear that these calls mobilized the crucial senior vote for Chiles. In one of the closest elections in Florida history, Chiles captured 2,135,000 votes to Bush's 2,071,000, winning by only 64,000 votes. Voter breakdown revealed that Chiles won the election with very strong support among traditional Democrats, many of whom resided on Florida's southeast coast. He carried Broward County, with its largest city of Fort Lauderdale, by 125,000 votes and Palm Beach County by 73,000 votes. He also defeated Bush in his home county of Miami-Dade by 17,000 votes, capturing the African-American and suburban white vote, while Jeb took the Cuban vote. Although some of the Cracker counties voted for Chiles, most chose Bush.[27] Chiles celebrated election night with a coonskin cap on his head, but he should have celebrated by playing shuffleboard with retirees at one of the large retirement complexes in southeast Florida. It was there that he won reelection.

Seniors and Florida

Seniors came to Florida in search of paradise in the 1950s. Their numbers increased dramatically in the 1960s as word spread among retirees, and advertisers promoted the ideas that there really was a Fountain of Youth in Florida, and that the state offered them a longer and healthier life in their retirement years. The year-round warmth, sunny climate, and balmy ocean breezes allowed seniors to spend much of their time outdoors, which in turn prolonged their health and well-being. By the mid-1980s, the senior population had swelled to 17 percent of the state population, up from 12 percent in the 1960s, and seniors had become a major force in state politics.

Whether from the Northeast or the Midwest, retirees had an impact on state politics that went well beyond their numbers. They had matured in an era when voting mattered and when decisions at the ballot box had monumental consequences for the nation, ultimately determining its response to the Great Depression, to the events of World War II, and to the Cold War. As a consequence, they took voting seriously and showed up at the polls for local, state, and national elections. The *Wall Street Journal* reported in 1984 that condo leaders like Jack Babich, a seventy-four-year-old retired restaurant owner and head of the West Delray Democratic Club, could turn out 85 percent to 95 percent of the voters in his condo. "Mr. Babich assembles squads of retirees who telephone all the registered voters in a condo and give rides to polling places. A palm card, which lists the candidates Mr. Babich has endorsed, is left on every doorknob." "Its small-time Tammany Hall," commented Evelyn Ostrow, a seventy-year-old New Yorker known in the area as "Mrs. Democrat." When Sidney Krutick, who resided in a retired condominium community of fourteen thousand, told the commissioners of Palm Beach County that he and his fellow retirees wanted a fire department closer to their condominium, they got the fire department. Karen Marcus, a recently elected county commissioner, observed: "God help you if you cross them. You can't win an election without the condo vote."[28]

The U.S. Census Bureau and the State Division of Elections reported in 1998 that seniors constituted 18 percent of the state's population but 24 percent of the voting-age population and 27 percent of the state's registered voters. Exit surveys during the 1998 gubernatorial election revealed that retirees constituted 32 percent of all voters, a stunning figure when compared to that for all other age groups. And when those aged sixty and older were lumped together, they represented a staggering 42 percent of the voters in that election. The political scientist Susan MacManus, who has closely examined senior voting in Florida, observed that seniors often account for 50 percent of the vote and higher in such counties as Charlotte, Citrus, Highlands, Pasco, and Sarasota, where they constitute more than one-third of the population. MacManus also found that during the 1990s seniors began electing their own to various local, county, and state positions.[29] Part of this development reflected the longer life span of seniors and their better health during retirement years. With more time on their hands, seniors searched for activities more purposeful than golf or a game of bridge, and some viewed politics as an attractive alternative. Senior voters also saw other seniors as more responsive to their interests and thus more likely to pursue their public-policy goals. Most liked Chiles because of his age—he was sixty-four when reelected in 1994—and they chuckled over his reference to himself as the "he-coon," a southern reference to the oldest, wisest raccoon. But they preferred him over Bush because he was more attuned to their needs and more willing to address issues of state growth that worried them.[30]

Many retirees had tired of the state's continuous growth and constant development, and the impact it was having on their lives. Mac Stipanovich, a Republican pollster and political adviser to Republican governors, observed that retirees wanted stability in their new location because they did not want to move again. "That leads to a drawbridge mentality," he contended, "that once they've come here, they don't want anybody else to come along and spoil it."[31] Stipanovich felt that their concerns worked to the advantage of the Republican Party. But seniors also wanted to preserve Florida's pristine environment, which had drawn them to the state in the first place, and they liked Chiles because of his strong commitment to the environment. Many joined forces with various environmental groups such as the Florida Defenders of the Environment, and they occasionally led them, as in the case of Manatee 88. Marjorie Carr founded the Florida Defenders of the Environment in 1969, an organization devoted to defeating the Cross-Florida Barge Canal, a mammoth, multimillion-dollar project traversing central Florida that threatened the area's ecosystem. The group, aided by the support of many retirees, presented convincing scientific and economic evidence that persuaded the federal government to abandon the project in 1971. Similarly, Gloria Rains, a retiree living in St. Petersburg, mobilized friends and neighbors to join her in creating Manatee 88 to block offshore oil drilling in Florida and to block the use of orimulsion in power electrical plants. Orimulsion, a bitumen-and-water mixture mined in Venezuela, proved to be highly toxic to the environment, and Rains and her supporters were able to block its use in Florida.[32]

The political clout of retirees did not always endear them to other residents, who felt that they acted like bullies on some issues and often prevented communities from addressing the needs of families and children. New tax initiatives to address public school needs, for example, proved nearly impossible to enact in many south Florida communities in the 1980s and 1990s because of opposition from seniors.[33] However, retirees were not one-issue voters, and they were not hesitant about changing their votes from one party to the other if they did not like a candidate's position on the issues. The pre-1970 retirees were overwhelmingly Democrats back home, remaining that way in Florida. The post-1970 retirees were largely Republican in their home states and typically voted Republican in Florida, but they tended to be less doctrinaire than the earlier Democratic generation of retirees. While those who resided in isolation from other Floridians in places like the Villages, south of Ocala, were much more likely to maintain their Republican ties, others who resided in cities and suburbs were more unpredictable because their concerns about such issues as traffic, health care, and the environment often outweighed party ties.

Chiles's Second Term and the Victory over Big Tobacco

Despite Chiles's victory over Bush, he confronted a legislature in 1995 in which Republicans had taken control of the Senate for the first time in the twentieth century, with twenty-two of the forty seats, and narrowed the gap in the House to only six votes with sixty-three Democrats and fifty-seven Republicans. Limited in what he could accomplish legislatively, Chiles spent much of his last four years doing battle with the tobacco companies. When he took office in 1991, the state entered a brief but steep economic slump. Chiles recalled: "One of the first actions I had to take before I was actually inaugurated was a plan that cut back all agencies a certain percent. I think we had to actually do it twice because our revenue was not coming in."[34] Chiles asked his aides to find out the reasons for the recession and its particular impact on Florida. His staff reported back to him that sales-tax revenues were down substantially, but also that health-care costs had increased by over 20 percent a year. Chiles asked his aides, "What in the world is the occasion for this huge health care cost?"[35] Part of the problem, they told him, was that the state operated on a fee-for-service, which meant that whatever a doctor or a laboratory ordered, it was paid for by Medicaid for Medicaid patients. But the other startling figure that caught their eyes and the governor's attention was the $400 million Florida paid to Medicaid recipients each year for tobacco-related illnesses. "Now, that's a huge sum of money," Chiles observed, "and especially so when you are cutting all kinds of programs."[36] Chiles challenged his staff to see if there was a way to change this situation and what the state could do to recover some of that money. In the course of these discussions, staff members noted that the smoker has a choice with regard to smoking, but the state had no choice but to pay for patient treatment.

Faced with a health situation that had been actively encouraged by the tobacco industry over many years, Chiles did not hesitate to sue the major tobacco companies (other states would follow Florida's lead). The decision particularly appealed to Chiles's populist values. "As we got into that a little bit," Chiles recalled, "we started seeing that the same defense that tobacco was using against individuals, they would attempt to try to use against the state. And we thought, that is not fair, we ought to have a level playing field in which they should not be able to say to us—what they said to the smoker—the warning was on the pack in that the state did not have those kind of choices. So that is where the idea for the Medicaid Liability Law came from."[37]

The Medicaid Liability Law passed quickly through the legislature with surprisingly little debate. Chiles was subsequently accused of using chicanery to get the measure through the legislature by not making fully clear to legislators his intention to use this law to sue the tobacco industry. When Republicans became aware of the governor's intentions, they set about to dismantle the legislation. That set the stage for the most difficult part of this battle for the governor, to sustain legislative support for the law. Major tobacco companies and their allies cried foul when the governor sought to use the new law against them, and they urged legislative supporters to repeal the law. In the 1993 legislative session, tobacco supporters successfully pushed through legislation to repeal the law, but Chiles vetoed the measure at the end of the session. Tobacco interests, in response, hired a small army of lobbyists to maintain legislative support on behalf of repeal and spent enormous sums of money on legislators and advertisements to ensure its repeal.

The Republican Party, which pursued tort reform as part of its political platform, urged its legislative members to repeal the law. Much like the party's decision to oppose Askew's corporate income-tax proposal in 1971, Republicans opted again to side with big business in this conflict, alienating many potential working-class and middle-class voters in the process. Joining Republican leaders was Associated Industries of Florida, an organization of major businesses. Spokespersons for Associated Industries alleged that the law allowed the state great latitude to go well beyond Big Tobacco and sue other legitimate businesses like milk producers and orange juice producers and anyone else who made a product that might adversely affect the public's health.

But Chiles's forces had the better of this argument and the support of voters when both the governor and Attorney General Bob Butterworth reminded reporters and Floridians that tobacco was the only product that killed people when used as directed. To strengthen his hand, Chiles also issued an executive order pledging that he would only use the law against the tobacco industry. Unsure of whether he could continue to sustain his veto with opposition from the Republican Party and Associated Industries, Chiles agreed with aides: "If we were going to sustain this veto, it had to be something akin to the hallmark of my administration or anybody's relationship with me as Governor for the rest of my term, so to speak." Unlike his proposal for tax reform, for which Chiles had failed to fight, he came to regard the battle against Big Tobacco as a moral crusade, the last one he would engage in as a politician, and one that, if he were successful, would help generations of Floridians. But how to win it politically was the major question. "We basically felt that the Senate was where we had to operate," Chiles recalled. "That body was smaller. There were too many House members. We thought we would have a better chance in the Senate. So we slowly went about trying to pick up members who would sustain the veto."[38]

Chiles campaigned to convince Floridians and, through them, a sufficient number of Republican senators to sustain the veto. Most Floridians resented the tactics of the tobacco industry and its efforts to pressure legislators. Moreover, despite Republican Party efforts to derail Chiles's plans, key Republican senators also expressed concern about the behavior of the tobacco industry and the degree to which its products had jeopardized the health of many Floridians. Most had relatives who had suffered physically from years of smoking. Chiles traveled extensively throughout the state for his program and gained the support of many antismoking groups, including the medical community, which publicly endorsed the governor's efforts. Chiles recalled: "It was pretty dramatic at the time. But that allowed us then to go forward with our suit."[39]

The lawsuit was filed by Attorney General Butterworth's office in 1995 to recover Medicaid dollars that paid for health problems resulting from tobacco products and to protect children from the industry's practice of selling products through Joe Camel–type marketing and advertising. As the suit progressed, Chiles noted, "We began to see a lot of things they [the tobacco industry] had known, and how long they had known, and what some of their practices are, so we then amended our suit to allege racketeering under a RICO statute and to demand punitive damages." This information and the resulting decision turned out to be one of the most important developments in the suit, because the judge subsequently ruled that the state was limited to Medicaid damages for only three years. But once the state was permitted to sue under RICO, it was able to ask for triple the amount of damages. Chiles and Butterworth recalled, "We were fortunate in that we had a very able judge: very disciplined, very studious, who paid attention to all the pleadings very carefully."[40]

On August 25, 1997, the tobacco industry, fearing the worst, decided to seek an out-of-court settlement with the state in the amount of $11.3 billion—the largest such settlement in history; other states would subsequently reach their own settlements with the industry, some of which would be larger. But Florida's was the first and set the precedent for the others. The judge ordered that $200 million be devoted to a two-year effort to dissuade youths from smoking cigarettes, which Chiles strongly supported, committing $70 million of the settlement toward the reduction of tobacco consumption through aggressive antitobacco marketing, coupled with a comprehensive combination of community and school-based efforts. The goals of the program focused on changing attitudes about tobacco, empowering youth to lead community involvement against tobacco, reducing accessibility and availability of tobacco to youth, and reducing youth exposure to secondhand smoke.[41] In the aftermath of the court's decision, Chiles observed, "A number of the lawmakers who fought us the hardest when we were trying to pass the act, bring the suit, and prevent the repeal of the act, were the first to say that when we won the suit, 'We want to spend the money for this, or we want to spend the money for that.'"[42] Opponents of the governor were not finished, however, and they challenged the legality of the state's Medicaid Liability Law before the Florida Supreme Court. The judges subsequently ruled on behalf of the governor, although by the narrow margin of 4 to 3.

The tobacco fight was the highlight of Chiles's last four years in office. On most other matters, he struggled in vain. With Jeb Bush waiting in the wings, Republicans felt confident that the governorship would be theirs in 1998. The consequence was that in Chiles's last four years he focused most of his energies on building upon his legal victory against Big Tobacco by pursuing programs to help families, seniors, and children. It was also in these areas where he could gain bipartisan support. State Senator John Grant, Republican from Tampa, admired Chiles's populist values, noting: "He didn't do things because they were political, he did them because he believed in them. And the most important issues to him were not partisan issues—children and health and speaking up for people who couldn't necessarily speak up for themselves."[43]

The End of an Era

The conclusion of Chiles's two terms in office marked the end of a remarkable period of Democratic leadership. Askew, Graham, and Chiles governed Florida for twenty-four years, each holding office for two consecutive terms and providing the state with remarkably strong, honest, and progressive leadership. All three regarded LeRoy Collins, the only other Democrat to serve two terms as governor in the twentieth century, as their political mentor. It was Collins's efforts to modernize Florida, to guide the state through the tumultuous events of the 1950s and 1960s, and to offer Floridians a better vision of themselves that inspired these three men. Although native white Floridians would turn against Collins for his progressive racial leadership, Askew, Chiles, and Graham never flinched in their support of a biracial society. And they persuaded a majority of middle-class voters that this was the proper course for their state. They benefited in this regard from the massive migration of northerners and business interests into the state, most of whom exhibited little tolerance for racial violence and discrimination.

Askew, Chiles, and Graham were all born before World War II, and all but Askew were born in Florida; Askew's mother moved the family to Pensacola when he was a young boy. They were part of a generation that helped the nation achieve political and economic prominence in the world, and these three sought to ensure that Florida and Floridians would benefit from the nation's rise to power. All but Graham served in the military; all became lawyers; and all served as state legislators before they became governors. Despite the ambitions of each man and despite their political competitiveness, the three worked closely together and became good friends. They brought a style of leadership to the state that had not been seen previously. Their ability to build a relationship of trust with Floridians from all backgrounds, to address the status of both poor white and poor black Floridians, to reach out to Cubans fleeing oppression in their homeland, and to seek long-term solutions to Florida's needs had no counterpart in state history prior to their election. And not least, their commitment to making state government transparent to Floridians through the Sunshine Law, public records disclosure, and limits on campaign spending helped build a relationship of trust and confidence in state government. It was a remarkable twenty-four years of gubernatorial leadership that had been inspired by the political courage and integrity of LeRoy Collins. Lawton Chiles observed poignantly: "That group all came through some common experiences. I guess there is some change of the times coming now."[44]

After those years of strong Democratic leadership, Buddy MacKay stood as the obvious successor to the Askew-Graham-Chiles triumvirate. MacKay, who served as lieutenant governor under Chiles, lacked the personal appeal of Askew, Chiles, and Graham, however. But it may well have been that no Democrat could have succeeded these three men. Twenty-four years is, after all, a long time for a particular party and a particular style of leadership to dominate any state. Few parties or leaders last that long. And, as Chiles observed, voter attitudes had shifted to favor the Republican Party and many aspects of the party's political agenda, despite Democratic achievements over the years. With their control of the state legislature secured, Republicans confidently prepared to nominate Jeb Bush once again for governor of Florida in 1998.

7

From Blue to Red

The Era of Jeb Bush and Republican Hegemony

A very bright, attractive, and passionate political figure, Jeb Bush gave the Florida Republican Party a badly needed star quality, much as Reubin Askew had done for Democrats in the 1970s. Bush looked like his mother, had the same gracious style of his father, but his politics more closely resembled those of Barry Goldwater, Ronald Reagan, and Newt Gingrich. Jeb fully embraced the values of the new Republican Party—its commitment to limited government and low taxes, its denunciation of government bureaucrats, its pledge to resurrect the historic principles that had made the nation great, and its opposition to affirmative action and to many of the social and cultural values that "liberal" Democrats had foisted on the country in the 1960s. "I have the luxury of hindsight," he declared when asked to compare his philosophy of government with that of his father. "People moving into the political fray now naturally have a different view of the effectiveness of government programs."[1]

The gubernatorial election of 1994 introduced Jeb Bush to Floridians, and most liked what they saw. Bush's energy and sense of mission mobilized Republicans as no one had previously, and his conservative values and rhetoric helped coalesce the thinking of conservative Democrats, Republicans, and many new voters. For Jeb Bush, good government was an oxymoron, and the less government, in his view, the better. Conservative audiences cheered when he pledged to eliminate many state offices and abolish the state Department of Education.[2]

Jeb's Florida Roots and Political Activism

Like so many Floridians, Bush and his family were quite new to the state, having lived in Florida for only fourteen years when he ran for governor in 1994. Jeb and his wife, Columba, moved to Miami in 1980, when they were twenty-seven and twenty-six, respectively, to work on his father's unsuccessful first presidential campaign. When the party's nomination went to Ronald Reagan, Jeb and Columba opted to stay in Miami. During Bush's years in Miami, he was involved in many different entrepreneurial pursuits, including working for a mobile phone company, serving on the board of a Norwegian-owned company that sold fire equipment to companies building the Alaska oil pipeline, becoming a minority owner of a professional football team (the Jacksonville Jaguars), buying a shoe company that sold footwear in Panama, and getting involved in a scheme to sell water pumps in Nigeria.[3]

Not much went well financially until Jeb took a job in real estate with Armando Codina, a thirty-two-year-old Cuban immigrant and self-made American millionaire. Bush met Codina in 1979, when both were working to help elect Ronald Reagan as president and Jeb's father as vice president in 1980, and the two developed a close friendship. Codina had made a fortune in a computer business and then formed a new company, IntrAmerica Investments Inc., to pursue real estate development opportunities. He invited Bush to join his investment firm. The addition of Jeb Bush made good sense for the company, and the firm's name was soon changed to the Codina-Bush Group. As one Miami developer commented, hiring Jeb Bush was "like hiring General Norman Schwarzkopf. He'll command attention." There was not a better time to invest in real estate in Miami, with the immigration of people from the Caribbean and Latin America flooding into the city and with relatively low property values because of city's economic problems in the 1970s and early 1980s. The Codina-Bush Group became one of South Florida's leading real estate development firms, and Bush received 40 percent of the firm's profits. In June 1993, Bush sold his share of the company that he and Codina had built for over $1 million to pursue his political ambitions.[4]

Bush got his start in Florida politics as the chairman of the Miami-Dade County Republican Party, where he played an important role in increasing GOP registrations from under 100,000 to 240,000 in five years and in coordinating Bob Martinez's successful 1986 campaign in Miami-Dade.[5] In return, Martinez appointed Bush as Florida's secretary of commerce. But Bush served only two years in this position before resigning in 1988 to work on his father's successful presidential campaign.

During this campaign, Bush came under the tutelage of Lee Atwater, his father's controversial and highly successful campaign manager. Atwater had been brought on board to convince Republicans that George Herbert Walker Bush represented the party's conservative values and was the rightful heir to Ronald Reagan. Atwater's opponents characterized him as "the Darth Vader of the Republican Party," "the happy hatchet man," and "the guy who went negative for the sheer joy of it." But Atwater had been given an assignment to convince Republicans and voters that Bush was tough enough to be a strong conservative president. In the process of doing so, he gained the respect and support of the entire Bush clan, from Barbara to George W. and Jeb. He also served as political mentor for George W., Jeb, and Karl Rove during the campaign and became a close friend of all three.[6]

The Bush presidential campaign in 1988 called for a series of conservative measures highlighted by a proposed voucher system in education, a new Social Security proposal to allow individuals to manage their own retirement account, the random testing of high school students for drugs, and a welfare-to-work proposal, entitled "if you don't work, you don't get paid." Much of the campaign, however, focused on Bush's commitment to "no new taxes" and his personal attacks against Bush's opponent, Massachusetts Governor Michael Dukakis, portraying him as a poster boy for the liberal left and a weak-kneed northeastern liberal who was "soft on crime." Bush's hard-hitting advertisements went right for the jugular and were designed to appeal to voter concerns about rising crime rates. A widely shown Bush television ad pictured Willie Horton, a burly black criminal who was serving a life sentence, being furloughed from a Massachusetts prison; following his release, Horton had raped and assaulted a young woman. The ad castigated Dukakis for supporting a furlough program for hardened criminals like Horton. The intensity of the negative ads in this campaign led political writers David Gergen and E. J. Dionne to observe: "America has suffered through nasty presidential campaigns in the past; it has endured more than its share of shallow campaigns; it has frequently watched with some embarrassment as one candidate pummeled another against the ropes and there has been no referee to leap in and stop the fight. But rarely have all of those elements come together in the same campaign, as they did in 1988."[7] While history suggests that Gergen and Dionne may have overstated their case, the success of the Bush 1988 presidential campaign made it a model for subsequent negative Republican campaign ads at the state and national levels. Both sons, George W. and Jeb, took much away from their experiences in 1988 that they subsequently incorporated into their own campaigns for political office.

Following the campaign, Jeb returned to Florida to serve as campaign manager for the election of Ileana Ros-Lehtinen, the first Cuban American to serve in Congress. After losing the 1994 gubernatorial election to Chiles, Bush pursued policy and charitable interests, which kept his name before the public and strengthened his conservative credentials. During this period, he launched the Foundation for Florida's Future, which served as a think tank for conservative ideas and which sought to shape conservative public policy in the state. Bush was something of a policy wonk, and the foundation proved an effective vehicle for him to further develop his conservative ideas.

Preparing for 1998 and the Gubernatorial Campaign

During the years between the 1994 and 1998 gubernatorial campaigns, Jeb deliberately set about to soften his image. Bush's inexperience and glib responses in the 1994 campaign often got him in trouble; for example, when he was asked what he would do to help black Floridians, he responded, "probably nothing." In fairness to Bush, he had actually said: "It's time to strive for a society where there's equality of opportunity, not equality of results. So I'm going to answer your question by saying: 'probably nothing.'"[8] In retrospect, he regretted saying "probably nothing." But Bush learned quickly from his mistakes, and public ire at his brazenness became an important part of his political education. It would be a mistake, however, to think he changed his political beliefs or his determination to dismantle government because of such criticism.

After 1994, Bush made it clear to Floridians that his brand of conservatism did not exclude African Americans and other minorities. Both he and his brother felt their approach to government offered black and ethnic Americans greater opportunity than the liberal, highly regulated, and bureaucratic programs of the Democratic Party. Subsequently he championed Republican efforts to establish charter schools and then cofounded the first charter school in Florida with T. Willard Fair, a well-known local black activist and head of the Greater Miami Urban League. Fair initially doubted Bush's intentions but soon became one of his strongest supporters. The Bush-Fair venture was located in an area of Dade County plagued by poverty. Bush's purpose was to provide for greater engagement by black parents in the education of their children and to demonstrate to black and white Floridians that charter schools offered a meaningful alternative to public schools that typically failed the children of the poor.[9]

His volunteer activities, the achievements of the charter school, and his partnership with Fair helped smooth out the rough edges of his political personality. He dramatized the new Jeb Bush in September 1997, when he had a single black woman from Liberty City, with her child in tow, file his paperwork for the gubernatorial election. All these actions helped strengthen his statewide reputation and revealed a more astute and seasoned candidate as he entered the 1998 campaign against Democrat Buddy MacKay.[10]

While Bush entered the race with significant momentum, MacKay struggled from the outset to energize the Democratic Party's base. Much of his message to voters sounded like the same old Democratic proposals at a time when the public sought new ideas to address rising crime rates, economic stagnation, and the failings of public schools. Even Jews and African Americans, among the most loyal of Democrats, were apathetic about MacKay's candidacy and his message. He did not help his cause in the debates, looking stiff and uncomfortable in front of the camera, while Bush had vastly improved his public-speaking delivery and enhanced his knowledge of the issues.

Bush had also moderated his tone. For example, he courted environmentalists by proposing an expansion of Florida's land-preservation program that would cost state taxpayers $1 billion. And he vowed to push for full funding for Everglades restoration, then estimated to cost state and federal taxpayers $8 billion. These were the promises of a savvy politician who came to realize that many retirees and wealthy residents had been attracted to the state by its environment and did not want it plundered.

The gubernatorial election was seldom in doubt. Early polls showed Bush with a substantial lead, and that remain unchanged throughout the fall campaign. Most agreed that MacKay was a talented, experienced, and able candidate, but few expressed enthusiasm about his candidacy, and he was unable to persuade them otherwise. Bush captured 55 percent of the vote to MacKay's 45 percent and beat MacKay in literally every part of the state, and among all constituent groups with the exception of black and Jewish voters. Bush, however, increased his vote total only slightly from 1994 to 1998. In 1994, he received 2 million votes in his loss to Chiles, and in 1998, he received 2.1 million votes. The Democratic vote total revealed that MacKay had failed to invigorate the party's base. In 1994, Chiles and MacKay obtained 2.1 million votes, but in 1998, MacKay garnered only 1.77 million votes, or nearly 364,000 votes fewer than the Chiles-MacKay ticket in 1994.[11]

The Jeb Bush Revolution

At his inaugural in January 1999, Bush issued a clarion call for a conservative political revolution. The differences between the new governor and his Democratic predecessors could not have been more obvious. "While our government has grown larger," Bush told his audience, "so, too, has the crushing weight of taxes, regulations and mandates on Florida's families and entrepreneurs. As we address these great challenges into the next century, we need not only ask 'What's new?' we should more often ask, 'What's best?' For the things that are best will endure, and the things that are merely new will soon become old and discarded." Stressing a theme that had been popularized in the Reagan administration and had been an important part of his father's administration, Bush told listeners: "What endures are Faith, family, friends—these are what's best. These will endure. We should trust in these more than we trust in government."[12]

In Bush's view, state government had become too powerful and too intrusive. "The best and brightest ideas do not come from the state capital," he emphasized, "but from the untapped human capital that resides in our diverse communities." In a statement that angered many Democrats, Bush harkened back to comments by former Governor LeRoy Collins: "Government cannot live by taxes alone or by jobs alone or even by roads alone. Government, too, must have qualities of the spirit. Truth and justice and fairness and unselfish service are some of these. Without these qualities there is no worthwhile leadership, and we grapple and grope in a moral wilderness."[13] But, as Democrats quickly pointed out, Bush failed to note that Collins did not see state government as a festering problem. In fact, Collins relied heavily on his powers as governor and the authority of state government to advance the cause of racial equality in Florida. Bush's aim in referring to Collins, however, was to silence liberal critics by suggesting that Collins, too, agreed with the principle of limited government.

In a plea to Floridians, Bush asked that they join him in making fundamental changes to state government, declaring "I want state government to be an ally, not an adversary of positive change within each community. I want to protect people, not bureaucracies. I want state government to be more respectful of the earnings of Florida's families, not more desirous."[14]

Aiding him in his plans to overhaul state government was a Republican-dominated legislature. At the time of Bush's inauguration in 1999, Republicans held majorities in both houses, with 25 of the 40 seats in the Senate and 73 of the 120 seats in the House. Moreover, Republican leaders gave Jeb Bush credit for the party's political rise to state leadership. He was not only governor, he was also party leader, and they were ready and eager to follow his leadership. Not since Reubin Askew assumed the governorship in 1970 had a governor enjoyed the political following among members of his own party as did Jeb Bush. In his first message to the state legislature in March 1999, he reiterated the vision expressed in his inaugural:

- A state with a world-class educational system that does not leave a single child behind;

- A state with safe neighborhoods where children can play and elders can live without fear;

- A state where abused and neglected children, the developmentally disabled and frail elders receive the help they need in a compassionate way;

- A state where our urban cores flourish, providing hope and opportunity to those who need it most;

- ◆ A state where our natural resources are sustained for the benefit and enjoyment of future generations;
- ◆ And a state where government takes less of our money.

Calling his legislative agenda "Resources, Reform and Relief," he promised "resources and reform for education and social services, and relief for Florida's taxpayers." To make his point on the need for social service reform and funding, he quoted from a letter from a mother with a disabled child who wondered what would happen to the child if she, the mother, passed away. Bush characterized the system, as he would frequently do when speaking about state agencies and state government, as "drowning in an ocean of federal lawsuits, waiting lists, and obsolete bureaucracy."[15]

Bush signaled the beginning of his conservative revolution with the "A+ Plan for Education." Within the neoconservative movement, public school reform stood near the very top of the list because of its importance in maintaining the nation's competitive edge. Aided by Lieutenant Governor Frank Brogan, a former school teacher and principal, Bush focused heavily on accountability measures for public schools, competition with the private sector through the development and expansion of charter schools, and vouchers for poor families to attend such schools. He told legislators that "while our plan recognizes that our schools need more money, we must also recognize that our money needs more accountability."[16]

School improvement held particular importance in the state, which was growing dramatically and being populated by people from diverse backgrounds, many of whom had special language needs, and by new businesses that were eager to have a pool of educated workers. Student performance in Florida's public schools had declined steadily over the previous decade, despite the infusion of additional state funds. The problems in Florida were not unique to the state; they existed in most Sun Belt states where the pressures from population growth and diversity were substantial. Whites as well as middle-class black parents in Florida worried that the deteriorating condition of the public schools and the absence of school discipline would negatively affect the education of their children. They demanded that schools be improved and teachers and principals be held accountable.[17]

As his plan unfolded and accountability measures were developed, the governor pushed through the legislature the nation's first voucher program in 1999 and with it a dramatic expansion of the charter school movement. Bush sold the voucher plan to Floridians not only as providing healthy competition for the public schools but as a way to offer the children of the poor and working classes an alternative to bad schools and bad teachers. Public school students, who earned a failing grade in two out of four years, would receive vouchers to attend private schools.

The rhetoric of the voucher program and charter school movement promised a little something to everyone. Within Hispanic communities, charter schools enabled children to retain aspects of their culture and language. For whites and evangelicals, these schools promised their children a better educational environment, opportunities to impart their cultural values, and a reduction in the number of black children, whom they held responsible for many of the classroom problems. And for black families, charter schools also offered an alternative to public schools that had often failed their children and over which they had no control and little influence.[18]

The Bush education initiatives dramatically expanded the state's involvement in public education. In this sense, the plans seemed inconsistent with Bush's commitment to reduce the role of state government in the lives of Floridians and to allow communities to determine the content of the curriculum. But Bush and aides rationalized these steps as essential to achieving their reforms. In the governor's view, public education had become too important to leave to the educators and too essential to Florida's future to risk decentralizing control and accountability. Bush dramatically reorganized and downsized the Florida Department of Education and ordered it to focus the school curricula on reading, writing, and mathematics. Through his secretaries of education and the chair and members of the State Board of Education, all of whom he had appointed, Bush kept his hands firmly on the controls of educational reform. As one political leader observed, Bush brooked no disagreement over his proposed reforms—"It was Jeb's way or no way."[19]

While the public generally accepted Bush's commitment to accountability and competition, they insisted that more be done financially to improve public education. Despite the governor's reforms, Florida still ranked forty-eighth in the nation in per-student funding, and voters recognized that the public schools would never improve until more funds were directed their way. In 2004, voters adopted a class-size amendment to the state constitution, limiting kindergarten through third grade to eighteen students per teacher, fourth through eighth grades to twenty-two students per teacher, and ninth through twelfth grades to twenty-five students per teacher. The state had until 2010 to meet those goals and provide the necessary funding. Bush opposed the amendment and subsequently sought to have the legislature overturn it, but voters had been persuaded that public education was in crisis and needed a radical overhaul, even if it cost them more in taxes. The class-size amendment was one of Bush's few political setbacks as governor—the other being the decision by the Florida Supreme Court in January 2006 to strike down the voucher system. The justices ruled that it undermined the public schools and violated the Florida constitution's requirement of a uniform system of free public education.[20]

Beyond his educational reforms, Bush maintained his campaign pledge to reduce taxes and proposed a $1.2 billion tax reduction in his first term. Some legislators, mostly Democrats, asked how he proposed to increase funding for education and social services while simultaneously cutting taxes. That would become clearer during the legislative session, as he worked closely with the Senate leadership and its president, Toni Jennings, and the House leadership, particularly his ally and friend Speaker John Thrasher, to cut funding and privatize many other state operations. Thrasher was a strong supporter of Bush's antigovernment message and met almost daily with him to implement his legislative program. Jennings, a native Floridian, exercised a bit more independence from the governor as was the tradition of the Senate, but in the area of educational reform and tax cuts, Jennings and her Republican colleagues signed on with the governor.

From the outset of his administration, it was evident that Bush's vision for state government and his role as political leader differed dramatically from those of Democrats Askew, Graham, or Chiles. These three embraced the central role of government in addressing the fundamental needs of citizens. Public education, crime prevention, the welfare of children, health care for the elderly, and environmental protection ranked high on any list of government obligations for Askew, Graham, and Chiles. All three men also valued the state's civil servants as the backbone of good government. While Bush was inclined to agree with them in the areas of public education, crime prevention, health care, and environmental protection, he believed the private sector could perform many of these functions more efficiently and economically than the state, and he had a much more negative view of state bureaucrats, often singling them out for the deficiencies of government.

Bush saw himself as part of a conservative revolution, as the head of this movement in Florida, and as responsible for disassembling government and privatizing its activities wherever it served the state poorly or added significantly to the costs of government. He invested enormous personal energy and dedication to his role as governor, party leader, and political reformer. To this extent he also differed from Askew, Graham, and Chiles, who did not regard their roles as quite this extensive or revolutionary. The three Democrats sought to build upon reforms of state government and improve its assistance, accountability, and responsiveness to citizens. By contrast, Bush regarded government as frequently the enemy of the people and had no doubt that his view of government was the correct one.

Bush surrounded himself with young people whom he charged with carrying out his vision for the state. Political commentator Carl Hiaasen accused Bush of recruiting "some real low-voltage hacks to Tallahassee" to oversee his administrative changes.[21] By and large Bush did not include senior, experienced aides among his staff members because he felt that he did not need their political guidance. This frustrated a good many aides, such as Ken Plante, who were top political advisers to Bush in his campaign and when he first took office. But like Plante, many walked away from their jobs after a year or two. When asked by the governor why he had resigned, Plante observed that it was obvious the governor did not want or need his advice.[22] Bush's style in this regard also differed dramatically from Askew, Graham, and Chiles, who typically surrounded themselves with very talented and experienced administrators who were encouraged to offer alternative points of view on policy initiatives. Bush, however, had little time for political debate and opposing views; he was on a mission to reshape and restructure the State of Florida. Jim King, Republican senator from Jacksonville, said of Bush's persona in his first term, it was "like a front-end loader: Bam, here I come." To state Senator Frederica Wilson, a Miami Democrat, he was "King Jeb," an arrogant monarch.[23]

But to whom did Bush listen? Most of his aides, as noted, were in their twenties and thirties and thus quite inexperienced in government. They did whatever the governor asked of them, and they echoed his views on policy matters, but he did not turn to them for advice. Bush did listen to Speaker Thrasher, and the two became very close, but Bush seemed most interested in the views of his former business associates in Miami-Dade. Bush spoke regularly with Codina and other business leaders as well as developers in Miami-Dade and in other sections of the state, and he had a clear preference for their views on government over those of state politicians. The governor also had a very close relationship with his brother George W. Bush, governor of Texas. The two Bushes spoke almost daily on the telephone, compared notes on legislative and political initiatives, and had their staffs meet and work together on major policy issues.

Jeb, for example, borrowed heavily from his brother's decision to eliminate affirmative action in admissions to the state university system on November 9, 1999. The Texas Bush had been forced to eliminate affirmative action in university admissions when the Fifth U.S. Circuit Court of Appeals ruled in the *Hopwood* case in 1996 that it was unconstitutional for Texas public colleges and universities to use race as a condition of admission. The program designed by the staff of the Texas Bush, therefore, guaranteed admission of the top 10 percent of Texas high school graduates to the public university of their choice in Texas. Although Florida was not affected by the *Hopwood* ruling, opponents of affirmative action led by Ward Connerly—a California businessman, a Republican, and a leading spokesman of the California-based American Civil Rights Coalition, an organization that sought to eliminate affirmative action programs nationally—were pursuing what they called the "Florida Civil Rights Initiative," which would amend Florida's constitution and eliminate the use of affirmative action in university admissions. Although in general sympathy with the efforts of Connerly, Jeb Bush worried that the initiative would sharply divide Floridians, create substantial problems for his leadership, and disrupt his efforts to woo black and Hispanic voters. Tom Slade, Republican Party chairman, warned fellow Republicans that the initiative was unpalatable to minorities. "Connerly's initiative has the appearance of a move that would disaffect certain segments of our society," Slade said. "That may be more perception than reality, but in politics, perception is reality."[24]

Shortly after taking office, Bush directed his aides to work with his brother's staff in Texas and develop a plan to end affirmative action in

Florida without disadvantaging African-American students. The Florida Bush plan differed from the Texas plan in that it proposed to offer automatic admission to Florida's universities for the top 20 percent of the state's high school graduates, regardless of their standardized test scores. Bush had even persuaded state Senator Daryl Jones, a prominent African American from Dade County, that the plan would aid black students, and Jones agreed to endorse the plan once it was formally announced.

The announcement of his One Florida initiative was indicative of the governor's style of leadership in many ways. As the One Florida initiative took shape, little discussion occurred outside the governor's inner circle, nor was there consultation with university officials to obtain their input. Dr. Adam Herbert, chancellor of the state university system and an African American, was a close ally of the governor and had served as cochair of the governor's inauguration program. Herbert had also hired Dr. Charles E. Young, former chancellor of the University of California at Los Angeles, as interim president of the University of Florida. Young, who had led UCLA when Proposition 209 had been approved by California voters, eliminating affirmative action from the admissions process at state universities, had substantial experience with the challenges faced by California universities in the wake of Proposition 209. At both UCLA and the University of California, Berkeley—the most competitive universities in the California university system—African-American enrollment had plummeted in the aftermath of Proposition 209, suggesting that much the same might happen in Florida. Significantly, neither Bush nor Herbert ever consulted Young to discuss the governor's plans, the challenges it posed to maintaining diversity in the state system, or changes that universities would need to implement once affirmative action had been eliminated. As was his wont, Bush decided what he intended to do and had no interest in having it debated.[25]

Bush proved extremely effective in staging important media events such as the unveiling of his plan to eliminate affirmative action. On such occasions, he typically surrounded himself with key figures from Florida and elsewhere who were expected to praise his initiative. The governor made the announcement to the press, emphasizing why his initiative was crucial to the state, then took a few questions, and concluded with some final remarks. Standing alongside him for the affirmative action announcement were Chancellor Herbert, Speaker of the House John Thrasher, College Board President Gaston Caperton, and D. J. Miller, president of D. J. Miller and Associates, the state's professional education consultants. Caperton attended because Bush proposed having the state partner with the College Board to improve college preparation for students at low-performing high schools, an arrangement that would provide millions of dollars to the company but offer little benefit to students. As soon as the governor finished his remarks, Herbert marched to the microphone as scripted and praised the governor's decision with a prepared statement: The elimination of affirmative action, he declared, "acknowledges Florida's past but also connects us to Florida's future." Speaker John Thrasher likewise praised the initiative and pledged his support in obtaining legislative funding for Bush's plan.[26] In these events, the Bush team exhibited a mastery of and control over the public relations process that marked his eight years in office.

Such events also revealed a governor who knew what he wanted, was determined to get his way, and would brook no opposition. It was not only the governor's power as the state's chief executive that intimidated potential critics but also his extraordinary influence with the Republican-led legislature, which, through funding programs and state regulations, directly impacted potential opponents. Bush's take-no-prisoners style made his leadership particularly daunting. For example, among university presidents, who depended on the governor and the legislature for much of the funding for their universities, criticizing the governor was not a realistic option.

Of the university presidents, only Young expressed reservations about the plan and its potential impact on the diversity of the student body at the University of Florida. He warned that the implementation of One Florida would significantly reduce the number of African-American students as it had done at UCLA and Berkeley. Black legislators and black leaders in the state echoed Dr. Young's concern and denounced the governor's One Florida initiative as a direct attack on the black community. Bush deeply resented Young's criticism, in part because it appeared to convince Senator Jones to withdraw his endorsement and inspired two African-American legislators, Kendrick Meek of Miami and Tony Hill of Jacksonville, to conduct a sit-in in the governor's office, where they vowed to remain until he rescinded his executive orders enacting One Florida. Angry at the legislators but unable to punish them, the governor singled out Dr. Young and the University of Florida, using his line-item veto to cut its construction budget for 2000–2001 and letting Young and other potential opponents know that he was not someone to be trifled with.[27]

By the time Bush formally implemented his One Florida plan with all its particulars in March 2000, many of the state universities had completed their admission decisions for the fall of 2000. Young's warning initially seemed irrelevant when the University of Florida's freshmen class was the most diverse in its history. What Floridians failed to realize was that One Florida had not been implemented soon enough to affect freshmen admissions at the University of Florida in 2000. The full impact of One Florida, in fact, would not be felt at the University of Florida and in the state university system until the fall of 2001, when President Young's warning came true: African-American enrollment fell dramatically, just as it had previously at UCLA and Berkeley.[28]

Critical Developments that Amplified Bush's Power

Bush adroitly asserted his gubernatorial leadership in such a dramatic and forceful manner in this and in other areas and got away with it because of four important developments. First, the Republican Party controlled the state legislature. Linked to this development was the second factor, Republican dominance of the state cabinet in 1999. In Florida, many executive functions are carried out by the state's principal officers sitting as the cabinet. Bush's leadership might have been limited by a cabinet that was controlled by Democrats, as it had been for all of the twentieth century up to 1999. But as with the Republican legislature, Bush enjoyed the full support of the Republican majority in the cabinet. Also enhancing the power and authority of the governor, voters supported a constitutional amendment in 1998 that consolidated the cabinet positions from six to three.

The original cabinet positions included the attorney general, agriculture commissioner, commissioner of education, comptroller, secretary of state, and treasurer/insurance commissioner. This amendment took effect in 2003. Under the reforms adopted, the secretary of state and education commissioner became appointed officials under the governor, who would oversee their respective agencies, while the positions of the comptroller and the treasurer/insurance commissioner/fire marshal were combined into the position of the chief financial officer. The cabinet, for example, lost oversight of the Florida Department of Education, including management of K-12 education and the community college system, both of which were shifted to the new Florida Board of Education.

A third development strengthening Bush's leadership was the adoption by voters of a constitutional amendment limiting legislative terms to eight years. More popularly known as "Eight Is Enough," this amendment forced out of office more than half the experienced members of the state House and the state Senate in 2000. They were replaced with newly elected, mostly Republican representatives and senators, who readily deferred to Bush. As a result, Bush enjoyed a commanding influence in legislative affairs that had no parallel in Florida politics in the twentieth century. The fact that Bush also headed the party that had been out of power for so long aided his negotiations with the state legislature and especially with its new members. Republican Party chief Tom Slade, and his successor, Al Cardenas, reinforced the governor's primacy by insisting on party discipline so that new legislators would not go off on political tangents, jeopardizing the governor's leadership and placing the party at risk.

Fourth, Bush's aides commenced a thorough housecleaning of Democratic officeholders, replacing them with Republicans or abolishing the agency that employed them. In higher education, Bush eliminated the State Board of Regents, which oversaw the university system, and replaced it with a Board of Education, which oversaw all public education in the state from kindergarten through university. He also appointed boards of trustees at each state university and all members of the Board of Education and boards of trustees, who were frequently selected not for their expertise in education but for their loyalty to the governor and the party.

These developments occurred alongside Bush's use of technology to communicate more personally as well as more effectively with Floridians. Where Lawton Chiles and Bob Martinez used television and Bob Graham relied on his Workdays, Bush took advantage of the Internet to reach out to voters and circumvent the press. Bush was not only a policy wonk, he was something of a technology wonk and was fully comfortable in using his handheld Blackberry to respond rapidly to Floridians daily. Additionally, he and his aides sent supporters a weekly update on his activities and key policy and legislative issues via the Web site jeb@jeb.org. Bush also bypassed the press by communicating directly with television news reporters, who were much less likely to ask difficult questions, and whose reports were consumed far more widely by the public than newspaper stories. When communicating through the press, Bush typically wrote "letters to the editor" to convey his position on policy matters, ensuring that his remarks would not be abbreviated by editors. No governor of his generation or in Florida history used these various means of communication as effectively as Bush.

Bush also cut a commanding image on television and in person. Although Fidel Castro snidely referred to him as the chubby younger brother of the president, Bush was strikingly tall, with a large head and clean-cut features that photographed well on television. As he gained experience, he became much more comfortable and effective in public speaking and in interacting with the public and the press. He could turn on the charm when he wanted, and his aides became very effective in mobilizing a crowd when he visited local communities. Moreover, he was also a policy junkie, especially on issues of concern to neoconservatives, and he became very comfortable in discussing such issues with the public. His fluency in Spanish gained him a large following among Florida's Hispanic community, in particular.

Although Bush's politics were often to the right of many Floridians, he managed to mask the differences and presented his policies to the public in a manner that seemed to reflect conventional thinking.[29] For example, Floridians were very sympathetic to public school reform and to the implementation of accountability measures. They were less convinced of the voucher system and his stunning expansion of charter schools, including those with religious affiliations, and the absence of accountability measures for these programs. In fact, most Floridians were oblivious to the charter school developments, which flew under their radar screen, receiving little mention from the governor. His approach, however, was much more radical than the public realized. Bush, who was well aware of what he was doing, chose instead to emphasize the healthy competition that charter schools provided for public schools and the opportunities they afforded minority children, rather than the extent to which they were eligible for public funds; that they were heavily segregated; and that they lacked accountability measures. Those Floridians who wanted their children in schools that emphasized their cultural values or were almost entirely white had few concerns about these aspects of the governor's initiatives.

The absence of accountability among charter schools represented but one example of the manner in which Bush governed Florida in his first term in office. Since the end of segregation, no governor had been as intrusive as Bush in state and local affairs or had so altered the manner in which the state carried out its business. From the reorganization and restructuring of public education, to the admissions process at universities and the dismantling of many state agencies, Bush's personal hand was involved in every aspect of these initiatives. Wherever possible, Bush sought to curtail or eliminate the role of government and replace it with the private sector. For example, he gutted funding and staff levels at the Department of Community Affairs, which had oversight for growth management, one of the most critical areas confronting Florida.[30] His most ambitious private contract went to Convergys to manage all state personnel functions. He continued to support the company even after it failed to cut paychecks accurately for state employees and misreported their benefits. Bush subsequently sought to push through an ambitious program to outsource the management of Medicaid benefits, but lawmakers balked at the scope of this initiative following the problems with Convergys and confined a pilot program to Broward and Duval counties. In most cases, the public had little or no input into these developments; indeed, many of these matters were not discussed by Bush in his political campaigns. Because of the state's ongoing massive population growth, most citizens were oblivious to the magnitude of the changes taking place.[31]

Coinciding with Bush's efforts to reduce the size and scope of state government was his commitment to reduce state taxes for Floridians. Whether it was through tax holidays, which enabled Floridians to shop on weekends or for a week without paying the state sales tax, or by cutting taxes to business and industry, Bush pushed tax reductions in every area and in every legislative term. He claimed proudly that he had reduced taxes by $18 billion over eight years and vetoed another $2 billion in legislative pork projects, earning the nickname among legislators as "Veto Corleone." He also placed most state appropriations on a nonrecurring basis, so that they could be reduced or eliminated in any legislative session. The governor's political philosophy remained rooted in the principle that government had a very limited purpose and that the private sector served the public much more effectively and efficiently than government. In many ways, his philosophy represented a throwback to the late nineteenth century, when big corporations first took root in America and when politicians embraced a laissez-faire approach to government operations and regulations. Despite the national corporate scandals at Enron, WorldCom, and other corporations in the early twenty-first century, Bush was much more likely to forgive and forget such behavior as the exception rather than the rule in the business world. An error by a state employee or state agency, however, often became justification for condemning the entire agency and state bureaucrats.

In the midst of his first term, as he unveiled his conservative revolution, Bush found himself at the center of his brother's presidential campaign and faced with the realization that Florida would decide the outcome of the closest presidential election in the twentieth century.

8

The Presidential Election of 2000

What Happened in Florida?

From the onset of the presidential campaign of 2000, two things were obvious: the election would be very close, and Florida would be at the epicenter of the contest. In a campaign between two of the nation's most prominent political families, Al Gore and George Bush both believed they would capture Florida and the presidency. Depending on how one counted the ballots in Florida, both were right.[1]

At the outset of the campaign, Republicans confidently predicted that Bush would carry the state and with it the general election. After all, Jeb had captured the governorship decisively in 1998, and state Republicans had been victorious in the majority of local and statewide races since 1996. But polls suggested throughout the campaign that Florida was a toss-up. Tim Russert, NBC's national political commentator, predicted the night before the election that the outcome would be determined by: "Florida, Florida, and Florida."[2]

What accounted for the closeness of the 2000 presidential election in Florida, when Republicans had dominated local and statewide races in the previous four years?

The most obvious answers were the substantial number of registered Democrats in Florida, the popularity of the outgoing Clinton administration among certain segments of the state's population, and the presence of Senator Joseph Lieberman of Connecticut, the first Jewish candidate for Vice President, on the Democratic ticket. Despite substantial Republican gains in Florida, Democrats still enjoyed a 350,000-plus lead in the number of registered voters, and although many Democrats had voted Republican in state and local contests, no one could be sure they would do the same in a presidential contest, especially when the outgoing administration enjoyed broad support in the heavily populated areas of southeast Florida. Moreover, the national Democratic Party recognized the structural weaknesses of the state party in Florida and, rather than rely on local party officials, sent many of its top people to organize the Gore campaign in Florida. Together with the assistance and advice of Bob Graham and his aides, the Gore campaign was well prepared for the obstacles they faced in Florida.

Aiding Gore as well were news reports and comments from Bush insiders that George W. Bush, like his father before him, was weighing plans to offer a private investment alternative to Social Security. The plan was sufficiently vague that Bush was hesitant to describe it during the campaign except to note that it would be for future generations. Gore seized on the issue and warned seniors nationwide and in Florida that Bush's election would threaten their benefits. "The Bush plan would turn Social Security into a grab bag where everyone is out for himself," Gore told supporters and seniors in south Florida. The Social Security issue was not unlike the Medicare issue that former governor Lawton Chiles had exploited to defeat Jeb Bush narrowly in the 1994 gubernatorial contest. Gore also benefited from his selection of Lieberman who became Gore's strategic weapon in mobilizing Jewish voters in southeast Florida. Jewish voters subsequently turned out in record numbers to support Lieberman and Gore.[3]

A series of other developments of no small significance occurred in Florida prior to this campaign and served to place the state at the epicenter of this election. The migration of 6 million new residents into the state during the previous two decades created a Florida that looked like the rest of the nation—with sizable populations of southerners, northerners, midwesterners, blacks, whites, Hispanics, various other ethnic groups, and, last but not least, retirees. The writer Michael Paterniti observed that Florida offered "a close reflection of the nation's ethnic breakdown. Where 75 percent of Americans today are white, in Florida 78 percent are white. Where nearly 13 percent are Hispanic, in Florida 17 percent are. And where 12 percent are black, in Florida 14 percent are."[4]

Additionally, like the nation as a whole, Florida was closely divided between Democrats and Republicans, with Democrats more frequently casting ballots for Republicans in the past decade than Republican voters did for Democrats. Because Republicans had risen to challenge Democrats for political control in the state so recently, the vast majority of Republican voters tended to remain loyal to the party and to its candidates. This trend was also true nationally, as Republicans emerged from the shadows of the Democratic Party in the 1980s to challenge it for national political leadership.

But Florida differed from the other states also because so many residents were newly arrived, and they tended to see themselves as residents of a particular city or region of the state first, and as state residents second. Communication through the many state newspapers and television stations reinforced their local orientation because such information was distributed locally and regionally through these multiple media hubs rather than through one large media hub as in most states. In this sense, Florida was much like California, another physically large state with a substantial population and a media network spread throughout the state. But unlike Californians, Floridians shared little sense of what it meant to be a Floridian, and the absence of a common identity made it very difficult to appeal to voters statewide.

The Politics of the Elian Gonzalez Case

In addition to the regional divisions that existed in the state, fissures also developed among Hispanics. Nowhere were their disagreements more in evidence, for example, than in the case of Elian Gonzalez, and the results of this case profoundly influenced the presidential election in Florida. Elian, a six-year-old, survived an escape to freedom from Cuba in a voyage that resulted in his mother's death. Rescued by the Coast Guard, he was taken in by the Cuban community in Miami; his father, who had remained in Cuba, demanded that his son be returned to him. His relatives in Miami, however, refused to part with him and allow him to be reared in "a Communist nation." Because Elian was orphaned and not a citizen, the matter worked its way up to the attorney general of the United States, Janet Reno, who was herself a native of Miami and whose family had resided there for several generations.[5]

The ensuing political battle over Elian set native against immigrant, the authority of the federal government against that of the family and ethnic community, communism against democracy, and Hispanic against Hispanic. The national media, sensing both a human-interest story and one that could influence both national and international politics, descended on the community like a pack of hungry wolves. Camera lights flooded the Miami neighborhood from dusk to dawn. The Gonzalez case rekindled all the pent-up anger Cubans had toward Fidel Castro and about their exile status. Most Americans and Floridians, as well as those in the other Hispanic communities of Miami-Dade County, however, did not appreciate the underlying frustrations of Cuban Americans; they saw only a battle royal unfolding over an innocent child who, they believed, was being used as a foil for continuing Cuban-American resentment toward Fidel Castro. Most felt the boy should be with his father, who was his closest surviving relative, and they indicated as much when polled. No one, however, relished the image of heavily armed federal government agents descending on the house where Elian stayed and removing him to Cuba and his father.[6]

The events in Miami highlighted the problem of grouping all Hispanics together. This was even truer for Florida than for other communities in states like Texas and California, where the preponderance of Hispanics/Latinos were from Mexico. In Florida, Cubans constituted slightly less than a majority of Hispanics in 2004, but they constituted the single-largest element within the diverse Hispanic community. The largest of these other communities were Puerto Ricans, Colombians, Nicaraguans, Mexicans, Peruvians, Hondurans, and Dominicans. In addition, Jamaicans and Haitians, who were not Hispanic, constituted a growing segment of the population in Miami-Dade, and they, along with most non-Cuban Hispanics, largely identified with the Democratic Party because of its social programs and the foreign policy of President Clinton. In this regard they differed significantly from Cuban voters in Miami. Cubans bolstered the Republican Party because of its fierce anticommunist stance. Most other Hispanics regarded Republican foreign policy as hostile to the independence of the Latin American nations and inconsistent with the nation's democratic values. They generally admired the foreign policies of Presidents Jimmy Carter and Bill Clinton, who had supported free, democratic elections, self-determination of nations, and regional cooperation.

The issues confronting their respective native countries and the policies of the United States toward those nations frequently shaped the political affiliation of Hispanic immigrants. So while some described Miami as the only city with its own foreign policy, it was a city that, in fact, had multiple foreign policies. The concerns about Fidel Castro that dominated the Cubans' worldview did not resonate with other Hispanic residents of Miami. In domestic affairs, the newer immigrants looked to government for unemployment assistance, worker protection, employment retraining, child support, and educational loans. They viewed the Democratic Party as more supportive of such programs and thus more likely to assist them as they adjusted to American society. But would they vote? That was the question of great concern to Gore's camp. First-generation non-Cuban Hispanics (with the exception of Puerto Ricans) and Haitians voted much less often than Cubans because they remained most interested in developments in their native lands, to which they traveled on a regular basis. How their vote would play out in Florida in the presidential election of 2000 was anyone's guess.

Such was not the case for Cuban Americans, however, who deeply resented the actions of the Clinton administration in seizing Elian and returning him to his father in Cuba. The Elian case had unified their community as few other incidents could have, and they held everyone in the Clinton administration responsible for the attorney general's decision—and that included Al Gore. The presidential election of 2000 gave them a chance to vent their anger at the Clinton administration, and they did so en masse against Gore.[7]

The Presidential Campaign in Florida

The two presidential candidates spent a great deal of their time in Florida. Bush and Gore each visited the state over thirty times. Surrogates for both candidates, including family members, spent additional time in Florida. Neither candidate followed Richard Nixon's ill-advised 1960 strategy of pledging to campaign in all fifty states. The 2000 race would be decided by a handful of swing states, and the candidates invested their time in those states, with Florida and its twenty-five electoral votes among the most crucial.

Both sides also had permanent staff members located in key sections of the state and invested large sums of advertising money in Florida. Both also sought to energize their political base in the state. With the advice of the political strategist Karl Rove and his brother Jeb, George W. highlighted his stance on cultural issues, noting his opposition to abortion; his support of mandatory parental consent and notification before a minor could obtain an abortion; his insistence on a "litmus test" for Supreme Court nominees; his opposition to same-sex marriages (Gore also opposed same sex-marriages for religious reasons); and his opposition to quotas and racial preferences. Bush also repeatedly referred to his tax-cut proposals, including elimination of the estate tax (a very popular proposal with many seniors); a 10 percent tax deduction for two-earner families; a pledge to veto any income-tax increase; and a ten-year, $1.3 billion tax cut. Bush's cultural agenda played very well in Florida, where Roman Catholics and evangelicals praised his opposition to abortion and gay rights, and his pro-family stance. Seniors cheered his tax-relief proposals, and whites welcomed his elimination of quotas and racial preferences.[8]

The strategic thinking of Rove and Jeb Bush aimed at energizing the president's political base among evangelicals, military retirees, Cubans, and Blue Dog Democrats. If successful, both men felt the president would carry Miami, southwest Florida, the I-4 corridor, Jacksonville and north Florida, and, consequently, the state. Jeb was confident that his brother would win Florida, if not strongly then certainly comfortably, and he placed his own reputation on the line in making this prediction. His confidence was understandable, given his substantial victory two years earlier and the general decline of the Democratic Party in the state. But Gore was not Buddy MacKay, whom Jeb had defeated, and Gore's advisers had a wealth of campaign experience, with many having served on Clinton's election staff in 1992 and 1996.

To help ensure his brother's victory, Jeb worked with his staff and the state elections office to make sure that Ralph Nader got on the ballot in Florida. Republicans felt certain that Nader would take votes away from Gore in Florida, increasing the likelihood of George W.'s victory in the state. Patrick Buchanan, the conservative columnist who appeared on the ballot as well, posed a threat to Bush's support among the state's most conservative voters. What impact the two third-party candidates would have on the outcome was unclear, but political experts contended that Nader would draw more votes away from Gore than Buchanan would from Bush.

For Gore and his aides, their strategic plan involved pumping significant sums of money into the state to pay for media spots and working closely with Senator Bob Graham and his staff members to mobilize Democrats. Bob Squier was a key campaign adviser to Gore, and he had worked with Graham in developing his famous Workdays program. Squier knew Florida well. In his view, the keys to a Democratic victory were to mobilize the Democratic base—including seniors, women, African Americans, and union workers—behind Gore, turn out a large vote in southeast Florida among Jewish voters and seniors, split the I-4 corridor, register new or lax black voters, and assist these groups in getting to the polls. To do so, Gore emphasized his and his party's long-term commitment to civil rights reform; affirmative action; Social Security; economic growth and development; budget responsibility, highlighting a projected $4.65 billion budget surplus; environmental protection; health care; and educational reform and enhancement. Gore also played the class card heavily, blasting Republicans for espousing the interests of the rich and big business, and generally ignoring the well-being of families and workers, the health needs of average Americans, and the environment. Gore's campaign offered a persuasive message to working- and middle-class voters in Florida, especially when combined with the economic achievements of the Clinton administration. If Gore could generate a large Democratic vote along the southeast coast from Palm Beach County to Miami-Dade County, he might well carry the state. With Lieberman's assistance, that appeared quite likely north of Miami-Dade, but neither Gore nor his aides anticipated the hostility his campaign encountered in the Cuban community of Miami-Dade. Repeated trips to Miami had only generated more resistance to the Gore's candidacy.[9]

Both campaigns focused time and money on the I-4 corridor and, in particular, on Orlando, to secure critical votes. A large Puerto Rican residential development in Osceola County, just to the south of Orlando, and a substantial in-migration of northerners into Orlando put this entire area into play for both parties. By the 2000 election, this substantial population of Puerto Ricans, who were Democrats in their native land, registered Democrat in Florida. Alongside this Puerto Rican immigration, the relocation of many northern Democrats into Orlando threatened to move Orange County into the Democratic presidential column for the first time since Franklin Roosevelt ran for reelection in 1944. Anyone who thought this region of the state would vote like it had for over fifty-five years over-looked these important demographic changes.

As the campaign entered its final days, Gore and Bush spent increasing time in Florida, where polls varied widely on who would win and thus who would be the next president of the United States. Rove felt confident that Bush would capture Florida, but Jeb was not so certain, and he directed Republican campaign funds toward a massive, last-minute telephone appeal to potential supporters. Taped telephoned messages from George Bush, Jeb, and their parents, George Herbert Walker Bush and Barbara Bush, as well as live calls from supporters, were received by potential Republican voters in the last week of the campaign. The entire Bush clan also visited the state on the last weekend prior to election day, November 7, appearing in various cities and towns individually and collectively. But the Gore-Lieberman forces were not sitting idly by. They, too, unleashed a barrage of telephone messages to supporters and campaigned in Florida right up to election day.[10]

To the amazement of most professionals, Gore opted not to utilize the assistance of outgoing President Bill Clinton, despite the closeness of the race and Clinton's popularity among seniors, African Americans, and immigrant groups in Florida. As with so many vice presidents who operated in the shadow of the presidency, Gore wanted to prove to himself, the public, and Clinton that he could win on his own. Gore also worried that Clinton might jeopardize his candidacy, given the president's recent scandalous behavior and the belief among some Democrats and independents that the nation needed new leadership that was both ethically and morally responsible. The vice president struggled unsuccessfully throughout the campaign, according to the political and legal reporter Jeffrey Toobin, to find a way "to embrace Clinton's political legacy and to reject the president's personal misdeeds."[11] Not selectively utilizing the president's campaigning skills proved to be a major political miscalculation by Gore, much as it had been by Richard Nixon, when, in 1960, he refrained from seeking the campaign support of the extremely popular President Dwight Eisenhower until the last two weeks of that election. The evidence suggests that Clinton would have been a major asset to Gore in selected counties in Florida where the president remained enormously popular.

On the evening of November 7, as television news broadcasters competed to be the first to call the election, it became apparent that Florida was pivotal and that the results were anything but clear. The Associated Press declared Vice President Al Gore the victor in Florida, based on Voter News Service (VNS) projections from exit polls. The major television networks also called Florida for Gore between 7:50 and 8:00 p.m., before the ballots had been tallied in west Florida, which was on central standard time. What followed was like something out of a Woody Allen movie. Dan Rather of CBS News asserted: "Let's get one thing straight right from the get-go. . . . We would rather be last in reporting returns than to be wrong. . . . If we say somebody has carried a state, you can pretty much take it to the bank." Between 8:00 p.m. and 2:20 a.m., Rather called it for Gore, then Bush, then undecided, then Bush. Dave Barry, syndicated columnist for the *Miami Herald*, said that the networks must be getting their news from the same source: the Psychic Friends Network.[12]

Rather was not alone in calling the election erroneously. All news networks were confused about the results because all relied on exit polling by the Voter News Service. And VNS was wrong for a good reason—the exit polls in Palm Beach County suggested that Gore supporters had voted in extraordinary numbers and carried the county decisively for him, thereby ensuring his victory statewide. But the actual votes in the county revealed something quite different, that conservative columnist Patrick Buchanan had won a surprising number of votes in Palm Beach County and Gore had not done as well as exit polls predicted.[13] In the early morning hours, Tom Brokaw of NBC News apologized to viewers and acknowledged that broadcasters did not know who had won the election in Florida and thus who would be the next president of the United States.

As evening turned into morning on November 8, Bush appeared to take a decisive lead in Florida. Some estimates had Bush leading Gore by fifty thousand votes, and between 2:16 and 2:20 a.m., networks projected Bush as the winner in Florida and the forty-third president of the United States. On learning the size of Bush's lead and the consensus of broadcasters and his staff members, Gore called Bush to concede the election and left his hotel in Nashville, Tennessee, for the War Memorial Plaza, where he planned to publicly concede the election and thank his supporters. As Gore's motorcade drove across town, his advisers received word from supporters in Florida that the vote totals were inaccurate and the election was much closer than the networks suggested. In the hectic minutes that followed, they desperately sought to reach Gore and stop him from conceding the race. When they finally reached his aides at the War Memorial Plaza, the vice president abruptly got back in his car and returned to his hotel without addressing his supporters. He then called Bush, and, in a conversation that was awkward for both men, he retracted his concession.[14]

As more accurate election reports emerged, they showed that fewer than one thousand votes separated Bush and Gore in Florida. Between 3:57 and 4:15 a.m., networks also retracted the projection that Bush had won the state. The presidency remained undecided, with the final margin showing Bush leading Gore in Florida by only 1,784 votes. The totals had Bush with 2,909,135 votes (48.8 percent) to Gore's 2,907,351 (48.8 percent), with other candidates receiving 139,616 votes (2.4 percent). At this point, the intense competition between the two state parties for political control of the state and for the presidency became grist for public scrutiny. It was not democracy's finest hour.

Postelection Developments

A full machine recount of votes was ordered by the State Department of Elections, which was required by Florida Election Code 102.141 when the margin of victory was 0.5 percent or less. Florida Governor Jeb Bush announced on November 8 that he was officially recusing himself from the process, but his role was not as transparent as his statement made it appear, especially when many of his principal aides took leave, with his approval, to facilitate George W.'s victory in Florida.[15]

With the outcome in doubt, both sides hired prominent state and national attorneys to represent them in the recount that followed. And interestingly, they both hired two former secretaries of state to direct their forces in Florida: Gore hired Warren Christopher, secretary of state under President Carter, and Bush hired James Baker, secretary of state under his father. Both Gore and Bush were well represented by Christopher and Baker in this process, but Baker proved the more adept politically. His experience in managing George Herbert Walker Bush's presidential campaign in 1988 and his broad-based background in state and national politics gave the Bush forces a clear-cut advantage in the process that followed. The author Jeffrey Toobin viewed the differences in the following way: "The Republicans were more organized and motivated, and also more ruthless in their determination to win. From the very beginning, the Democratic effort was characterized by a hesitancy, almost a diffidence, that marked a clear contrast to the approach of their adversaries."[16]

The preliminary nationwide popular vote numbers on November 9 revealed just how critical Florida was to the final outcome and how close the election was: Gore led the popular vote 48,976,148 to Bush's 48,783,510, but Bush had won twenty-nine states with 246 electoral votes, while Gore captured eighteen states plus the District of Columbia for a total of 260 electoral votes. With Florida and its 25 electoral votes in the undecided column, neither candidate had sufficient electoral votes to claim victory.

Immediately following the first official election results in the state, Clay Roberts—a Republican who had been appointed director of the Division of Elections in the secretary of state's office when Katherine Harris was elected secretary of state in 1998—notified the election supervisors in the sixty-seven counties to commence an official recount in compliance with the state constitution.[17] Sixty-four of Florida's sixty-seven counties quickly retabulated their votes, and Bush's lead over Gore shrunk to 362 votes in an unofficial tally by the Associated Press.

The public review of voting irregularities focused initially on Palm Beach County, where voters complained on election day that the ballot was confusing and that they may have voted for the wrong candidate. Theresa LePore, supervisor of elections in Palm Beach County for nine years and president-elect of the Florida State Association of Supervisors of Elections, had received complaints on voting day from "a couple of very elderly gentlemen" who came in around midmorning to complain about the ballot. Somewhat later, her office received a number of angry calls from voters and Democratic Party officials expressing concern about the configuration of the punch-card ballots (or butterfly ballots), because the names of the presidential candidates did not line up directly with the punch holes.[18]

Local Democrats, including LePore, felt certain that there was a significant voting problem when results from predominantly Jewish precincts showed that presidential candidate and conservative columnist Pat Buchanan had received a surprisingly large number of votes. The *Palm Beach Post*'s subsequent review of the discarded ballots revealed that 5,330 votes were cast for the presumably rare cross-party combination of Gore and

Buchanan, compared with only 1,631 for the equivalent cross-party combination of Bush and Buchanan. That alone would have decided the contest in Florida. Past voting records indicated that these precincts should have gone decisively for Gore, especially with the large number of Jewish voters and with Lieberman on the ticket. Although Bush spokesman Ari Fleischer asserted on November 9, 2000, that, "Palm Beach County is a Pat Buchanan stronghold and that's why Pat Buchanan received 3,407 votes there," Buchanan's Florida coordinator, Jim McConnell, dismissed the statement immediately, calling it "nonsense." Jim Cunningham, chairman of the executive committee of Palm Beach County's Reform Party, added: "I don't think so. Not from where I'm sitting and what I'm looking at." Cunningham estimated the number of Buchanan supporters in Palm Beach County at between four hundred and five hundred. Asked how many votes he would guess Buchanan legitimately received in Palm Beach County, he said: "I think 1,000 would be generous. Do I believe that these people inadvertently cast their votes for Pat Buchanan? Yes, I do. We have to believe that based on the vote totals elsewhere." On November 9, Buchanan himself acknowledged, on the television morning news show *Today*, that "when I took one look at that ballot on Election Night . . . it's very easy for me to see how someone could have voted for me in the belief they voted for Al Gore."[19]

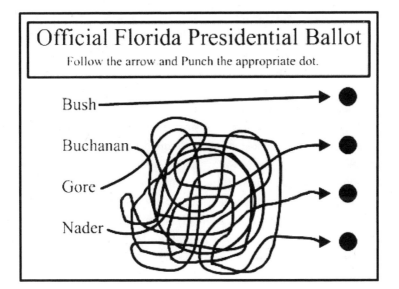

Despite the obvious problems with the ballot in Palm Beach County, there was little that local officials or state officials could do about it. LePore, who had created the ballot with a larger font so that the county's many elderly voters could read the names on it easily, wished she could do it over, but she recognized that was impossible. Moreover, a new election could not be held just in Palm Beach County, and if the punched ballots did not correctly identify the candidate for whom voters had intended to vote, it was impossible to determine what their intentions had been. Dexter Douglass, who had been hired by Gore to represent him in Florida, agreed: "When you looked at it, there was just no way that you could effectively do anything with that. It was great political fodder and it was really an illegal ballot, but so what?"[20] Although no one yet realized it, the butterfly ballot in Palm Beach County and the inability of local or state officials to correct the results from its use effectively sealed the outcome. There would not be enough clearly marked ballots remaining for Gore to overcome Bush's statewide lead.

Following the retabulation in sixty-four of the sixty-seven counties, Gore's team made a strategic decision to request a hand count of presidential ballots in four heavily Democratic Florida counties (allowed under Florida Election Code 102.166)—Palm Beach, Broward, Miami-Dade, and Volusia. These four counties had cast a total of approximately 1.8 million ballots. Gore's advisers decided against demanding a full recount in all sixty-seven counties, believing that the public would not accept such a request, that many election offices would not support such a recount, and that the process would take too long and thus alienate Americans anxious for a decision.[21] But their strategy to seek a recount in these four heavily Democratic counties appeared excessively partisan to many Americans, and it called into question Gore's motives. On November 11, the Bush camp sought a federal injunction to stop hand recounts of ballots in several Florida counties because of alleged equal protection and other constitutional violations.[22]

As the battle for Florida unfolded, Gore's supporters were convinced that the ballots were there to elect their candidate if they could only be counted properly. Bush's aides felt equally strongly that a recount along the lines proposed by Gore's advisers was inherently unfair to their candidate. In their view, either all ballots had to be hand-recounted or none should be, and they preferred the latter since Bush held the lead.[23] The closeness of the contest and the importance of the outcome led to a political don-nybrook between Republicans and Democrats for most of the next thirty days and highlighted the thin margin and passionate differences between the two parties in Florida and the nation.

Enter Secretary of State Katherine Harris, who had constitutional responsibility for the elections process in Florida. Harris had also been one of eight cochairpersons of the Committee to Elect George W. Bush in Florida, but unlike Jeb Bush, she refused to recuse herself from the post-election process, claiming that her role was largely ceremonial during the campaign, that she would not recount ballots, and thus she could not influence the outcome of the election. But in an election this close, her rulings on any aspect of the election and the recount could well determine the victor. Moreover, there was no question but that she favored Bush's victory.

Harris's initial ruling convinced Gore's advisers that she was inherently partisan and could not be relied on to act fairly and impartially. On November 13, she announced that she would not extend the 5:00 p.m. eastern standard time November 14 deadline (Florida Election Code 102.112) for certifying election results. Her decision did not affect the counting of overseas absentee ballots, which had a November 17 deadline. Volusia County officials immediately sued to extend the certification deadline, and lawyers for Palm Beach County and the Gore campaign joined the suit. Bush lawyers partnered with the state in seeking to block the extension. In the immediate wake of the legal challenge by Volusia County, U.S. District Judge Donald Middlebrooks, former general counsel to Governor Reubin Askew, issued his ruling on November 13, rejecting Bush's attempt to stop manual recounts in Florida.[24]

Although Harris followed the letter of the law, many questioned her unwillingness to be more flexible given the closeness of the election, the controversies surrounding it, and the crucial nature of the results in Florida. What also angered and frustrated state and national Democrats and others was her persistent ignorance of state election law. In response to question after question from reporters, Harris revealed that she was either badly informed or simply incompetent. Lucy Morgan, senior reporter for the *St. Petersburg Times* and Pulitzer Prize winner, commented pointedly: "On balance, she probably was not a very good public official. I think she didn't know anything about election law."[25] As questions about her competence alongside questions about her partisanship were raised, reporters and voters came to doubt her ability to oversee the postelection process fairly. More questions emerged following the contentious 2000 recount, when e-mails on Harris's computer revealed that she had been in contact with Jeb Bush during the recount, contrary to both their claims. The *Miami Herald* reporter Meg Laughlin discovered that e-mail messages sent to Jeb Bush from Harris had been deleted after the recount. Harris then had the operating system of her computer changed, a procedure that erased all its data. "What was odd about what she did," said Mark Seibel, an editor at the *Miami Herald*, "was that they installed an old operating system—not a new one—which makes you wonder why they did it."[26]

While George W. Bush's campaign aides kept a discreet public distance from Katherine Harris, they worked behind the scenes to build support for the embattled secretary of state. It was not in their interests to have her credibility thoroughly damaged and thus have Bush's victory in Florida disputed further. On November 15, a Republican Governors Association official sent an e-mail to Elizabeth Hirst, Jeb Bush's press secretary, with contact information for Harris. "Our governors are being requested by Austin to call or send strong messages of support ASAP to Ms. Harris in Florida," wrote the official, Kirsten Fedewa. Hirst wrote back to say she couldn't "receive these messages or act upon them" because the Florida governor had recused himself from any deliberations involving his brother's election. Dana Milbank, a *Washington Post* reporter, wrote, "The e-mails between Bush aides show an office continuing to administer the humdrum business of the state but also keenly interested in—and sometimes seeking to influence—the fate of the Republican presidential nominee."[27]

Despite the criticism of Harris and concerns about Jeb Bush's behavior, Lucy Morgan doubted that Harris had any communications of significance with either Bush. She noted that the governor personally disliked Harris, and he may well have doubted her competence. Morgan commented that the *St. Petersburg Times* had hired a company to examine the hard drives on Harris's computer and "found very little that we had not already found in public records requests made at the time of the election."[28] Dexter Douglass, a member of the Gore legal team, also found nothing improper about Jeb Bush's behavior. "What would you expect him to do?" Douglass asked. "I would have been very shocked if he had not been involved in decision-making. I don't think there is anything wrong with it either."[29]

The accusations against Bush, Harris, and other state Republicans notwithstanding, Democrats were not virtuous in this process. Both parties in Florida had a lot at stake in the outcome of this election, and both played political hardball in seeking victory for their candidate. The role of Attorney General Bob Butterworth in the postelection process, for example, was seldom referred to, but he was as engaged in this process as Jeb Bush. The *St. Petersburg Times* published an article about his efforts to pressure the judge in Volusia County to recount the ballots in a way that favored Gore. In that story Morgan wrote: "He was calling down there, trying to intimidate him into recounting those votes in a certain way, and sending him written opinions on it that were unsolicited and contrary to those being put out by the Division of Elections. The intriguing thing is that his own website said he didn't issue opinions on elections."[30] With so much riding on the outcome, both sides overstepped their responsibilities and the legitimate roles of their office.

At the end of the day on November 14, Harris announced the vote totals: Bush's vote margin of victory in Florida was now down to 300 votes, which was significantly less than the 1,784-vote margin he had immediately after the election. Harris agreed to give two heavily Democratic counties, Miami-Dade and Palm Beach, until 2:00 p.m. Wednesday to explain, in writing, why they proposed to add hand recounts after the 5:00 p.m. deadline. But the following morning, heavily Democratic Broward County decided that it also would conduct a full manual recount. Harris interceded to halt these developments, petitioning the Florida Supreme Court to stop the manual recounts in Miami-Dade, Broward, and Palm Beach Counties.

At a press conference on November 15, Al Gore offered George Bush a compromise. He agreed to forgo any further legal challenges if Republicans agreed to a hand recount in all of Florida's sixty-seven counties. Bush rejected the offer, pointing out correctly that there was no assurance that a manual recount would be as accurate, or any more accurate, than the machine tabulation. This was particularly true with ballots that had chads. (As the world came to know, chads are paper particles created when holes are made in a computer-punched tape or punch card, and hanging chads result from incompletely punched holes.) When such ballots were handled frequently, the chads often dislodged or were sufficiently damaged that they became difficult for a machine or a person to read. At the same conference, Gore proposed a face-to-face meeting with Bush, which the governor rejected as of little use until the election was decided. Bush iterated what became his mantra: "The votes of Florida have been counted. They have been recounted."[31]

Although Gore and his advisers advocated counting all the ballots, they discussed challenging the military ballots, many of which had arrived beyond the state's deadline and some of which were unsigned. But this strategy was fraught with danger for Gore. With the nation at war in Iraq and Afghanistan, Americans on both sides of the political divide felt the troops should be given every opportunity to vote, and the system ought to be flexible enough to ensure their ballots counted. The overseas absentee ballots had, in fact, tripled Bush's lead in Florida to 930 votes. As the Gore proposal to challenge these ballots circulated among supporters, it was leaked to a Bush aide. Baker and his assistants saw a great public relations opportunity and immediately denounced Gore for even considering such action, calling it unpatriotic. Retired General Norman Schwarzkopf, a national hero in the Desert Storm campaign in Iraq and strong supporter of Bush, publicly berated Gore officials for their plan, calling it a sad day when military personnel, who were defending the nation abroad, were denied the right to vote because of a legal technicality.[32]

Stung by the criticism, Gore's forces sent vice-presidential candidate Joseph Lieberman before the national media, where he announced the commitment of the Gore campaign to count all military ballots.[33] The Gore-Lieberman forces had allowed themselves to become ensnared in a foolish maneuver, which created the public impression that they were determined to win the election at any cost. In truth, they could have and perhaps should have questioned some of the military ballots, which were unsigned, but once they allowed Republicans to define their position in opposition to all such ballots, there was only one way to extricate themselves. Public opinion, which had been running in favor of Gore, now shifted to favor Bush.

But that momentum proved fleeting, as it would throughout this thirty-six-day process. On November 21, the Florida Supreme Court, which was dominated by Democratic appointees—six of the seven had been appointed by Chiles and one by Graham—ruled unanimously that counties still conducting manual recounts of ballots should continue. The justices also dismissed Harris's decisions during the previous week, calling them "unreasonable," "unnecessary," "arbitrary," "contrary to law," and "contrary to the plain meaning of the statute." The court came just short of calling her incompetent and biased. The one-paragraph order did not say, however, if those votes could be added to Florida's final tally. The court set November 26, a Sunday, or early November 27, as the deadline for certifying the election.[34] Palm Beach County resumed hand-counting ballots, and Miami-Dade and Broward elections officials followed suit.

Cameras, reporters, and the public watched as officials in Palm Beach tried to determine whether a partially attached chad was a vote for a particular candidate or a nonvote. It was not a pretty sight for the world's oldest democracy, and Florida and Florida voters became the object of public ridicule in the process. Late-night talk-show host Jay Leno announced: "Last night Vice President Al Gore addressed the nation. A lot of folks in Palm Beach, Fla. missed it because they couldn't find the right channel on their remotes." Caricatures of election officials examining ballots with mystified looks on their faces appeared in newspapers around the world, leading many to wonder about the stability of the world's oldest democracy.

As the recount progressed, both sides positioned themselves to ensure the best outcome for their candidate. The Democrats, for example, had requested that Palm Beach County conduct a 1 percent manual recount. Republicans countered with a request for another machine count. Palm Beach officials decided that, given the controversy surrounding the election, they would do both. But that didn't end the political machinations. The Democrats wanted the 1 percent recount in three particular precincts that were heavily elderly and Democratic. The canvassing board agreed but also selected one other precinct to review, which Gore's aides opposed. The results of this recount gave Gore nineteen more votes, and Democrats proceeded to request a full manual recount of the entire county, contending that their candidate might well pick up sufficient votes in the six hundred precincts in the county to win Florida and the election. Their conclusion was highly doubtful, however, since Gore did not have nearly as much support in the other precincts as he had in the ones that had been recounted. The *Late Show* host and comedian David Letterman warned, "If the recounts don't stop, here's my fear—sooner or later there's going to be a winner."[35]

When the courts ordered the Supervisor of Elections office to proceed with a full manual recount, officials representing both candidates resorted to every legitimate tactic at their disposal to aid their respective candidates. Supervisor of Elections LePore observed that Republicans sought to disrupt and delay the process by objecting repeatedly to contested ballots, requiring that those ballots be placed into a pile to be reexamined further. At the end of the recount, she noted that over half the ballots had been objected to and needed to be reviewed once again. LePore commented: "[we] had to look at each of those, and when we were looking at them, we had three attorneys from each side behind us, watching what we were doing. They had a court reporter there reporting everything."[36] Charging that the protests disrupted the recount effort, the Democrats sent a letter to the U.S. Justice Department asking for an investigation. In Miami-Dade, the local Republican Party mobilized supporters, who descended on the Supervisor of Elections office and delayed and disrupted the proceedings. As officials gathered to commence the recount in the county, a substantial crowd of young Republicans, many of them working for George W. Bush or other prominent Republicans, tried to block their paths, shouted insults at them, and generally hampered the proceedings. It was near-chaos, and officials had to wait until police arrived before they could do anything.

Republican leaders in Florida had, meanwhile, tired of the rulings by the Florida Supreme Court and examined ways to deliver the election to Bush. In a stunning announcement on November 29, Florida House Speaker Tom Feeney, a close political ally of Jeb Bush, stated that a special session of the Florida Legislature would be called December 12, at which time it would be asked to certify the twenty-five electors for George W. Bush that had been initially certified by Secretary Harris. Jeb Bush, who apparently urged Feeney not to pursue this matter, nevertheless praised the state Republican initiative as an "act of courage." On November 30, a Republican-controlled Florida legislative panel voted to recommend convening a special session of the Florida Legislature to designate the state's twenty-five electors.[37]

Despite this highly questionable constitutional development, events shifted to the courts, which asserted their authority in this increasingly wacky and politically charged election. On December 8, the Florida Supreme Court reversed, in a 4 to 3 split decision, a lower court rejection of the statewide manual recounts of undervotes. The Florida Supreme Court decision stunned both sides when the justices went well beyond ordering recounts of 12,300 undervotes in Miami-Dade and Palm Beach Counties, which Gore had sought, directing that a manual recount of undervotes in all counties where a hand recount had not occurred commence immediately. The court also directed the lower court to add to Gore's tally the 168 votes in Miami-Dade and 215 in Palm Beach from earlier hand counts excluded from the certified count. Gore and his supporters were ecstatic; the justices had given them more than they had anticipated. The added votes immediately narrowed Bush's statewide lead from 537 votes to just 154. As a result of the court's decision, it was estimated that 45,000 undervotes statewide would have to be counted.[38]

But, as with so much in this postelection controversy, the highs and lows occurred quickly. Four days after the Florida Supreme Court decision came the fateful day for Gore forces. Early on December 12, Republicans in the Florida House met and, as their leaders promised, voted to appoint the state's twenty-five electors for George Bush. Two Democrats joined their Republican colleagues in the 79 to 41 vote.

The Decision of the U.S. Supreme Court and the Conclusion of the 2000 Election

The much more critical decision came later in the day when the U.S. Supreme Court, in a 5 to 4 ruling, effectively ended the election and Al Gore's quest for the presidency. The justices in the majority reversed the ruling of the Florida Supreme Court decision that ordered a statewide recount of undervotes, stating that differing vote-counting standards from county to county and the lack of a single judicial officer to oversee the recount violated the equal-protection clause of the Constitution. The majority opinion effectively precluded Gore from attempting to seek any other recounts on the grounds that a recount could not be completed by December 12, in time to certify a conclusive slate of electors. "It is obvious that the recount cannot be conducted in compliance with the requirements of equal protection and due process without substantial additional work," the majority ruled. The Court remanded the case to the Florida Supreme Court "for further proceedings not inconsistent with this opinion." In delivering their opinions, the justices were as divided as the voters and the two parties. In a blistering dissent, Justice John Paul Stevens wrote:

"One thing . . . is certain. Although we may never know with complete certainty the identity of the winner of this year's presidential election, the identity of the loser is perfectly clear. It is the nation's confidence in the judge as an impartial guardian of the rule of law." Justice Stephen G. Breyer echoed Stevens: "In this highly politicized matter, the appearance of a split decision runs the risk of undermining the public's confidence in the Court itself."[39]

The divided rulings of the Florida Supreme Court and the U.S. Supreme Court and the fact that the two courts had Democratic and Republican majorities, respectively, added to the view of many that the decisions had been politically motivated and that the outcome did not reflect the will of the people in Florida or in the nation. In particular, a number of experts questioned the decision by the U.S. Supreme Court to intercede in what they perceived as largely a state matter. And they noted that both Federal Judge Don Middlebrooks and the Eleventh Circuit Court of Appeals ruled that the recount was a state issue.[40] But Barry Richard, attorney for Bush, felt strongly that the inconsistencies and the absence of a uniform standard in the vote-counting process made this an "elementary Fourteenth Amendment equal-protection" case. Richard observed, "It was perfectly consistent with what the U.S. Supreme Court has always done."[41]

On December 13, Gore brought the drama to a close, announcing shortly after the Supreme Court's ruling that he accepted the decision and George Bush's election as the forty-third president of the United States, and Bush pledged in his acceptance speech to provide reconciliation and unity to a divided nation.[42]

It was over! The nation had a new president, and many in the public seemed more relieved than angry. Many Gore loyalists remained convinced that their candidate had won Florida and had thus won the election and that only the politics of the "banana republic" had prevented their candidate from obtaining office. Bush loyalists felt equally certain that their candidate had been victorious and alleged that it had almost been stolen by a liberal Democratic State Supreme Court. They were confident that any count of the ballots would confirm that Bush had won, albeit narrowly, a majority of the ballots cast in Florida. But the evidence is as sketchy as the outcome.

A subsequent review of the ballots by the *Miami Herald* led to the conclusion that Bush would have won in any statewide recount. What the

Herald could not do and what no one else could determine was how voters in Palm Beach County meant to vote and would have voted if it had not been for the "butterfly ballot." Most assume that voters in key precincts in Palm Beach had cast ballots for Buchanan that were clearly intended for Gore, and that alone would have ensured Gore's victory in Florida. The *Palm Beach Post* conducted a review of all the undervotes in Palm Beach County alone and determined that Gore would have netted 784 new votes in the county using an undervote standard similar to the one employed in Broward County. If that standard was used in Miami-Dade and other sections of the state, it appears likely that Gore would have won.[43] Certainly the vice president would have been victorious if Ralph Nader had refrained from running. Nader received 97,488 votes in Florida, and by most estimates Gore would have received at least one out of every one hundred Nader votes, thus ensuring him a comfortable victory.

To what degree was the election outcome in Florida a microcosm of the nation in 2000? Clearly election day and the postelection events bore little relationship to developments elsewhere. But a comparison of voter preferences in the state with those nationally reveals that they paralleled one another in remarkable ways. Besides the fact that the election was the closest since 1876, it was also the first in the twentieth century in which the losing candidate captured the popular vote and lost the presidency. In Florida, voters split sharply as they did in most of the nation, with most senior, Jewish, Hispanic, African-American, and women voters casting ballots for the Democratic Party, while most rural, Cuban, white male, and evangelical voters embraced Bush. Catholic voters divided their votes between Gore and Bush, while Catholic Floridians cast slightly more votes for Bush because of support from Cuban voters. Urban and suburban voters also split their votes, depending on where they resided in the state and nation. For example, in southeast Florida and in the Northeast and West Coast cities of the United States, voters went for Gore. But in southwest Florida, in the South, and most of the Midwest, voters cast their ballots for Bush. Gore did better with voters who were the least and best educated in Florida and the nation, while Bush attracted voters with some community college and college education and with incomes over $50,000. So, despite the chaos and confusion in Florida, its voters reflected developments nationally as well as the views of voters nationally. And they were as polarized about who should govern the nation for the next four years. The entire election played itself out on the Florida stage in a comedy/drama that was, in many ways, reminiscent of Shakespeare.[44]

What did the election say about Florida and national politics? The election revealed, as few others have, the extent of the political chasm in Florida and the nation. The political goals articulated by Bush and Gore were so substantially different that they offered Americans and, of course, Floridians a clear-cut choice about the direction of the nation. The closeness of the vote in Florida spoke to the relative parity between Democrats and Republicans and voter schism over Democratic and Republican positions on cultural, economic, and political issues. Seldom have the two parties been so divided, and seldom have voters in Florida and in the nation been so conflicted.

9

So What Does the Future Hold
for Florida?

The drama of the presidential election overshadowed other momentous political developments in Florida. For the first time in state history, Floridians not only helped elect a Republican president, they also voted in a Republican congressional majority, a Republican governor, a Republican cabinet, and significant majorities in both houses of the state legislature. Republicans, in fact, enjoyed such a huge majority in the House of Representatives that Democrats had little voice in committee deliberations or in drafting legislation. The Democratic Party had not experienced anything like it previously, and it was unclear when the party would be positioned to challenge the Republican Party again.

Ironically, as the nation remained transfixed by the 2000 election, Bill Clinton and Jeb Bush met with the press at the White House to sign the Comprehensive Everglades Restoration Plan. The proposed public works project would be the largest ever undertaken by the nation. The legislation, passed unanimously by the Florida Legislature and overwhelmingly by Congress, was a remarkable political feat, considering the longtime enemies, from developers to environmentalists to sugar-cane growers, who formed a coalition to support it. That political arch-foes Clinton and Jeb Bush should appear together as leaders of this environmental reform effort said a great deal about Bush's political maturation and his realization that Republicans could retain power in Florida only if they avoided being seen as partners with developers in plundering the state's fragile environment.[1]

The 2002 Gubernatorial Election

In 2002, Jeb Bush ran for reelection with widespread public support and the full backing of his party. The election of his brother as president gave Jeb a prominence that no state Republican or Democrat had enjoyed previously. The attack on the World Trade Center and the Pentagon by terrorists on September 11, 2001, rallied the nation behind President Bush, and Jeb's close familial and political relationship with his brother further strengthened his political standing. Jeb was also well regarded by many in Republican circles as a leading spokesperson for the national neoconservative movement. His political achievements were often featured as examples of how to reduce the size and scope of state government. The family name alone gave him enormous stature; after all, who else had two immediate relatives elected president of the United States? But Jeb Bush was a political force in his own right.

The 2002 gubernatorial election highlighted the popularity of Jeb Bush and his policies, while also signaling the dwindling fortunes of the Democratic Party. Many urban and suburban residents, as well as Cubans and an increasing number of recent retirees, prized the governor's efforts to control state spending, champion tax holidays, combat crime through mandatory prison sentences, and eliminate state bureaucratic waste and inefficiency. Those who had moved to Florida from such high-tax states as Minnesota, Michigan, Massachusetts, and New York welcomed Bush's opposition to new taxes and his advocacy of smaller, less costly, and more efficient government. They were joined by native whites who also valued low taxes and had historically resented intrusive government that pursued social and environmental reforms, often at their expense. Through the force of his personality and political leadership, Jeb Bush, much like Ronald Reagan, brought these voters together in a powerful statewide coalition.[2]

Democrats would have been wise to avoid an intraparty squabble in selecting a candidate to challenge Bush. But such was not the case. Bill McBride, almost unknown in state political circles, opposed Janet Reno, former attorney general of the United States in the Clinton administration, for the nomination. Although a native of Florida, Reno had been away from the state for a long time, and she carried considerable political baggage from her days in the Clinton administration. Some Clinton loyalists, in fact, blamed her for the appointment of Kenneth Starr as special counsel to investigate the president, while Republicans felt that she failed the nation as attorney general by not pursuing an indictment against the president. And most Cubans despised her for deciding to seize Elian Gonzalez from the home of relatives in Miami and returning him to his father in Cuba. Many Republicans secretly wanted Reno to get the nomination so the election would pit the Bush forces against the Clinton camp. But that was not to be the case. McBride and Reno ran neck and neck in a strange role-reversal campaign, with Reno, the experienced and better-known candidate, traveling the state in her red pickup truck seeking grass-roots support in the manner of Lawton Chiles, while McBride sought to curry the favor of party leaders and Democratic interest groups—snatching many surprise endorsements, including that of the teachers' unions. In a very close primary, McBride edged past Reno by fewer than five thousand votes, but neither candidate created much enthusiasm among Democrats.[3]

On paper, McBride looked like a worthy opponent for Jeb Bush. The son of a working-class family in rural Leesburg, where he became a high school football star, McBride won a scholarship to the University of Florida in Gainesville. After graduating from Florida at the height of the Vietnam War, McBride joined the Marine Corps and earned a Bronze Star in Vietnam, complete with a "V" for valor. Upon his return to the States, McBride enrolled at the University of Florida College of Law, and after graduation he joined the Tampa law firm of Holland and Knight, one of the oldest and most respected in the state, where he rose to become its managing partner in 1992. While McBride had been involved in Democratic politics as a donor, fund-raiser, and delegate to the national convention in 1984, he was a virtual political unknown, having never held or run for office, when he decided to challenge for the governorship. He and his wife, Alex Sink, who served as president of the Bank of America's Florida operations, were, however, regarded by many as one of Florida's most influential couples.

Throughout the campaign, McBride played up his modest background and even sought to recapture some of the down-home southern charm of the "He-Coon" of Florida politics, Lawton Chiles. But McBride lacked the political reputation of Chiles, was uncomfortable and often awkward on television, and ineffective in the debates against Bush. McBride's legal abilities had clearly not been honed in the give-and-take of courtroom trials. His biggest failing, however; was his inability to develop a message that offered a corrective to Bush's conservative agenda. Instead, McBride came across as a tired liberal spokesman for the party's special interests, calling for improved salaries for teachers, higher salaries for state employees, special programs for black citizens, and a more ambitious environmental agenda, all without explaining how he proposed to pay for them.[4]

Bush, in his third gubernatorial election, had significantly honed his campaign skills. He hammered away at McBride's "liberal" agenda and the potential cost to taxpayers. During the debates, he asked McBride repeatedly to explain how he intended to pay for his programs, while McBride dodged the question and refused to acknowledge that additional taxes would be necessary. "With his bobbing and weaving and not saying anything specific, he won't have a chance to lead, in my opinion," Bush told viewers. Bush won easily, taking 56 percent of the popular vote, defeating McBride by nearly 650,000 votes, and winning sizable majorities in all but the most devout Democratic counties of Alachua, Leon, Gadsden, Palm Beach, and Broward. Bush's support came from nearly all major voting blocs including seniors, evangelicals, Catholics, Hispanics, rural white voters, and suburban and urban voters, and every section of the state. The results said as much about McBride's shortcomings as a candidate as it did about Bush's personal popularity and the appeal of his message.[5]

While Republicans celebrated Bush's reelection and the party's standing in the state, a close examination of the election results revealed that many Floridians were not fully on board with Bush's agenda. As the incumbent candidate, the brother of a very popular president at the time, and with a dominant party and a weak opponent, Jeb Bush should have captured 60 percent of the vote or more. Askew and Graham, for example, had done so when they were reelected as governor in 1974 and 1982 respectively. So why hadn't Bush done better?

The results suggested that many Floridians still had reservations about Bush's support for big business, his dismantling of state government, his unwillingness to address growth issues, and his meddling with public schools together with his support for vouchers. Opponents included African Americans, non-Cuban Hispanics, Jews, schoolteachers, urban voters in central and southeast Florida, and retirees residing in southeast Florida. Neither did leading environmentalists trust him, despite his support for Everglades restoration. This coalition of voters continued to offer the state Democratic Party hope if not victory in statewide elections. Perhaps more significantly, Jeb's personal popularity had not resulted in a watershed re-alignment of voters.

The Presidential Campaign of 2004 in Florida

Led by Governor Bush and armed with millions in campaign contribu-tions, state and national Republicans were determined not to repeat the 2000 election fiasco in Florida. Bush and Karl Rove, the president's cam-paign adviser, enlisted over one hundred thousand volunteers to ensure President Bush's reelection in 2004. Armed with a new centralized data-base called Voter Vault, Rove and his assistants targeted Republican sym-pathizers who were viewed as "unreliable," or "lazy," voters but had voted Republican when they did go to the polls or who resided in communities that were strongly Republican. Voter Vault enabled the party to tailor mes-sages directly to these voters. The president and Rove also aimed at mak-ing inroads among Jewish, African-American, and non-Cuban Hispanic voters, whose overwhelming support had been such an enormous asset to Gore in 2000.[6]

With issues of national security, the war on terrorism, and support for the troops in Iraq dominating the headlines, Bush and his supporters de-scended on areas of traditional Republican strength in Tampa, Sarasota, Miami, and Pensacola, as well as Democratic strongholds in Alachua, Palm Beach, and Volusia Counties. Door-to-door visits by young people, personal and taped telephone calls from the Bush family, and carefully coordinated campaign visits by the president to urban and rural areas of the state generated enormous attention. Voters in Florida rallied to the president during this war on terrorism. Much like voters from previous generations who rallied to support a third term for Franklin D. Roosevelt at the outbreak of World War II and Lyndon Johnson during the build-up of the Vietnam War in 1964, most voters considered it unpatriotic to oppose Bush in 2004. The president also benefited from the candidacy of Republican and Cuban-born Mel Martinez of Orlando for Florida's U.S. Senate seat. Martinez, the first Cuban to seek a U.S. Senate seat in Florida, generated enormous interest among Hispanic voters, most of whom, Bush aides believed, would vote for the president as well. Sergio Bendixen, a Democratic pollster, acknowledged the skillful work of both Bushes in raising the profile of the Republican Party among Hispanics by actively courting their support, addressing them in Spanish, and building a close affiliation with Cuban leaders in the state.[7]

Although Democratic candidate John Kerry had served in Vietnam and been highly decorated, many voters felt closer ties to the sitting president and more confident in his ability to defend the nation against international terrorism. The latter proved especially so after some Vietnam veterans openly criticized Kerry's service in Vietnam as self-promotional. His liberal record and close association with Senator Ted Kennedy from Massachusetts also did not help him with many voters in Florida, who regarded Kennedy as the apostle of big government and liberalism. While Kerry handled himself well in the debates with Bush, his personal aloofness and smugness did not appeal to voters. He was also unable to persuade them he would serve the nation effectively in time of war or that his domestic programs offered solutions to the nation's most pressing problems.[8]

With the war against terrorism weighing heavily on the minds of voters and aided by a very adroit campaign, Bush won a record 3,964,522 votes in Florida and increased his margin of victory by 5 percent over the 2000 election. Much of the president's additional support in Florida came from new voters and those who had not voted in recent elections, especially in rural and exurban areas of the state. The new exurban voters, who lived in residential areas beyond the suburbs and who sought better housing, enhanced schools, less crime, and a better overall quality of life, had been heavily courted by Rove and Jeb Bush to the party. The president also drew strong backing from active and retired military personnel, evangelicals in both Protestant and Catholic churches, Cuban and non-Cuban Hispanics who came out to vote for Martinez and, as predicted, also voted for Bush, urban and suburban voters, and seniors in southwest and central Florida. Despite Kerry's membership in the Catholic Church, religious leaders actively opposed his candidacy because of his support for abortion and gay rights.[9]

In the aftermath of the campaign, some scholars asserted that the South and much of the Sun Belt had been lost to Democrats for at least a generation, but the results, in fact, suggested that the Democratic Party continued to be a significant factor in statewide elections in Florida.[10] Despite his defeat, Kerry received 3,583,544 votes in Florida, over 650,000 votes more than Gore received in 2000. Democrats could also take some consolation in carrying Orange County, home to Orlando and at the center of the I-4 corridor, repeating Gore's victory in 2000 and suggesting that the I-4 corridor was tilting to the Democrats. Bob Graham, as well informed about state politics as anyone, contended that national and international developments made it very difficult for any Democrat to defeat President Bush. He argued that Floridians "just felt more comfortable with President Bush than they did with Senator Kerry. President Bush was able to convey a sense of strength, leadership, and purposefulness as it relates to the war on terror and the war in Iraq."[11] In his view, the 2004 election was an aberration.

Republican Successes and Democratic Aspirations

Graham's assessment of the election may have been correct, but the evidence suggested that the Republican victory reflected a growing trend among Florida voters. However one measured the results of the 2004 vote in Florida, when combined with the results from 2000 and 2002, they represented a major advance for Republicans and a disappointing setback for Democrats.

As with the national party, state Democrats struggled to find a new vision that went beyond the social, economic, and political programs of the New Deal and the Great Society and that would draw middle-class voters back into the Democratic fold. But Democrats struggled, often unsuccessfully, to get beyond the special interests of its constituent groups. Reporters Tom Hamburger and Peter Wallsten observed of Democrats, "They rallied to defend Social Security and other progressive reforms of the past, but they offered no coherent answer to the hottest issues of the moment: rapid globalization, growing economic disparities, and the soaring cost of health care."[12]

Republicans meanwhile offered a coherent message that had broad voter appeal: promising a smaller, less intrusive, and more efficient government, lower taxes, a strong national defense, welfare reform, educational reform and accountability, an aggressive defense of the nation against international terrorism, and the retention of values that, according to the

GOP, had historically defined the nation. At the same time, Republicans successfully caricatured the Democrats as proponents of big government, increased government spending, special interests, and cultural radicalism. Party leaders also capitalized on public perceptions that Democrats were soft on the national defense needs of the nation and on crime. Ronald Reagan expressed it most convincingly to voters in 1981 when he asserted that federal programs under Democratic leadership had grown too large and were suppressing the freedom of Americans and threatening the nation's democracy.[13] It was a message that gained broad support among many middle-class and upper-class whites, who were concerned about expanding government, the mounting federal debt, the threat of terrorism, and rising taxes. The Democratic Party struggled to find common ground among its constituent groups and offset the appeal of the Republican message.

Republicans also enhanced their appeal to supporters and independents by developing their own think tanks, led by the Heritage Foundation, the Cato Institute, and the American Enterprise Institute. These think tanks performed a significant role in challenging the Democratic agenda at every level and in positioning the Republican Party programmatically and intellectually with middle-class Americans. In Florida, both the James Madison Institute and Jeb Bush's Foundation for Florida's Future proved forceful and effective proponents of a neoconservative Republican agenda. Democrats at the state level had no counterpart to the James Madison Institute or Bush's Foundation for Florida's Future.

At the community level in Florida, concerns about crime and schools played an important role in driving many whites into what were perceived as safe neighborhoods and suburbs and into the Republican Party. Whites of more modest means fled such areas as Pine Hills in Orlando, which had become increasingly black and poor, because of perceptions about crime and schools. Teenagers from Pine Hills, for example, attended Jones High School in Orlando, which in 2005–6 received its fourth "F" (failing) grade in a row in the state's school-grading program. Families that could afford to do so relocated to Deltona, an "instant" exurban community to the north and east of Orlando, where they have voted Republican because of lingering concerns about schools and crime as well as taxes. Many similar developments occurred in Tampa Bay, Miami, Fort Myers, Fort Lauderdale, and Jacksonville, pushing both middle-class whites and blacks into the suburbs and, for most whites, into the Republican Party. But one must be careful about generalizing too broadly about exurban voters. For example, most middle-class and educated non-Cuban Hispanics and whites in the suburbs adjacent to Fort Lauderdale and Miami continued to vote for Democratic candidates, reflecting their political values, their belief in the efficacy of government, and their voting habits.[14]

Moreover, despite state and national political developments and the popularity of Jeb Bush, the Democratic Party remains a force in statewide elections. Democrat Bill Nelson, for example, defeated Republican Bill McCollum, a staunch neoconservative and congressional leader in the impeachment efforts against Bill Clinton, for the U.S. Senate seat by over 280,000 votes in 2000. Democrat Betty Castor lost narrowly to Republican Mel Martinez in the 2004 U.S. Senate race by 70,000 votes at the same time that President Bush defeated Kerry by almost 500,000 votes. Most political writers contend Castor would have defeated Martinez, despite Republican allegations that she was soft on terrorism, if the election had occurred in a nonpresidential year.

Aiding the efforts of moderate Democrats in Florida, the national Democratic Leadership Conference (DLC) campaigned to rejuvenate the party by urging supporters to look and think beyond the political agenda of the Great Society. The DLC operated much like a shadow government in opposition to Republican leadership and simultaneously sought to reform the Democratic Party so that it would be better positioned to defeat the Republican Party in state and national contests. DLC members argued that, until the party embraced such moderate reforms as lower taxes, a balanced budget, economic growth, government efficiency, and a stronger military defense, Democrats would continue to lose state elections in the South and the presidential election to Republicans. DLC critics in the party argued, however, that the organization offered little more than a watered-down version of the Republican neoconservative "Contract for America" and threatened to undermine the progress made by minorities and women. Only Bill Clinton proved skillful enough to win over liberal Democrats and then reach out to a national audience with a moderate, middle-of-the-road message that borrowed liberally from Republicans.[15] The political columnist Martin Dyckman observed of this intraparty squabble, "Trouble is, moderate policy is easy to conceptualize but hard to adopt." He added: "There is no organization like Britain's shadow government to give coherent voice to the opposition. The out-party doesn't have the semblance of one until it selects a presidential nominee, by which time it is about two years too late and the special constituencies are once again controlling the agenda."[16]

In Florida, despite the prominence of Lawton Chiles and Bob Graham in the DLC, the Democratic Party has struggled to rebuild its image. Its failures have resulted from political proposals that seemed to offer little more than piggybacking on those of Republicans and a chaotic state organization. With regard to the latter, Scott Maddox, former mayor of Tallahassee and a once-promising figure in Democratic circles, bollixed the job of state party leader badly when he used the office to raise funds for his own gubernatorial campaign in 2006. When his opponents complained, Maddox withdrew sheepishly as party leader and subsequently as a candidate. In the wake of Maddox's departure, Democrats turned to Karen Thurman as its director. Thurman, former congresswoman from north Florida and a Clinton-style Democrat, faces a daunting task in resurrecting the party. With party fortunes at their lowest ebb, there appears to be plenty of opportunity to pursue institutional change. But state Democrats are hardly united in their assessment of what needs to be done, and Thurman must convince Democrats in southeast Florida, where the party remains strongest, that she has the ability to reinvigorate it. Such internal squabbling between Democrats from north and south Florida, however, continues to tear at the fabric of the party and prevent it from mounting a well-organized challenge to Republicans.

Also seeking to revitalize the party is a small group of mostly Democratic stalwarts, led by Jon Mills, former Speaker of the Florida House of Representatives, and Martha Barnett, former president of the American Bar Association. Calling themselves the Florida Forum for Progressive Policy, the group has taken up the challenge posed by political writer Dyckman, developing an Internet-based dialogue among Democrats and moderates about the failures of Republican leadership in Florida and the antidemocratic agenda of their initiatives. The forum members have embraced Bill Clinton's advice, which is to find solutions to critical problems that make sense for the nation rather than to focus on ideology. At this date, it is unclear whether Thurman's leadership and the work of forum members will coincide or conflict. Moreover, it is unclear at present where Bob Graham, the leading figure in the state party despite his retirement from the Senate, stands on Thurman's leadership of the party and on the role of the Florida Forum.

Emerging Republican Divisions and the Terri Schiavo Case

Although the Republican Party appears likely to remain the majority party for the immediate future, it faces some of the same challenges that Democrats encountered when they dominated state politics. Such control makes it difficult for the party to maintain a consistent and uniform message and to avoid internal conflicts. Gone as Republican Party boss is Tom Slade, who helped establish and maintain party discipline, and his successor, Al Cardenas, has operated largely in the shadow of Jeb Bush. In the 2006 legislative session, intraparty squabbling broke into the open when Senator Alex Villalobos of Miami opposed Bush's efforts to weaken the class-size amendment approved by voters and to restore tuition vouchers for students, which had been declared unconstitutional by the state Supreme Court. Bush maneuvered behind the scenes with Senate Republicans to strip Villalobos of his election to the majority leader's position in the Senate and then actively campaigned against Villalobos in his bid for reelection in 2006. In a fund-raising letter, Bush wrote that Villalobos "has abandoned our party's principles and lost his way." But voters rejected Bush's appeal and reelected Villalobos. Several Republicans condemned Bush's actions as dictatorial and politically dangerous.[17]

As Bush neared the end of his second term as governor and was ineligible for reelection, party discipline went into a free fall when Katherine Harris ran for the U.S. Senate seat in the fall of 2006, despite active public opposition from the Governor, and candidates Charlie Crist and Tom Gallagher slugged it out in a no-holds-barred contest for the Republican gubernatorial nomination. In the blink of an eye, the discipline of the Bush years seemed to disappear.

The success of the party has also posed a challenge in restraining the arrogance of power by political leaders. Such was the case when Republican legislative leaders ignored the U.S. Constitution and proposed to select Florida's twenty-five electors for George W. Bush in the 2000 election and when Governor Bush interceded in the life-and-death struggle of Terri Schiavo in 2005. Theresa Marie "Terri" Schiavo lived in Florida when the effects of bulimia caused her heart to stop briefly, resulting in substantial brain damage in 1990. As she had left no written directive, her husband, Michael Schiavo, sought to remove her feeding tube, testifying in court that she had told him she did not want to be kept alive artificially. Her parents, however, challenged her husband's contention, claiming that she remained responsive and initiating a long and controversial court battle to keep her alive.

The conflict between family members became a public event when Governor Bush joined forces with Schiavo's parents in 2005, vowing to do "everything within my power" to restore Schiavo's feeding tube. Subsequently President Bush, Republicans in Congress, and the U.S. Justice Department chose to side with Governor Bush and Terri Schiavo's parents. President Bush signed a bill passed by Congress in mid-March that pushed the battle over Schiavo from state courts to federal courts. And the Justice Department filed three "statements of interest" supporting the parents in each court action. These steps constituted part of a dizzying series of legal maneuvers launched at the state and federal levels to prolong Schiavo's life. The actions by the governor, the president, and Republicans in Congress appeared designed to strengthen political support among evangelicals and other religious supporters. At a federal appeals court in Atlanta, one judge rebuked the White House and lawmakers for acting "in a manner demonstrably at odds with our Founding Fathers' blueprint for the governance of a free people—our Constitution." "Any further action by our court or the district court would be improper," wrote Judge Stanley Birch Jr., who had been appointed by President Bush's father.[18]

Like Judge Birch, the public was deeply troubled by the politicization of this family battle over the life of a dying woman. Real-life television dramas may well have appealed to the prurient interests of some Americans, but the debate over a feeding tube and the possible life or death of a young woman caused most great consternation. When politicians sought to inject what was perceived as their political agenda into this highly personal family matter, most Floridians and Americans recoiled.

On March 23, Pinellas-Pasco Circuit Judge George Greer denied a petition from the state Department of Children and Families and Governor Bush to take Terri Schiavo into state custody. Greer also denied a petition from the Florida Department of Children and Families to investigate allegations that Terri Schiavo's husband, Michael, had abused her. Such allegations had been considered and dismissed several times in the fifteen years that Terri Schiavo had been incapacitated.[19]

The Republican-controlled Florida Senate also had enough and on Wednesday, March 24, 2005, rejected, by a vote of 18 to 21, a bill that would have restored Schiavo's feeding tube. But the governor refused to yield to the courts or the legislature, and on Wednesday afternoon, he argued that new information suggested that Schiavo's condition might have been misdiagnosed, and that she may not, after all, be in a persistent vegetative state. "This new information raises serious concerns and warrants immediate action," Bush contended to reporters, although he never presented any new information.[20] The political scientist Susan MacManus said of Bush's announcement: "He is a very ideologically consistent person. He made no bones about that from the first day he ran for office. Those of us who watch him think this is Jeb, and how he truly believes and what he truly believes, and this may be one of those instances where he's putting politics aside."[21] MacManus may well have been right, but Bush was wrong in his diagnosis. Terri Schiavo died March 31 at the age of forty-one, and the autopsy revealed on June 15 that she was blind and that her brain had shrunk to about half the normal size for a woman her age.

Even after her death, Bush persisted. He asked prosecutors to examine Michael Schiavo's role in his wife's initial collapse, suggesting that Schiavo may have delayed his emergency call for help and this delay led to her vegetative state. Reporter Bob Herbert of the *New York Times* expressed the views of many following the governor's request when he quoted lawyer Joseph Welch's statement to U.S. Senator Joseph McCarthy during the Army-McCarthy hearings, "Have you no sense of decency, sir, at long last?" Herbert added, "I would ask the same question of Florida's governor, Jeb Bush."[22] The autopsy also "found no evidence that she was strangled or otherwise abused." Several Republicans washed their hands of the matter, led by state Senator Nancy Argenziano from Crystal River, who told the press: "That the brain was half the size, that she couldn't have been fed, that she was blind . . . really said that we played politics with this issue and shame on us."[23] Bush finally agreed to drop the matter.[24]

For all his achievements in mobilizing a strong Republican base in Florida and for his successes in public school accountability, privatizing government, economic growth and diversification, environmental protection, and tax reform, Bush has too often been tripped up by ideology and partisanship, by his support for big business at the expense of the public interest, and by his commitment to his brother's presidency. The Schiavo case was but one example of where his ideology got in the way of governing the state. The failings of several of Bush's appointees reflected his tendency to appoint friends and allies to office rather than competent and experienced professionals. James Crosby, state corrections secretary, appears headed to prison for kickbacks from vendors. Jerry Regier and two of his assistants at the beleaguered Department of Children and Families lost their jobs for accepting favors from contractors and violating Bush's ethics policy. And the Department of Management Services served as a revolving chair for six Bush secretaries who were suppose to oversee a vast array of outsourcing ventures. State Senator Argenziano characterized the situation as "a never-ending supply of secretaries and directors who had to leave under bad circumstances."[25]

The Election of 2006 and Beyond Jeb

Much of the gubernatorial rhetoric in 2006 swirled around Jeb Bush's eight years in office. This was not the first time one of the parties faced the challenge of replacing such a powerful and influential governor. In 1978, when Reubin Askew stepped down after two terms as governor, Democrats struggled to identify someone of his stature to replace him. Republicans faced the same dilemma in 2006. And although neither candidate generated the passion among Republicans that Jeb did, they both identified their campaigns with him.

Unlike Bush, the two candidates for the Republican nomination, Attorney General Charlie Crist and Chief Financial Officer Tom Gallagher were longtime Florida political operatives. Crist had run against Bob Graham for the U.S. Senate when he was barely thirty-two years old and held a variety of state offices subsequently, and Gallagher had sought the governorship on three previous occasions. Both contended they were best suited ideologically to assume the mantle of leadership from Jeb, and each of their Web sites featured prominent photographs of them with Bush.

Evangelicals and neoconservatives favored Gallagher, and he highlighted his commitment to family values and his opposition to taxes, gay marriage, and abortion, and asserted that Crist favored gay unions. But a poor showing in two debates and, most importantly, revelations that he had been day-trading in stocks of companies he was supposed to regulate crippled Gallagher's campaign. Crist gave as good as he got from Gallagher, frequently reminding Republicans of Gallagher's ethical lapses and other questionable decisions. Aided by a substantial lead in the polls, Crist focused mainly on his conservative credentials, his support for civil rights, and his work as attorney general in protecting homeowners from greedy insurance companies and contractors following the hurricanes of 2004 and 2005. Gallagher could not overcome questions about his integrity, and Crist crushed him by a margin of more than two to one in the primary election.[26]

Two relatively unknown Democrats—Congressman Jim Davis of Tampa and state Senator Rod Smith of Gainesville—vied for the nomination, and both campaigns denounced Jeb Bush's "radical conservative" agenda for Florida. The heavily favored Davis condemned Bush's role in the Terri Schiavo case, his efforts to unravel and privatize government, his opposition to funding class-size limits, his support for charter schools, and his tax breaks for the rich. But Davis, a forthright, intelligent, though uninspiring speaker, ran a lackluster campaign and appeared to rely on the endorsement of most leading Democrats to secure the party's nomination. Smith refused to go away, however, and demonstrated that he was a very effective political street fighter. A former hard-nosed prosecutor in north Florida and a Democratic leader in the state Senate, Smith was more conservative than Davis and emphasized his ability to work with Republicans to get things done for Floridians.

What appeared to be an open-and-shut primary suddenly turned into a dogfight that advantaged Smith. Davis couldn't seem to poll more than 30 percent of the Democratic vote, and Smith kept narrowing the gap. Aiding Smith's efforts was Davis's unwise decision to spend most of 2006 on the gubernatorial campaign trail, ignoring his congressional duties. It was a major mistake that would plague Davis in the primary and general election. Smith hammered at Davis's record in the first debate, asserting that he "hasn't earned a promotion to governor." Davis hung on to win the nomination, but by only 47 percent to 41 percent for Smith. And in an ominous development, Davis generated little enthusiasm for his candidacy among African-American voters and those in vote-rich southeast Florida.[27]

In the general election, Crist relied on a huge fund-raising advantage—a record $56 million in state contributions and donations from the national party—to launch ads immediately after the primary portraying himself as a middle-of-the-road Republican, even while selecting religious conservative Jeff Kottkamp from Cape Coral to secure his political right. Six-figure checks rolled in day after day from Disney, Princess Tours, Clear Channel Outdoor, Palm Beach Kennel Club, and U.S. Sugar to help finance Crist's public-relations campaign. By the time the financially strapped Davis was able to air his first ads in early October, Crist had already defined him as an absentee, a liberal, and a tax-and-spend Democrat. The experienced Crist noted, "In a state as big as Florida, if you're not on TV, you don't exist." Davis did not help himself by continuing his lackluster campaign. He repeatedly showed up late to gatherings and often revealed poor judgment when addressing an audience, as when he gave an antibusiness speech to the Council of 100, the state's leading business organization.[28]

Despite a skillful media campaign, a huge fund-raising advantage—$56 million to Davis's $15 million—and a big lead in the polls, Crist limped toward the finishing line. As with all Republicans in 2006, his campaign felt the effects of President Bush's falling ratings because of the unpopular war in Iraq and Republican congressional corruption charges, especially accusations that Florida Congressman Mark Foley had made sexual advances toward male pages. But Crist also fared poorly in the two debates with Davis, getting his facts incorrect about the state murder rate and his role in the Terri Schiavo case, and angering Republicans by failing to appear alongside President Bush at a campaign-ending rally in Pensacola. None of this helped Crist, but it still was not enough to save the lackluster, cash-strapped Davis. Crist captured southwest, central, and north Florida decisively and took 52 percent of the vote to 45 percent for Davis. Although Davis won by significant margins in Miami-Dade, Broward, and Palm Beach Counties, the turnout was very low, and he lost the important I-4 corridor, including Orange and Volusia Counties, which had voted Democratic in 2000 and 2004.[29]

Could Democrats have captured the governorship with a stronger candidate than Davis? There is some evidence that the party might well have won given the softness of Crist's support and widespread voter anger over the leadership of the national Republican Party. In the same election, for example, Democrat Alex Sink, a rising star in the party, defeated a formidable Republican opponent, former Senate President Tom Lee, for the position of chief financial officer by over three hundred thousand votes. She also received more state votes than Charlie Crist and won her race by stressing nonpartisan competence and experience. U.S. Senator Bill Nelson also won reelection by over 1 million votes against Republican opponent Katherine Harris. But it is difficult to draw any conclusions from that race since Harris's candidacy was crippled from the outset by opposition from Governor Bush and public questions about her competence. Democrats did capture seven seats in the state House of Representatives, narrowing the Republican majority to seventy-eight Republicans to forty-one Democrats, and two additional congressional seats, so that there are now nineteen Republicans and eight Democrats.[30]

Unlike Jeb Bush's victories in 1998 and 2002, Crist's comparatively modest results did not provide long enough coattails to pull Republican cabinet-level candidates to victory. As noted, former Senate President Tom Lee lost to Alex Sink. And Republicans Bill McCollum and Charles Bronson ran ahead of Crist in winning, respectively, the attorney general and agriculture commissioner offices.[31]

Crist's limitations as a candidate pose potential challenges for his efforts to maintain party discipline after Bush and to build a governing coalition. The governor's leadership, his role in helping to elect many state Republicans, his standing within the national party because of his relationship to the president, and his personal popularity in the state gave Jeb Bush a position of influence that Crist will find impossible to duplicate. Following Bush's retirement from office, party squabbles and personal ambitions are likely to magnify themselves further and undermine party unity.[32] Crist must deal immediately, for example, with Senate President Ken Pruitt and House Speaker Marco Rubio, both of whom are politically ambitious, have their own political agenda, and enjoy greater standing with Republicans in the legislature.

Moreover, Crist does not share Bush's libertarian philosophy nor his connections to the Christian right in Florida, despite the fact that he spent much of the primary and general election proclaiming himself as a Jeb disciple. Crist is, in fact, a much more pragmatic political figure and will struggle to build a coalition to address such difficult and costly issues as school funding, health care, and property taxes. The political consequences will be immense if Crist decides he must increase taxes to address state needs or bolster the state bureaucracy to address the shortcomings of privatization. Further compounding the challenges facing Crist, Bush did not surround himself with senior advisers, like Askew and Graham, who might have served a Crist administration well.

Of no small consequence, Crist faces the prospect of dealing with a state bureaucracy that has been seriously damaged by Bush's policies. Although Bush has expressed deep respect for public servants in his last year in office, he has been a leading critic of government employees throughout his administration, portraying them as the bane of state operations.[33] It is ironic that it was the Republican Party in the late nineteenth century that implemented civil service reform and Republican President Theodore Roosevelt who significantly expanded civil service to ensure that the nation had honest, experienced, and independent civil servants working for the well-being of the public. But state and national Republicans today believe that these employees are at the root of the problems with government. Recently Republicans, following a proposal from the governor, required that each state department, agency, and commission be abolished every eight years unless lawmakers vote to keep it in operation. That stance by Republicans persists in marked contrast to the party's historic position.[34] The effects of Bush's actions drove most middle-level managers out of state government because they saw no future in it. Without strong and effective civil servants, it is unclear how Crist or subsequent governors will meet the needs of citizens in a financial or political crisis, or how they will be able to respond constructively to Florida's massive growth.

At present, despite reservations about some of his legislative initiatives and administrative changes, Bush will leave office as one of Florida's most popular governors and perhaps the most influential governor in the modern era. He has redefined the state Republican Party, steered it sharply to the right, and persuaded a new generation of Floridians to embrace his conservative fiscal and social agenda. Reporter Tim Nickens of the *St. Petersburg Times* noted that one of his disciples, Speaker of the House Marco Rubio, has championed "100 innovative ideas for Florida's future," but "none of these ideas can be tied to a tax increase or expansion of government" because of the influence of Jeb Bush.[35]

Moreover, most newcomers to the state have embraced Bush's position on taxes, economic development, educational accountability, and crime prevention. Midwesterners and northeasterners, who continue to flood into Florida, have come seeking better jobs and economic advancement and have a built-in bias against new taxes that might limit their financial well-being. Not surprisingly, they have generally favored the Republican position on taxes.[36]

Significantly, neither party today resorts to racial overtures in seeking voter support because party leaders specifically and Floridians generally have largely accepted the racial and ethnic diversity of the state. Moreover, a booming state economy continues to offer opportunity without regard to one's race or ethnicity. Jane Healy of the *Orlando Sentinel* observed that many of the new upper-middle class neighborhoods in west Orange County are naturally integrating: "I am amazed that there are new neighborhoods that are attracting both middle-class blacks and whites, but it is happening."[37]

While these newcomers appreciate Bush's accomplishments and the ways they have benefited from them, many are not died-in-the-wool Republicans. They, in fact, are more interested in candidates who offer initiatives to improve job opportunities, lower property taxes, improve public education, and enhance the quality of life. Growth in southwest Florida has continued to benefit state Republicans as midwesterners locate there. Hillsborough and Pasco Counties, once swing counties, have become increasingly Republican and supported Bush and then Crist in recent gubernatorial elections. But Davis and Sink won by large margins in Broward and Palm Beach Counties as well as in Bush's home county of Miami-Dade, where northeasterners and non-Cuban Hispanics continue to locate and display a predilection toward the Democratic Party.[38]

Because migration and immigration patterns continue to redefine urban and suburban life in the state, they threaten the political stability and political expectations of both parties. For example, the growing Hispanic presence could pose a major problem for Republicans, despite the influence of Jeb Bush. Two exit polls showed Florida's fastest-growing demographic group of voters supported Davis over Crist.[39]

In cities throughout central and south Florida, large numbers of whites and blacks as well as Hispanics, Vietnamese, and Asians have moved into the inner city, attracted by an unemployment rate that is below 2.5 percent. Many of these new ethnic residents have purchased homes from whites who have fled the city because of concerns about crime, failing schools, immigration, and deteriorating neighborhoods. But, where whites saw problems, ethnics and immigrants see opportunities: the chance to purchase their own home at a reasonable price, a short commute to work, and public education for their children. They tend to be caught up in the pressures of daily living and adjusting to a new community and have little concern about the racial or ethnic makeup of their neighborhoods. As with other voters in the state, they are receptive to overtures from either Republicans or Democrats. A class appeal to these ethnic voters has had little effect, however, because they regard themselves first as Asian or Hispanic and also see themselves as nascent capitalists. Moreover, they continue to focus on developments in their native countries, and the role played by the United States in facilitating democracy and economic progress abroad. But it will take a stronger, better-funded, and better-organized Democratic Party to win their votes. Puerto Ricans, who moved into Osceola County and registered as Democrats, were subsequently ignored by local Democrats despite their support for Al Gore in 2000. As a result, they opted to vote for Jeb Bush in 2002 and President Bush in 2004. Exit polls suggest they supported Crist narrowly in 2006.[40]

Although Crist had over $56 million to spend on his campaign, he could not keep the "little-known Tampa congressman from the best Democratic gubernatorial showing in 12 years." The election results suggest that, despite the strength of the Republican Party and the popularity of Jeb Bush, it does not have a stranglehold on statewide races. They also indicate that Crist won the election along the I-4 corridor. If Davis had had more advertising money and run a better campaign, he could have done a more effective job of recruiting support in the towns and cities along the corridor. The growing importance of I-4 explains, in part, why every successful statewide candidate in 2006—Senator Bill Nelson, Governor Crist, Attorney General McCollum, and Chief Financial Officer Sink—resided in Tampa Bay or the Orlando area.[41]

And what about the state's senior population, which remains the singlemost influential group of voters in the state? Despite the threat of hurricanes, they continue to enter the state in search of an active, healthy lifestyle beyond retirement. They are most concerned about quality-of-life issues, personal expenses, and health care, and they welcome the absence of a "state income tax and the $25,000 homestead exemption."[42] Recent retirees, in particular, believe Republicans are more likely to restrain state spending and oppose new taxes. But to ensure they do so, seniors championed efforts to adopt constitutional amendment number 6 in 2006, which increased the homestead exemption in Florida from $25,000 to $50,000 for low-income seniors over sixty-five. The amendment passed by a 3½ to 1 margin in 2006.[43]

But not all retirees are solely focused on their self-interest. One resident of the Villages, one of the largest and more conservative retirement centers just south of Ocala, reflected the views of many northerners who retire to Florida: "I come from a high-tax state (Minnesota) with a good educational and cultural environment. . . . I must admit that I miss that here and would never have moved here simply to save money or to get away from a progressive government."[44] Like other voters, seniors are also concerned about such national developments as the war on terrorism, rising health-care costs, Social Security, immigration policy, the federal debt, and the economy. The challenge for Democrats is to persuade seniors that their proposals offer better solutions for both seniors and the state than does the low tax and antigovernment message of Republicans. So far, Democrats have not been able to do so.[45]

So what's to become of Florida and its politics in the coming years? For now, Floridians are reasonably content because the economy remains very strong, and tourists continue to flock into the state, helping to pay for many needs through the 6 percent sales tax. Jeb Bush and the state Republican Party have reaped the political benefits of a Pax-Florida. And their political message still resonates well with the desires and concerns of most Floridians. But will it last? As Carl Hiaasen cautions readers about the state and its politics, Floridians are unpredictable because they don't know or remember the past.[46] And it is not just senior citizens who are memory-challenged. In a state where change is a daily occurrence and where traditions find little traction, no politician or party in a state as dynamic as Florida can be smug about the future.

The one certainty is that growth will remain a constant and Floridians will muddle along without a clear-cut sense of themselves. As newcomers adjust to a new community, new neighbors and friends, and a new job, they will continue to be caught up in local and regional matters rather than state issues. The state's complex racial, ethnic, and age diversity promises to add further to its lack of identity and to obstruct consensus on public policy.

These dynamic social, cultural, and demographic developments have, not surprisingly, resulted in a political revolution in the state, that signaled the death knell of the Yellow Dog Democrats and paved the way for the Republican ascendancy. These developments have all occurred in a mere lifetime and helped Florida become a megastate in the process. How Floridians adjust to these developments will say a great deal about the state's political future. Because so few of these changes have deep roots and because few Floridians have a strong philosophical commitment to one party, personality still tends to trump party politics, making statewide election results uncertain and keeping Florida in play for both parties. That's not likely to change for the foreseeable future.

Notes

Introduction

1. *CBS News*, November 6, 2000. See also <politicalhumor.about.com/library/blratherisms.htm>; and Sabato, ed., *Overtime*.

2. Gannon, *Florida: A Short History*, 6.

3. Mormino, *Land of Sunshine, State of Dreams*, 2.

4. U.S. Bureau of the Census, U.S. Census: Florida, General Characteristics, Fact Sheet, 2005.

5. Reed, Kohls, and Hanchette, "The Dissolution of Dixie and the Changing Shape of the South," 221, 227.

6. Richard Patterson, quoted in Cobb, "We Ain't White Trash No More," 139.

7. Reed et al., 227.

8. Hiaasen quoted in Paterniti, "America in Extremis," 28–35, 66, 74.

9. U.S. Bureau of the Census, U.S. Census: Florida, General Demographic Characteristics, 2005; *St. Petersburg Times*, August 21, 2006.

10. "The Changing Face of Florida," *Gainesville Sun*, March 28, 2001.

11. Ibid.

12. U.S. Bureau of the Census, U.S. Census: Florida, General Characteristics, Fact Sheet, 2005.

13. *Florida Statistical Abstract, 2002, 2003*, 36th, 37th ed., Section 6.00, Labor Force, Employment and Earnings.

14. Hiaasen, from his interview by Steve Croft on the television show *60 Minutes*, April 17, 2005.

15. Kruse, *White Flight*; Lassiter, *The Silent Majority*, 4. There are many other excellent books on southern politics, the politics of race and class, and the emergence of the Republican Party to which this author is indebted. Briefly, and in no particular order, these include: D. T. Carter, *The Politics of Rage*; D. T. Carter, *From George Wallace to Newt Gingrich*; Edsall and Edsall, *Chain Reaction*; Phillips, *The Emerging Republican Majority*; Black and Black, *Politics and Society in the South*; Bartley and Graham, *Southern Politics and the Second Reconstruction*; Sugrue,

The Origins of the Urban Crisis; Fraser and Gerstle, eds., *The Rise and Fall of the New Deal Order, 1930–1980*; Novak and Zeliser, eds., *The Democratic Experiment*; Lublin, *The Republican South*; Rieder, *Canarsie: The Jews and Italians of Brooklyn against Liberalism*; Formisano, *Boston against Busing*; Frank, *What's the Matter with Kansas?*; Hamburger and Wallsten, *One Party Country*.

16. U.S. Bureau of the Census, U.S. Census: Florida, General Demographic Characteristics, 2005.

Chapter 1. From Darkness to Sunshine

1. Paterniti, "America in Extremis," 30–31.

2. William H. Rehnquist, *The Centennial Crisis: The Disputed Election of 1876* (New York: Knopf, 2004).

3. *Tampa Morning Tribune*, May 4, 1909; Ortiz, *Emancipation Betrayed*, xix.

4. Colburn and Scher, *Florida's Gubernatorial Politics*, 59–60, 73, 78.

5. Key, *Southern Politics in State and Nation*, esp. 82–105, 298–311.

6. Colburn and deHaven-Smith, *Government in the Sunshine State*, 10, 15; see also Ortiz, *Emancipation Betrayed*.

7. Cash, *The Mind of the South*; McWhiney, *Cracker Culture*.

8. Walter Fuller, quoted in William W. Rogers, "Fortune and Misfortune," 297.

9. Colburn and deHaven-Smith, *Government in the Sunshine State*, 28–29.

10. Winkler, *Franklin D. Roosevelt and the Making of Modern America*, 69.

11. Ibid., 72.

12. Gannon, *Florida: A Short History*, 104–6; see also Mormino, *Land of Sunshine, State of Dreams*, 308–9.

13. Mormino, "World War II," 325.

14. Arnold Harms, interview by David Colburn, November 22, 2005. Interview is part of the Veterans Oral History Project, Library of Congress. See also Gannon, *Operation Drumbeat*.

15. Mormino, *Land of Sunshine, State of Dreams*, 308.

16. Colburn and deHaven-Smith, *Florida's Megatrends*, 44.

17. Mormino, *Land of Sunshine, State of Dreams*, 129.

18. Ibid., 132.

19. Colburn and deHaven-Smith, *Florida's Megatrends*, 55.

20. U.S. Bureau of the Census, U.S. Census: Florida, General Demographic Characteristics, 2000.

21. Mormino, *Land of Sunshine, State of Dreams*, 141–42.

22. *St. Petersburg Times*, January 9, 1953.

23. MacManus, "Aging in Florida and Its Implications."

24. Lassiter, *The Silent Majority*, 11; see also Cobb, *The Selling of the South*; and Colburn and deHaven-Smith, *Florida's Megatrends*, 40, 41.

25. Colburn and deHaven-Smith, *Florida's Megatrends*, 41.

26. Jones, "No Longer Denied," 255.

27. *St. Petersburg Times*, October 14, 1960.

28. McCollough, *Truman*, 639.

29. Ibid., 667.

30. *St. Petersburg Times*, October 31, November 2, 3, 4, 1948.

31. Ibid., November 3, 4, 1948.

32. Lawson, Colburn, and Paulson, "Groveland," 300–301.

33. Colburn and deHaven-Smith, *Government in the Sunshine State*, 37, 38.

34. Lawson, Colburn, and Paulson, "Groveland," 315; see also Mormino, "A History of Florida's White Primary."

35. Ibid., 319–20. In 2005, Florida Attorney General Charlie Crist launched an investigation to determine who was responsible for the deaths of the Moores. The investigation had the flavor of a campaign ploy by Crist to obtain African-American support for his 2006 gubernatorial campaign. The investigation failed to identify those directly and indirectly involved in the murder of the Moores.

36. Colburn and Scher, *Florida Gubernatorial Politics*, 175–76.

37. Dyckman, *Floridian of His Century: The Courage of Governor LeRoy Collins*, 96–98; Colburn and Scher, *Florida's Gubernatorial Politics*, 223, 224.

38. Wagy, *Governor LeRoy Collins of Florida*, 87.

39. Rabby, *The Pain and the Promise*, 204–5; see also Colburn and Scher, *Florida's Gubernatorial Politics*, 230–31.

40. Colburn and Scher, *Florida's Gubernatorial Politics*, 102–3.

41. Luther H. Hodges, *The Business Conscience* (Englewood Cliffs, N.J.: Prentice-Hall, 1963); see also Chafe, *Civilities and Civil Rights*.

42. Wagy, *Governor LeRoy Collins*, 101.

43. Jacoway and Colburn, eds. *Southern Businessmen and Desegregation*.

44. Jacoway, "Taken By Surprise"; Colburn and Scher, *Florida's Gubernatorial Politics*, 231.

45. Wagy, *Governor LeRoy Collins*, 94.

46. Dyckman, *Floridian of His Century*, 91.

47. LeRoy Collins, interview by David Colburn and Richard Scher, February 12, 1975, Samuel Proctor Oral History Program, University of Florida, Gainesville, 38AB, 24; Colburn and Scher, *Florida's Gubernatorial Politics*, 226.

48. Wagy, *Governor LeRoy Collins*, 128–30.

49. Ibid., 130.

50. Transcript of statewide television-radio talk to the people of Florida on race relations, March 20, 1960, 5, in box no. 4 (Speeches, March 17–April 13, 1960), LeRoy Collins Papers, University of South Florida, Tampa.

51. Wagy, *Governor LeRoy Collins*, 172.

52. Garrow, *Bearing the Cross*, 146–47.

53. Lassiter, *The Silent Majority*, 229–30.

Chapter 2. Racial Protest and the Emergence of Fault Lines in the Democratic Hegemony

1. Chafe, *Civilities and Civil Rights*, 91–141.

2. Ibid., 116–18.

3. Rabby, *The Pain and the Promise*, 93.

4. Ibid., 91.

5. Ibid.

6. Ibid, 98.

7. Ibid., 118.

8. Ibid., 102; Dyckman, *Floridian of His Century*, 194–95.

9. Dyckman, 194; Rabby, *The Pain and the Promise*, 107–8.

10. Wagy, *Governor LeRoy Collins*, 135–39; Colburn and Scher, *Florida's Gubernatorial Politics*, 231.

11. Dyckman, *Floridian of His Century*, 194–97.

12. Rabby, *The Pain and the Promise*, 110.

13. Ibid.; Dyckman, *Floridian of His Century*, 196.

14. Colburn and Scher, *Florida's Gubernatorial Politics*, 81; Dyckman, *Floridian of His Century*, 196.

15. *Tampa Tribune*, May 10, 1956; *Miami Herald*, May 16, 1956.

16. Dyckman, *Floridian of His Century*, 199.

17. Ibid.; Wagy, *Governor LeRoy Collins*, 139–42.

18. Dyckman, *Floridian of His Century*, 199–200; *St. Petersburg Times*, November 10, 1960.

19. Wagy, *Governor LeRoy Collins*, 143.

20. Rabby, *The Pain and the Promise*, 128.

21. Ibid.

22. Colburn, *Racial Change and Community Crisis*, 178–79; T. Branch, *Pillar of Fire: America in the King Years, 1963–65*, 33–41.

23. Colburn, *Racial Change and Community Crisis*, 139–43.

24. Ibid., 62–64, 87–89.

25. Jacoway, "Taken by Surprise," 39–40; Colburn, *Racial Change and Community Crisis*, 151–53.

26. Colburn, *Racial Change and Community Crisis*, 148.

27. Colburn and Scher, *Florida's Gubernatorial Politics*, 230; Foglesong, *Married to the Mouse*, 55.

28. Kirkpatrick Sale, *Power Shift: The Rise of the Southern Rim and Its Challenge to the Eastern Establishment*, 112–15; Edsall and Edsall, *Chain Reaction*, 38–43.

29. Edsall and Edsall, *Chain Reaction*, 37.

30. Reubin O'D. Askew, interview by Julian Pleasants, May 8, 1998, Samuel Proctor Oral History Program, University of Florida, Gainesville, FP1 Reubin Askew, 54; Colburn and Scher, *Florida's Gubernatorial Politics*, 81–82.

31. *Tampa Tribune*, April 7, 1965; Colburn and Scher, *Florida's Gubernatorial Politics*, 82.

32. Claude R. Kirk Jr., interview by Julian Pleasants, October 29, 1998, Samuel Proctor Oral History Program, University of Florida, Gainesville, FP74 Claude R. Kirk Jr., 75–76.

33. Mathews and Prothro, *Negroes and the New Southern Politics*, 394.

34. Claude R. Kirk Jr., interview by Julian Pleasants, October 29, 1998, Samuel Proctor Oral History Program, University of Florida, Gainesville, FP74 Claude R. Kirk Jr., 76.

35. Colburn and Scher, *Florida's Gubernatorial Politics*, 83.

36. Jane Healy (vice president and editorial page editor, *Orlando Sentinel*), interview by David Colburn, June 5, 2006.

37. *Tampa Tribune*, November 2, 1966.

38. Ibid., November 7, 1966; *Tampa Times*, November 9, 1966. See also Colburn and Scher, *Florida's Gubernatorial Politics*, 83–84.

39. Kelly and Harbison, *The American Constitution*, 945–51; *Gainesville Sun*, July 27, 2004.

40. *Tampa Times*, November 9, 1966; Ralph Turlington, interview by Jack Bass and Walter DeVries, May 18, 1974, original in the Southern Historical Collection, Library of the University of North Carolina at Chapel Hill, S.O.H.P. #4007, A-61, copy in the Samuel Proctor Oral History Program, University of Florida, Gainesville, FP55, 19.

41. Wagy, *Governor LeRoy Collins*, 194, 196.

42. Dyckman, *Floridian of His Century*, 141–46.

43. Wagy, *Governor LeRoy Collins*, 193.

44. Ibid.; Dyckman, *Floridian of His Century*, 246.

45. Wagy, *Governor LeRoy Collins*, 193; Dyckman, *Floridian of His Century*, 247–48.

46. Edsall and Edsall, *Chain Reaction*, 77–79; Carlson, *George C. Wallace and the Politics of Powerlessness*, 144.

47. Lassiter, *The Silent Majority*, 232, 233, 238; Kruse, *White Flight*; see also Phillips, *The Emerging Republican Majority*.

48. Wagy, *Governor LeRoy Collins*, 194; Dyckman, *Floridian of His Century*, 249.

49. Dyckman, *Floridian of His Century*, 248; Wagy, *Governor LeRoy Collins*, 194.

50. Dyckman, *Floridian of His Century*, 241.

51. "Howard Carries Varied History," *St. Petersburg Times*, September 27, 1998.

52. Dyckman, *Floridian of His Century*, 251.

53. *Miami Herald*, November 7, 1968.

54. Lassiter, *The Silent Majority*, 232–38.

55. *New York Times*, January 8, 1967, April 7, 30, May 6, 1967; *Miami Herald*, July 19, 26, 1967; Colburn and Scher, *Florida's Gubernatorial Politics*, 269–70.

56. *Tampa Tribune*, April 6–11, 1970.

57. Reubin Askew, interview by David R. Colburn and Richard K. Scher, January 10, 1975, Tallahassee, copy in the author's possession.

58. Colburn and Scher, *Florida's Gubernatorial Politics*, 234–35.

59. See Blake, *Land into Water—Water into Land*.

60. Stanley I. Kutler, ed. *Abuse of Power: The New Nixon Tapes* (New York: Free Press, 1997); Philip B. Kurland, *Watergate and the Constitution* (Chicago: University of Chicago Press, 1978).

Chapter 3. Reubin Askew, Lawton Chiles, and the Reinvention of the Democratic Party

1. *Miami Herald*, September 15, 25, 1970.

2. *Tampa Tribune*, September 2, 5, 1970.

3. *Miami Herald*, August 22, September 17, 22, 1970.

4. Ibid., September 17, 1970.

5. Colburn and Scher, *Florida's Gubernatorial Politics*, 85–86.

6. Ibid., 86; *Miami Herald*, August 20, 1970.

7. Reubin O'D. Askew, interview by Julian Pleasants, May 8, 1998, Samuel Proctor Oral History Program, University of Florida, Gainesville, FP1 Reubin Askew, 90; see also *Miami Herald*, October 9, 10, 1970.

8. Colburn and Scher, *Florida's Gubernatorial Politics*, 86.

9. Lassiter, *The Silent Majority*, 267–68.

10. Reubin O'D. Askew, interview by Julian Pleasants, May 8, 1998, Samuel Proctor Oral History Program, University of Florida, Gainesville, FP1 Reubin Askew, 99.

11. Ibid.

12. Ibid., 106.

13. *Tampa Tribune*, June 27, 1973.

14. Reubin O'D. Askew, interview by Julian Pleasants, May 8, 1998, Samuel Proctor Oral History Program, University of Florida, Gainesville, FP1 Reubin Askew, 128.

15. Colburn and Scher, *Florida's Gubernatorial Politics*, 199–200.

16. Ibid.

17. Reubin O'D. Askew, interview by Julian Pleasants, May 8, 1998, Samuel Proctor Oral History Program, University of Florida, Gainesville, FP1 Reubin Askew, 128–29.

18. Ibid., 223.

19. *Tampa Tribune*, February 2, 1972; Colburn and Scher, *Florida's Gubernatorial Politics*, 217–18.

20. Reubin O'D. Askew, interview by Julian Pleasants, May 8, 1998, Samuel Proctor Oral History Program, University of Florida, Gainesville, FP1 Reubin Askew, 224.

21. Ibid., 225.

22. *Tampa Tribune*, January 6, 1971.

23. Sanders, *Mighty Peculiar Elections*, 6.

24. J. Carter, *Sharing Good Times*; Domin, *Jimmy Carter, Public Opinion, and the Search for Values, 1977–1981*.

25. Speech presented by Governor Reubin Askew at the Governor's Luncheon, Central Florida Fair, Orlando, Fla., February 21, 1972, Reubin O'D. Askew Papers, Office of the Governor, Florida State Archives, Tallahassee.

26. Lassiter, *The Silent Majority*, 310.

27. *St. Petersburg Times*, August 29, 1971.

28. Formisano, *Boston against Busing*, 107; see also Lassiter, *The Silent Majority*, esp. 121–97.

29. Reubin O'D. Askew, interview by Julian Pleasants, May 8, 1998, Samuel Proctor Oral History Program, University of Florida, Gainesville, FP1 Reubin Askew, 202.

30. Ibid., 242.

31. Ibid.

32. *Tampa Tribune*, March 15, 1972; *Miami Herald*, March 15, 1972.

33. See, most notably, Formisano, *Boston against Busing*; Lassiter, *The Silent Majority*; and Kruse, *White Flight*.

34. "Equality of Opportunity: Askew's Administration in Motion," memorandum, Reubin O'D. Askew Papers, Office of the Governor, State Archives, Tallahassee; see also Colburn and Scher, *Florida's Gubernatorial Politics*, 230.

35. Reubin O'D. Askew, interview by Julian Pleasants, May 8, 1998, Samuel Proctor Oral History Program, University of Florida, Gainesville, FP1 Reubin Askew, 253.

36. Ibid.

37. *Tampa Tribune*, June 2, 1974; Colburn and Scher, *Florida's Gubernatorial Politics*, 204.

38. Colburn and Scher, *Florida's Gubernatorial Politics*, 281, 286–87, 291.

39. Reubin O'D. Askew, interview by Julian Pleasants, May 8, 1998, Samuel Proctor Oral History Program, University of Florida, Gainesville, FP1 Reubin Askew, 251.

40. *New York Times*, November 6, 1978.

41. Lassiter, *The Silent Majority*, 226–37.

42. Reubin O'D. Askew, interview by Julian Pleasants, May 8, 1998, Samuel Proctor Oral History Program, University of Florida, Gainesville, FP1 Reubin Askew, 250; Colburn and Scher, *Florida's Gubernatorial Politics*, 86–87.

Chapter 4. An Era of Political Transition

1. Don Pride, interview by Jack Bass and Walter DeVries, May 18, 1974, original in the Southern Historical Collection, Library of the University of North Carolina at Chapel Hill, S.O.H.P. #4007, A-57, copy in the Samuel Proctor Oral History Program, University of Florida, Gainesville, FP46 Don Pride, 28.

2. Reubin O'D. Askew, interview by Julian Pleasants, May 8, 1998, Samuel Proctor Oral History Program, University of Florida, Gainesville, FP1 Reubin Askew, 250.

3. *Tampa Tribune*, October 1, 2, 4, 5, 1978; *Miami Herald*, October 6, 1978.

4. B. Graham, *Workdays*, 1–130; *Miami Herald*, October 6, 1978.

5. *Tallahassee Democrat*, September 14, 1978; *Tampa Tribune*, November 6, 8, 9, 1978; *Miami Herald*, November 9, 1978. For campaign results, see Florida Department of State, Division of Elections, November 7, 1978 General Election. For urban voting patterns in Florida, see Bartley and Graham, *Southern Politics and the Second Reconstruction*.

6. *The Florida Handbook*, 1979, 1981.

7. Phillips, *The Emerging Republican Majority*; see also Edsall and Edsall, *Chain Reaction*, 81.

8. Abby Goodnough, "Strange Brews Are Created in Melting Pot That Is Florida," *New York Times*, April 3, 2005.

9. Lassiter, *The Silent Majority*, 309–13.

10. Senator Bob Graham, interview by Samuel Proctor, Samuel Proctor Oral History Program, University of Florida, Oral History FP 50, 475.

11. Date, *Quiet Passion*.

12. *St. Petersburg Times*, December 13, 2004; Senator Bob Graham, interview by Samuel Proctor, Samuel Proctor Oral History Program, University of Florida, Oral History FP 50, 400.

13. Senator Bob Graham, interview by Samuel Proctor, Samuel Proctor Oral History Program, University of Florida, Oral History FP 50, 417–18, 421.

14. Ibid., 370.

15. See also Lassiter, *The Silent Majority*, 11. Lassiter notes the role of corporate leaders in the South, who led the effort "to transcend the burdens of the region's history through the twin pillars of rapid economic development and enforced racial harmony."

16. Reed, quoted in the interview with Graham by Samuel Proctor, Samuel Proctor Oral History Program, University of Florida, Oral History FP 50FP 50, 370.

17. Colburn and deHaven-Smith, *Florida's Megatrends*, 53; Senator Bob Graham, interview by Samuel Proctor, Samuel Proctor Oral History Program, University of Florida, Oral History FP 50, 394.

18. Graham notebook entry from Feb. 10, 2001, as quoted in the *New York Times*, June 4, 2003.

19. Ibid.

20. In his campaign for election to the U.S. Senate in 1982 and in subsequent reelections to the Senate, Graham consistently had strong support from seniors in Florida.

21. "Graham's Quiet Exit," *St. Petersburg Times*, December 13, 2004.

22. Ibid.

23. For more on Reagan, see Reeves, *The Triumph of Imagination*; D'Souza, *Ronald Reagan*; and Morris, *Dutch*.

24. Florida Department of State, Division of Elections, General Election, November 4, 1980, and November 6, 1984.

25. Edsall and Edsall, *Chain Reaction*, 137–39.

Chapter 5. Migration of the Middle Class, the Search for Community, and the Emerging Hispanic Presence

1. *Gainesville Sun*, March 5, 2006. For a more extensive look at the loss of community in America, see Putnam, *Bowling Alone*.

2. *Florida Trend Magazine*, April 2006, 28–103.

3. Colburn and deHaven-Smith, *Florida's Megatrends*, 54.

4. Paterniti, "America in Extremis," 31.

5. Colburn and deHaven-Smith, *Florida's Megatrends*, 44–45.

6. Juan Carlos Espinosa, interview by the author, September 16, 2005.

7. Mormino, *Land of Sunshine, State of Dreams*, 297.

8. Ibid., 129.

9. Mike Vogel, "Big Box Worship," *Florida Trend*, December 2005, 84–89; *Gainesville Sun*, March 5, 2006.

10. *Gainesville Sun*, March 5, 2006.

11. Ibid.

12. Miller, "Postdenominational Christianity in the Twenty-first Century," 205.

13. Ibid., 199.

14. Vogel, "Big Box Worship," *Florida Trend*, December 2005, 84–89.

15. Flynt, "Sidney J. Catts," 116; see also Flynt, *Cracker Messiah*; and Colburn and Scher, *Florida's Gubernatorial Politics*, 67–69.

16. Flynt, *Cracker Messiah*, 87.

17. Jon Nordheimer, "Florida Runoffs May Set Stage for a Close Contest for Governor," *New York Times*, September 30, 1986; see also Jon Nordheimer, "Florida Race Underscores Changes, *New York Times*, September 2, 1986; and Jon Nordheimer, "12,000 Votes Separate Democrats in Florida Race," *New York Times*, October 1, 1986.

18. Jon Nordheimer, "12,000 Votes Separate Democrats in Florida Race," *New York Times*, October 1, 1986.

19. Jon Nordheimer, "Florida Race Underscores Changes, *New York Times*, September 2, 1986.

20. Bob Martinez, interview by Julian Pleasants, March 23, 1999, Oral History Collection, University of Florida, FP73 Bob Martinez, 60.

21. Ibid., 62, 65, 68; Steve Bousquet, "Democrats Must Look for Pay Dirt in Palatka," *St. Petersburg Times*, September 21, 2002.

22. *The Florida Handbook*, 1987; Colburn and deHaven-Smith, *Government in the Sunshine State*, 69–71.

23. Mormino, *Land of Sunshine, Land of Dreams*, 285.

24. Ibid., 285–88, 293.

25. Colburn and deHaven-Smith, *Florida's Megatrends*, 56–58; Mormino, *Land of Sunshine, Land of Dreams*, 296.

26. George H. W. Bush, "Remarks at a Reception for Governor Bob Martinez in Orlando, Florida," November 1, 1990, George Bush Presidential Library and Archives, Texas A&M, Papers of President George H. W. Bush, 1990/1991, 1–4; Colburn and deHaven-Smith, *Government in the Sunshine State*, 71.

27. Senator Bob Graham, interview by Samuel Proctor, Samuel Proctor Oral History Program, University of Florida, Oral History FP 50, 449.

28. Colburn and deHaven-Smith, *Florida's Megatrends*, 59.

29. Ibid., 108.

30. Bob Martinez, interview by Julian Pleasants, March 23, 1999, Oral History Collection, University of Florida, FP73 Bob Martinez, 80.

31. Colburn and deHaven-Smith, *Government in the Sunshine State*, 71.

32. *Florida Times-Union*, June 1, 21, 24, 1931.

33. Colburn and deHaven-Smith, *Government in the Sunshine State*, 71.

34. *The Florida Handbook*, 1987, 1993.

Chapter 6. Holding Back the Republican Tide, but for How Long?

1. James LeMoyne, "Chiles Transforms Florida Campaign," *New York Times*, April 25, 1990; "Ex-Senator's Comeback Confuses Race in Florida," *New York Times*, April 15, 1990.

2. James LeMoyne, "Polls Show Chiles Leading in Florida," *New York Times*, September 2, 1990; "Chiles Wins Democratic Vote for Florida Governor," *New York Times*, September 5, 1990.

3. Clinton, *My Life*, 263–66, 365–66.

4. Florida Department of State, Division of Elections, September 4, 1990, Primary Election, Democratic Primary Election.

5. Ibid.

6. Lowry, "Bush: The Next Generation"; Bill Maxwell, "Lawton Chiles, 1930–1998: Florida's Crackers Lose a Kinsman," *St. Petersburg Times*, December 16, 1998; see also David Binder, "Lawton Chiles, Populist Florida Governor, Is Dead at 68," *New York Times*, December 13, 1998.

7. Bob Martinez, interview by Julian Pleasants, March 23, 1999, Oral History Collection, University of Florida, FP73 Bob Martinez, 82.

8. Kruse, *White Flight*, 10–11, 260. Kruse argues that "Newt Gingrich embodied the politics of the suburban Sunbelt." In Florida, the appeal was broader, however, extending into the rural Panhandle, where Crackers embraced the cultural conservatism of Republicans, and into the urban environs of Miami, where Cubans endorsed anticommunism, small government, and traditional cultural values.

9. Tyler Bridges, "GOP's Strategy Flips Florida Politics: Redistricting Plan Hurt Democrats," *Miami Herald*, December 1, 2002; see also "The Bipartisan Screw Job," *Weekly Planet*, August 24–30, 2005, 18–19; Hamburger and Wallsten, *One Party Country*, 40–43.

10. Hamburger and Wallsten, *One Party Country*, 42–43; Guy Gugliotta, "Blacks Join Forces with GOP on Remap," *Washington Post*, May 11, 1992; Bill Moss, "Redrawn Districts Help GOP, Minorities," *St. Petersburg Times*, November 15, 1992.

11. Tyler Bridges, "GOP's Strategy Flips Florida," *Miami Herald*, December 1, 2002.

12. Ibid.

13. Ibid.

14. Ibid.

15. Tim Nickens, "Chiles Leaves Footprints in Many Parts of Florida," *St. Petersburg Times*, December 13, 1998.

16. Lloyd Dunkelberger, "Never Defeated, Chiles Pulling No Punches," *Gainesville Sun*, 1994 Voter Guide, 5 (also at <www.afn.org/~sun/elect/nulawled.htm>).

17. Ibid.

18. Lowry, "Bush: The Next Generation"; Florida Department of State, Division of Elections, September 8, 1994, Primary Election, Republican Primary.

19. Lloyd Dunkelberger, "Never Defeated, Chiles Pulling No Punches," *Gainesville Sun*, 1994 Voter Guide, 1 (also at <www.afn.org/~sun/elect/nulawled.htm>).

20. Lowry, "Bush: The Next Generation."

21. Hamburger and Wallsten, *One Party Nation*, 62–63.

22. Lowry, "Bush: The Next Generation."

23. Tim Nickens, "Chiles Leaves Footprints in Many Parts of Florida," *St. Petersburg Times*, December 13, 1998.

24. Lucy Morgan, "He-coons and Dogs that Hunt. . . ." *Forum: The Magazine of the Florida Humanities Council* (Winter 2006): 30.

25. Patrick Cockburn, "Bush Campaign Ad Sparks Backlash," *Independent*, November 5, 1994; Hamburger and Wallsten, *One Party Nation*, 64.

26. Tim Nickens, "Chiles Leaves Footprints in Many Parts of Florida," *St. Petersburg Times*, December 13, 1998.

27. Florida Department of State, Division of Elections, November 8, 1994, General Election.

28. "South Florida Retirement Condominiums Are Emerging as Centers of Political Clout," *Wall Street Journal*, November 27, 1984.

29. MacManus, "Aging in Florida and Its Implications," 8–9, 18.

30. See also Tim Nickens, "Chiles Leaves Footprints in Many Parts of Florida," *St. Petersburg Times*, December 13, 1998; Lloyd Dunkelberger, "Never Defeated, Chiles Pulling No Punches," *Gainesville Sun*, 1994 Voter Guide, 1–5 (also at <www. afn.org/~sun/elect/nulawled.htm>).

31. Tim Nickens, "Chiles Leaves Footprints in Many Parts of Florida," *St. Petersburg Times*, December 13, 1998.

32. Craig Basse, "ManaSota Environmentalist Gloria C. Rains Dies," *St. Petersburg Times*, September 27, 2000.

33. Rosenbaum and Button, *The Aging and Florida's Local Governments*.

34. "Transcript of the Florida Tobacco Litigation Symposium—Fact, Law, Policy, and Significance," Florida State University College of Law. Copyright © 1998, *Florida State University Law Review*.

35. Ibid.

36. Ibid.

37. Ibid.

38. Ibid.

39. Ibid.

40. Ibid.

41. "The Smoke Settles," *Online NewsHour*, August 25, 1997, 1–2.

42. "Transcript of the Florida Tobacco Litigation Symposium—Fact, Law, Policy, and Significance," Florida State University College of Law. Copyright © 1998, *Florida State University Law Review.*

43. Tim Nickens, "Chiles Leaves Footprints in Many Parts of Florida." *St. Petersburg Times,* December 13, 1998.

44. Ibid.

Chapter 7. From Blue to Red

1. "A New Clump of Bushes," *Economist,* October 29, 1994, 1.

2. Lowry, "Bush: The Next Generation," 1–3.

3. Ibid.

4. Andres Viglucci and Alfonso Chardy, "Bush and Business: Fast Success, Brushes with Mystery," *Miami Herald,* October 5, 2002; Alecia Swasy and Robert Trigaux, "Jeb Bush Followed the Family Game Plan: Earn Your Fortune, Then Run for Office," *St. Petersburg Times,* September 20, 1998.

5. *Gainesville Sun,* May 27, 2006.

6. Brady, *Bad Boy;* James Herbert, "Lee Atwater's Sorrow for the Road Taken," *San Diego Union-Tribune,* May 19, 2006; E. J. Dionne, "President Supports Atwater in Furor over Foley Memo," *New York Times,* June 9, 1989.

7. Gergen and Dionne, "Election Campaign Strategy," 197.

8. Ellen Debenport, "GOP Candidates Glibly Hold Court," *St. Petersburg Times,* July 28, 1994; Lowry, "Bush: The Next Generation," 1; Hamburger and Wallsten, *One Party Country,* 63.

9. Hamburger and Wallsten, *One Party Country,* 68–69.

10. Ibid., 71.

11. Florida Department of State, Division of Elections, November 3, 1998, General Election.

12. Jeb Bush Inaugural Address, January 5, 1999 (also at <www.myflorida.com/eog/speeches_remarks/1–5–99_inaugural.html>).

13. Ibid.

14. Ibid.

15. Jeb Bush, State of the State Address, March 2, 1999 (also at <www.myflorida.com/myflorida/government/mediacenter/news/speeches/3-2-99_soaddress.html>).

16. Ibid.

17. Lassiter, *The Silent Majority,* 13–14, 45–46; Kruse, *White Flight,* 252–53.

18. Kent Fisher, "Public School, Inc.," *St. Petersburg Times,* September 15, 2002; Matthew I. Pinzer, "State Agency Will Say on Charter School Approval," *Miami Herald,* June 27, 2006.

19. *Gainesville Sun*, May 8, 2006.

20. Jon East, "Stakes Are High for Education Tests," *St. Petersburg Times*, March 5, 2006; *Gainesville Sun*, May 8, 2006.

21. *Gainesville Sun*, May 16, 2006.

22. Ken Plante, interview by the author, March 14, 2000.

23. *Gainesville Sun*, May 8, 2006.

24. Terry M. Deal and David S. Broder, "Affirmative Action Tears at Florida GOP," *Washington Post*, May 15, 1999.

25. William Yardley, "Bush Details Anti-Bias Plan," *St. Petersburg Times*, November 10, 1999.

26. Ibid.; *Tampa Tribune*, November 10, 1999.

27. Hamburger and Wallsten, *One Party Country*, 77–78.

28. Freshmen Enrollment, University of Florida, Fall 2001, State Department of Education, Tallahassee, Florida.

29. Steve Bousquet, "The Bush Legacy," *St. Petersburg Times*, December 29, 2006.

30. Dan DeWitt, "Growing Pains," *St. Petersburg Times*, February 27, 2006.

31. Joni James, "Did the Savings Balance the Cost?" *St. Petersburg Times*, December 30, 2006.

Chapter 8. The Presidential Election of 2000

1. See Toobin, *Too Close to Call*; Greenfield, *Oh, Waiter! One Order of Crow*; Correspondents of the *New York Times*, *36 Days*; and Pleasants, *Hanging Chads*.

2. *NBC News*, November 6, 2000.

3. Hamburger and Wallsten, *One Party Country*, 81.

4. Paterniti, "America in Extremis," 34. The total is over 100 percent because the census allowed people to identify themselves as multiple races.

5. "7 Months Later, Elian Goes Home to Cuba," *Washington Post*, June 29, 2000.

6. "A Year Later, Elian's Echoes Linger," *Washington Post*, November 26, 2000.

7. Toobin, *Too Close to Call*, 142–44.

8. Dan Balz, "Bush's Campaign Strategy Sets the Pace for 2000," *Washington Post*, July 4, 1999; "Bush, Gore Hone Post-Debate Strategy on the Campaign Trail," October 4, 2000, at http://edition.cnn.com/2000/ALLPOLITICS/stories/10/04/campaign.wrap/; see also Robert E. Denton, ed., *The 2000 Presidential Campaign: A Communication Perspective* (New York: Praeger/Greenwood, 2002).

9. Toobin, *Too Close To Call*, 148–52.

10. Hamburger and Wallsten, *One Party Country*, 81.

11. Toobin, 100–101, 226, 249–250; Pleasants, *Hanging Chads*, 10.

12. Pleasants, *Hanging Chads*, 3.

13. Toobin, *Too Close to Call*, 14–16.

14. Ibid., 22–25.

15. Dana Milbank, "E-Mails Show Jeb Bush's Office Keenly Interested," *Washington Post*, November 21, 2000.

16. R. W. Apple Jr., "Gore Campaign Vows Court Fight over Vote with Florida's Outcome Still up in the Air," *New York Times*, November 10, 2000; Toobin, *Too Close to Call*; see also www.c-span.org/campaign2000/Florida/ussupcourt.asp.

17. Toobin, *Too Close to Call*, 65.

18. Pleasants, *Hanging Chads*, 84.

19. *The Today Show*, November 9, 2000; see also http://archives.cnn.com/2000/ALLPOLITICS/stories/11/09/election.president/.

20. Pleasants, *Hanging Chads*, 238.

21. Toobin, *Too Close to Call*, 38.

22. Ibid., 50.

23. Ibid., 48–50.

24. Ibid., 100.

25. Pleasants, *Hanging Chads*, 100.

26. Ann Louis Bardach, "Hoodwinked: Why Is Florida's Voting System So Corrupt?" *Slate*, August 24, 2004 (also at <www.slate.com/id/2105524/>).

27. Dana Milbank, "E-Mails Show Jeb Bush's Office Keenly Interested," *Washington Post*, November 21, 2000; *Tallahassee Democrat*, November 20, 2000.

28. Pleasants, *Hanging Chads*, 101.

29. Ibid., 241–42.

30. Ibid., 101–2.

31. Toobin, *Too Close to Call*, 119.

32. Ibid., 130.

33. Pleasants, *Hanging Chads*, 10; Toobin, *Too Close to Call*, 130.

34. Quote from Toobin, *Too Close to Call*, 137; see also 126–28.

35. Ibid., 243–45.

36. Pleasants, *Hanging Chads*, 84.

37. Ibid., 125, 138–39.

38. Toobin, *Too Close to Call*, 236.

39. Ibid., 248–50, 264–67.

40. Pleasants, *Hanging Chads*, 239.

41. Ibid., 256.

42. Dan Belz, "Gore Calls 2000 Verdict 'Crushing,' Assails Court," *Washington Post*, November 15, 2002. Although Gore conceded the results following the Supreme Court's pronouncement, he "strongly disagreed with the Supreme Court decision and the way in which they interpreted and applied the law." "But," he added, "I respect the rule of law, so it is what it is."

43. Toobin, *Too Close to Call*, 167.

44. Larry J. Sabato, "The Perfect Storm," in Sabato, ed., *Overtime*, 97–110.

Chapter 9. So What Does the Future Hold for Florida?

1. Grunwald, *The Swamp*, 2.

2. Tim Nickens, "Jeb Bush's Long Shadow," *St. Petersburg Times*, March 5, 2006.

3. Florida Department of State, Division of Elections, September 10, 2002, Primary Election, Democratic Primary.

4. Adam Smith, "Behind McBride vs. Bush Is Battle of Media Consultants," *St. Petersburg Times*, October 13, 2002; Tim Padgett, "Why Jeb Bush Won Big," *Time Magazine*, November 6, 2002; Dana Kennedy, "The 2002 Elections: Florida," *New York Times*, November 7, 2002. See also <www.whoseflorida.com/mcbride. htm>.

5. Florida Department of State, Division of Elections, November 5, 2002, General Election.

6. Katharine Q. Seelye, "Kerry in Struggle for Democratic Base: Women," *New York Times*, September 22, 2004; Adam Nagourney and David M. Halbfinger, "Kerry Enlisting Clinton Aides in Effort to Refocus Campaign," *New York Times*, September 6, 2004; Christopher Drew and Abby Goodnough, "The 2004 Elections: Issues—Florida; It Was Our Turnout," *New York Times*, November 4, 2004; "Bush Secured Victory in Florida by Veering from Beaten Path," *New York Times*, November 7, 2004.

7. Hamburger and Wallsten, *One Party Country*, 160.

8. Adam C. Smith, "Rural Vote Gave State to Bush," *St. Petersburg Times*, November 14, 2004; Dan Balz, "Bush Wins Second Term," *Washington Post*, November 4, 2004; "How Bush Did It," *Newsweek*, November 7, 2004.

9. "Bush Secured Victory in Florida by Veering from Beaten Path," *New York Times*, November 7, 2004; "Hidden in Plain Sight," *Washington Post*, December 12, 2004; Hamburger and Wallsten, *One Party Country*, 154–55.

10. Robin Toner, "Southern Democrats' Decline is Eroding the Political Center," *New York Times*, November 15, 2004. Toner noted that only four of twenty-two U.S. senators from the old Confederacy were Democrats as a result of the election of 2004, the smallest number since Reconstruction.

11. "GOP Has Lock on South, and Democrats Can't Find Key," *Los Angeles Times*, December 15, 2004; "Bush Secured Victory in Florida," *New York Times*, November 7, 2004.

12. Hamburger and Wallsten, *One Party Country*, 232.

13. Ronald Reagan, First Inaugural Address, January 20, 1981; Reagan, State of the Union Address, February 4, 1986.

14. Jane Healy, interview by David Colburn, May 5, 2006; see 2000, 2002, and 2004 General Election Results, Florida Department of State, Division of Elections,

November 7, 2000, President, Senate, Representative and Cabinet results, November 5, 2002, Governor, Cabinet and Representative results; November 2, 2004, President, Senate, and Representatives results.

15. Bill Clinton's acceptance speech to 1992 Democratic Convention; see also Clinton, *My Life*, 419–41; and Lassiter, *The Silent Majority*, 320.

16. Martin Dyckman, "Voters Are Ready for Professionalism in Politics," *St. Petersburg Times*, October 9, 2005.

17. Bill Cotterell, "State Senator Blasts Bush in E-Mail," *Tallahassee Democrat*, August 29, 2006; see also Marc Caputo, "Miami Senator Appears to Have Lost Top Job," *Miami Herald*, February 9, 2006.

18. *MSNBC Reports*, March 31, 2005.

19. "Florida Judge Rejects State Custody Bid in Schiavo Case," CNN.com, March 24, 2005.

20. Ibid.

21. Adam Nagourney, "In a Polarizing Case, Jeb Bush Cements His Political Stature," *New York Times*, March 25, 2005.

22. *New York Times*, June 23, 2005, late edition, sec. A.

23. Chris Tisch and Joni James, "The State Attorney Will Review Discrepancies Concerning Terri Schiavo's Unexplained Collapse," *St. Petersburg Times*, June 17, 2005.

24. *New York Times*, June 23, 2005, late edition, sec. A, 19.

25. Steve Bousquet, "The Bush Legacy," *St. Petersburg Times*, December 29, 2006.

26. Florida Department of State, Division of Elections, Republican Primary, September 5, 2006.

27. Ibid.; Steve Bousquet and Alex Leary, "Davis Campaign Races the Clock, *St. Petersburg Times*, October 3, 2006.

28. Steve Bousquet and Alex Leary, "Davis Campaign Races the Clock, *St. Petersburg Times*, October 3, 2006; Jason Garcia and John Kennedy, "Charm, Costly Campaign Prove Winning Formula for Candidate," *Orlando Sentinel*, November 8, 2006; *Orlando Sentinel*, November 9, 2006; Steve Bousquet, "Even Gecko Outshone by Crist's Green," *St. Petersburg Times*, November 11, 2006.

29. *Orlando Sentinel*, November 9, 2006.

30. Ibid.; Adam C. Smith, "In Florida It's the I-4s Who Have It," *St. Petersburg Times*, November 12, 2006.

31. *Orlando Sentinel*, November 9, 2006.

32. Mark R. Howard, "Jeb's Legacy," *Florida Trend*, March 2005, 52–59.

33. Dan DeWitt, "Growing Pains," *St. Petersburg Times*, February 27, 2006.

34. Martin Dyckman, "Voters Are Ready for Professionalism in Politics," *St. Petersburg Times*, October 9, 2005.

35. Tim Nickens, "Jeb Bush's Long Shadow," *St. Petersburg Times*, March 5, 2006.

36. Jane Healy, interview by David Colburn, May 5, 2006.

37. Ibid.

38. Adam C. Smith, "In Florida It's the I-4s Who Have It," *St. Petersburg Times*, November 12, 2006.

39. Ibid.

40. Ibid.

41. Ibid.

42. John and Nancy Bell, interview by Robert Thompson, May 8, 2006, Lady Lake, Fla. Copy in the author's possession.

43. *Orlando Sentinel*, November 9, 2006.

44. Eleanor M. Strickland, interview by Robert Thompson, May 10, 2006. Copy in the author's possession.

45. "Key Race: Florida (Open)," *Washington Post*, June 22, 2006.

46. Paterniti, "America in Extremis," 35.

Bibliography

Archives and Collections

Charlton Tebeau Library. Archives. Historical Association of Southern Florida, Miami; Florida State Archives, Tallahassee.

Pepper, Claude. Papers. Florida State University, Tallahassee.

Southern Collection. University of North Carolina, Chapel Hill.

Special Collections. University of South Florida Library, Tampa.

State of Florida Archives. Tallahassee.

Yonge, P. K., Library of Florida History. University of Florida, Gainesville.

Government Documents

U.S. Bureau of the Census. *1940 to the Present*. Washington, D.C.: U.S. Government Printing Office.

Books and Articles

Akerman, Robert Howard. "The Triumph of Moderation in Florida Thought and Politics: A Study of the Race Issue from 1954 to 1960." Ph.D. diss., American University, Washington, D.C., 1967.

Barnett, Cynthia. "Too Little, Too Late." *Florida Trend* 46 (November 2003): 60–61.

Bartley, Numan V. *The New South 1945–1980*. Vol. 11 of *A History of the South*. Baton Rouge/Austin: Louisiana State University Press and the Littlefield Fund for Southern History, University of Texas, 1995.

———. *The Rise of Massive Resistance: Race and Politics in the South during the 1950s*. Baton Rouge: Louisiana State University Press, 1969.

Bartley, Numan V., and Hugh Davis Graham. *Southern Politics and the Second Reconstruction*. Baltimore: Johns Hopkins University Press, 1975.

Bass, Jack. *Unlikely Heroes*. New York: Simon and Schuster, 1981.

Bass, Jack, and Walter DeVries. *The Transformation of Southern Politics: Social Change and Political Consequence since 1945*. New York: Basic Books, 1976.

Belasco, Warren James. *Americans on the Road: From Autocamp to Motel.* Cambridge: MIT Press, 1979.

Bernard, Richard. "Sunbelt." In *Encyclopedia of Southern Culture*, 1126. Chapel Hill: University of North Carolina Press, 1989.

Bernard, Richard, and Bradley R. Rice, eds. *Sunbelt Cities: Politics and Growth since World War II.* Austin: University of Texas Press, 1983.

Black, Earl, and Merle Black. *Politics and Society in the South.* New York: Free Press, 2001.

———. *The Rise of Southern Republicans.* Cambridge: Harvard University Press, 2002.

Blake, Nelson Manfred. *Land into Water—Water into Land.* Tallahassee: University Presses of Florida, 1980.

Blakey, Arch Fredric. *The Florida Phosphate Industry: A History of the Development of a Vital Mineral.* Cambridge: Harvard University Press, 1973.

Blakey, Edward J., and Mary Gail Snyder. *Fortress America: Gated Communities in the United States.* Washington, D.C.: Brookings Institute Press, 1997.

Brady, John. *Bad Boy: The Life and Politics of Lee Atwater.* Reading, Mass.: Addison Wesley, 1997.

Branch, Stephen E. "The Salesman and His Swamp: Dick Pope's Cypress Gardens." *Florida Historical Quarterly* 80 (Spring 2002): 483–503.

Branch, Taylor. *Parting the Waters: America in the King Years, 1954–62.* New York: Touchstone, 1988.

———. *Pillar of Fire: America in the King Years, 1963–65.* New York: Simon and Schuster, 1998.

Braukman, Stacy Lorraine. "Anticommunism and the Politics of Sex and Race in Florida, 1954–65." Ph.D. diss., University of North Carolina, Chapel Hill, 1999.

Brazeal, B. R. "Some Problems in the Desegregation of Higher Education in the 'Hard Core' States." *Journal of Negro Education* 27 (1958): 352–60.

Breslauer, Ken. *Roadside Attractions: The Golden Era of Florida's Tourist Attractions, 1929–1971.* St. Petersburg: Type House, 2000.

Bretos, Miguel. *Cuba and Florida: Exploration of a Hispanic Connection, 1539–1991.* Miami: Historical Association of Southern Florida, 1991.

Brown, Loren G. *Totch: A Life in the Everglades.* Gainesville: University Press of Florida, 1993.

Brunais, Andrea. "Memories of a Child of the Space Program." *Forum* 20 (Winter 1997/98): 14–18.

Carleton, William G. "Negro Politics in Florida: Another Middle-Class Revolution in the Making." *South Atlantic Quarterly* 57 (1958): 419–34.

Carlson, Jody. *George C. Wallace and the Politics of Powerlessness: The Wallace*

Campaigns for the Presidency, 1964–1976. New Brunswick, N.J.: Rutgers University Press, 1981.

Caro, Robert A. *The Years of Lyndon Johnson: Master of the Senate.* New York: Knopf, 2002.

Carr, Patrick. *Sunshine States: Wild Times and Extraordinary Lives in the Land of Gators, Guns, and Grapefruit.* New York: Doubleday, 1990.

Carson, Rachel. *Silent Spring.* Boston: Houghton Mifflin, 1962.

Carter, Dan T. *From George Wallace to Newt Gingrich: Race in the Conservative Counterrevolution, 1963–1994.* Baton Rouge: Louisiana State University Press, 1996.

———. *The Politics of Rage: George Wallace, the Origins of the New Conservatism, and the Transformation of American Politics.* New York: Simon and Schuster, 1995.

Carter, Jimmy. *Sharing Good Times.* New York: Simon and Schuster, 2004.

Cash, W. J. *The Mind of the South.* Garden City, N.Y.: Doubleday, 1954.

Chafe, William H. *Civilities and Civil Rights: Greensboro, North Carolina, and the Black Struggle for Freedom.* New York and Oxford: Oxford University Press, 1980.

Chapman, Julia Sullivan. "A Southern Moderate Advocates Compliance: A Study of LeRoy Collins as Director of the Community Relations Service." Master's thesis, University of South Florida, 1974.

Christie, Terry L. "The Collins-Johns Election, 1954: A Turning Point." *Apalachee* 6 (1967): 5–19.

Clark, James C. "Civil Rights Leader Harry T. Moore and the Ku Klux Klan in Florida." *Florida Historical Quarterly* 73 (October 1994): 167–82.

Clark, Roy Peter, and Raymond Arsenault, eds. *The Changing South of Gene Patterson: Journalism and Civil Rights, 1960–1968.* Gainesville: University Press of Florida, 2002.

Clinton, Bill. *My Life.* New York: Knopf, 2004.

Cobb, James C. *The Selling of the South: The Southern Crusade for Industrial Development, 1936–1980.* Baton Rouge: Louisiana State University Press, 1982.

———. "'We Ain't White Trash No More': Southern Whites and the Reconstruction of Southern Identity." In *The Southern State of Mind,* edited by Jan Nordby Gretlund. Columbia: University of South Carolina Press, 1999.

Cohen, Lizabeth. *A Consumers' Republic: The Politics of Mass Consumption in Postwar America.* New York: Knopf, 2003.

Colburn, David R. "The Push for Equality: All Eyes on Florida, St. Augustine 1964." *Forum: The Magazine of the Florida Humanities Council* 28, no. 1 (Winter 1994/95): 22–29.

————. *Racial Change and Community Crisis: St. Augustine, Florida, 1877–1980.* 1985. Gainesville: University of Florida Press, 1991.

————. "Rosewood and America in the Early Twentieth Century." *Florida Historical Quarterly* 76 (Fall 1997): 175–92.

Colburn, David R., and Lance deHaven-Smith. *Florida's Megatrends: Critical Issues in Florida.* Gainesville: University Press of Florida, 2002.

————. *Government in the Sunshine State: Florida since Statehood.* Gainesville: University Press of Florida, 1999.

Colburn, David R., and Richard K. Scher. *Florida's Gubernatorial Politics in the Twentieth Century.* Gainesville: University Presses of Florida, 1980.

Collins, LeRoy. *Forerunners Courageous: Stories of Frontier Florida.* Tallahassee: Colcade, 1971.

————. "How It Looks from the South." *Look,* May 13, 1958.

Correspondents of the *New York Times. 36 Days: The Complete Chronicle of the 2000 Election.* New York: Times Books, 2001.

Crooks, James B. *Jacksonville after the Fire, 1901–1919: A New South City.* Gainesville: University Presses of Florida, 1991.

————. *Jacksonville: The Consolidation Story from Civil Rights to the Jaguars.* Gainesville: University Press of Florida, 2004.

Curl, Donald. *Mizner's Florida: American Resort Architecture.* Cambridge: MIT Press, 1984.

D'Alemberte, Talbot "Sandy," and Frank Sanchez. "A Tribute to a Great Man: LeRoy Collins." *Florida State University Law Review* 19 (Fall 1991): 255–64.

Danese, Tracy E. *Claude Pepper and Ed Ball: Politics, Purpose, and Power.* Gainesville: University Press of Florida, 2000.

Daniel, Pete. *Lost Revolutions: The South in the 1950s.* Chapel Hill: University of North Carolina Press, 2000.

Date, S. V. *Quiet Passion: A Biography of Bob Graham.* New York: Jeremy P. Tarcher/Penguin, 2004.

DeGrove, John M. *Land Growth and Politics.* Washington, D.C.: Planners Press, 1984.

Derr, Mark. *Some Kind of Paradise: A Chronicle of Man and Land in Florida.* New York: William Morrow, 1989.

Doherty, P. C. "Development and Impact of Legislative Involvement on Selected Aspects of State University System Operations." Vol. 1. Ph.D. diss., Florida State University, 1991.

Domin, Gregory Paul. *Jimmy Carter, Public Opinion, and the Search for Values, 1977–1981.* Macon, Ga.: Mercer University Press, 2003.

Douglas, Marjory Stoneman. *Voice of the River: An Autobiography with John Rothchild.* Sarasota: Pineapple Press, 1987.

Downey-Anderson, Charlotte. "The 'Coggins Affair': Desegregation and Southern Mores in Madison County, Florida." *Florida Historical Quarterly* 59 (April 1981): 464–72.

D'Souza, Dinesh. *Ronald Reagan: How an Ordinary Man Became an Extraordinary Leader.* New York: Simon and Schuster, 1997.

Dunn, Marvin. *Black Miami in the Twentieth Century.* Gainesville: University Press of Florida, 1997.

Dyckman, Martin A. *Floridian of His Century: The Courage of Governor LeRoy Collins.* Gainesville: University Press of Florida, 2006.

Edmonds, Bill. "Civil Rights and Southern Editors: Richmond, Little Rock, Tallahassee." Master's thesis, Florida State University, 1996.

Edmonds, Rick. "The Push for Equality: Journey to the Selma Bridge, LeRoy Collins." *Forum: The Magazine of The Florida Humanities Council* (Winter 1994/1995): 30–33.

Edsall, Thomas Byrne, and Mary D. Edsall. *Chain Reaction: The Impact of Race, Rights, and Taxes on American Politics.* New York: Norton, 1991.

Egerton, John W. *The Americanization of Dixie: The Southernization of America.* New York: Harper's, 1974.

———. *Speak Now Against the Day: The Generation before the Civil Rights Movement in the South.* Chapel Hill: University of North Carolina Press, 1995.

Encyclopedia of Southern Culture. Edited by Charles Reagan Wilson and William Ferris. Chapel Hill: University of North Carolina Press, 1989.

Espey, Ruth F. "The Anatomy of Defeat: The 1968 United States Senatorial Campaign of LeRoy Collins." Master's thesis, University of South Florida, 1974.

Evans, Jon. "The Origins of Tallahassee's Racial Disturbance Plan: Segregation, Racial Tensions, and Violence during World War II." *Florida Historical Quarterly* 79 (Winter 2001): 346–63.

Farris, Charles D. "Effects of Negro Voting upon the Politics of a Southern City: An Intensive Study, 1946–48." Ph.D. diss., University of Chicago, 1955.

Fischer, David Hackett. *Growing Old in America.* New York: Oxford University Press, 1977.

The Florida Handbook. Tallahassee: Peninsular, 1945–2005.

Florida Statistical Abstract 1990 to Present. Gainesville: University of Florida Press, 1991 to present.

Flynt, Wayne. *Cracker Messiah, Sidney J. Catts of Florida.* Baton Rouge: Louisiana State University Press, 1977.

———. "Sidney J. Catts: The Road to Power," *Florida Historical Quarterly* 49, no. 2 (October 1970): 108–39.

Foglesong, Richard E. *Married to the Mouse: Walt Disney World and Orlando.* New Haven: Yale University Press, 2001.

———. "When Disney Came to Town." *Washington Post Magazine*, May 14, 1994.

Formisano, Ronald P. *Boston against Busing: Race, Class, and Ethnicity in the 1960s and 1970s.* Chapel Hill: University of North Carolina Press, 1991.

Foster, Mark S. *Castles in the Sand: The Life and Times of Carl Graham Fisher.* Gainesville: University Press of Florida, 2000.

Frank, Thomas. *What's the Matter with Kansas?: How Conservatives Won the Heart of America.* New York: Metropolitan Books, 2004.

Fraser, Steve, and Gary Gerstle, eds. *The Rise and Fall of the New Deal Order, 1930–1980.* Princeton: Princeton University Press, 1989.

Gannon, Michael V., ed. *The New History of Florida.* Gainesville: University Press of Florida. 1996.

———. *Operation Drumbeat: The Dramatic True Story of Germany's First U-Boat Attacks along the American Coast in World War II.* New York: Harper and Row, 1990.

———. *Florida: A Short History.* Gainesville: University Press of Florida, 1993.

Garcia, Maria Cristina. *Havana USA: Cuban Exiles and Cuban Americans in South Florida, 1959–1994.* Berkeley and Los Angeles: University of California Press, 1996.

Garrow, David J. *Bearing the Cross: Martin Luther King, Jr., and the Southern Leadership Conference.* New York: William Morrow, 1986.

———. *Protest at Selma: Martin Luther King, Jr., and the Voting Rights Act of 1965.* New Haven: Yale University Press, 1978.

Gelfand, Mark I. *A Nation of Cities: The Federal Government and Urban America, 1933–1965.* New York: Oxford University Press, 1975.

Gergen, David, and E. J. Dionne. "Election Campaign Strategy: Conventions, VP Choices, and Debates," In *Campaign for President: The Managers Look at '88,* edited by David R. Runkel. Dover, Mass.: Auburn House, 1989.

Goldfield, David. *Cotton Fields and Skyscrapers: Southern City and Region, 1607–1980.* Baton Rouge: Louisiana State University Press, 1982.

Goodwyn, Larry. "Anarchy in St. Augustine." *Harper's*, January 1965, 74–81.

Graham, Bob. *Workdays: Finding Florida on the Job.* Edited by Lawrence Mahoney. Miami: Banyan Books, 1978.

Graham, Thomas. "The Flagler Era." In *The Oldest City,* edited by Jean Parker Waterbury, 181–210. St. Augustine: St. Augustine Historical Society, 1983.

Green, Ben. *Before His Time: The Untold Story of Harry T. Moore, America's First Civil Rights Martyr.* New York: Free Press, 1999.

Greenfield, Jeff. *Oh, Waiter! One Order of Crow: Inside the Strangest Presidential Election Finish in American History.* New York: Putnam's, 2001.

Grunwald, Michael. *The Swamp: The Everglades, Florida and the Politics of Paradise.* New York: Simon and Schuster, 2006.

Halberstam, David. "Claude Kirk and the Politics of Promotion." *Harper's*, May 1968.

———. *The Powers That Be.* New York: Knopf, 1979.

Hall, Kermit L. "Civil Rights: The Florida Version." *Forum: The Magazine of the Florida Humanities Council* 18, no. 1 (Winter 1994/1995): 10–13.

Hamburger, Tom, and Peter Wallsten. *One Party Country: The Republican Plan for Dominance in the 21st Century.* Hoboken, N.J.: Wiley, 2006.

Harney, Robert. "The Palmetto and the Maple Leaf: Patterns of Canadian Migration to Florida." In *Shades of the Sunbelt*, edited by Randall Miller and George Pozzetta, 21–40. Westport, Conn.: Greenwood Press, 1988.

Hartsfield, Annie Mary, and Elston E. Roady. *Florida Votes 1920–1962.* Tallahassee: Institute of Governmental Research, Florida State University, 1963.

Havard, William C., and Loren P. Beth. *The Politics of Mis-Representation: Rural-Urban Conflict in the Florida Legislature.* Baton Rouge: Louisiana State University Press, 1962.

———. "The Problem of Apportionment in Florida." In *Reapportionment and Representation in Florida*, edited by Susan A. MacManus, 21–76. Tampa: University of South Florida, 1991.

Herman, Harley. "Anatomy of a Bar Resignation: The Virgil Hawkins Story. An Idealist Faces the Pragmatic Challenges of the Practice of Law." *Florida Coastal Law Journal* 2 (Fall 2000): 77.

Hewlett, Richard Greening. *Jesse Ball duPont.* Gainesville: University Press of Florida, 1992.

Hine, Darlene Clark, ed. *Black Victory: The Rise and Fall of the White Primary in Texas.* Columbia: Missouri University Press, 2003.

Hughes, Melvin Edward, Jr. "William J. Howey and His Florida Dreams." *Florida Historical Quarterly* 66 (January 1988): 243–64.

Hurston, Zora Neale. *Mules and Men.* Philadelphia: Lippincott, 1935.

———. *Their Eyes Were Watching God.* New York: Harper and Row, 1937.

Hyde, Samuel C., Jr., ed. *Sunbelt Revolution: The Historical Progression of the Civil Rights Struggle in the Gulf South, 1866–2000.* Gainesville: University Press of Florida, 2003.

Iorio, Pam. "Colorless Primaries: Tampa's White Municipal Party." *Florida Historical Quarterly* 79 (Winter 2001): 297–318.

Jacobstein, Helen L. *The Segregation Factor in the Florida Democratic Gubernatorial Primary of 1956.* Gainesville: University of Florida Press, 1972.

Jacoway, Elizabeth. "Taken by Surprise: Little Rock Business Leaders and Desegregation." In *Southern Businessmen and Desegregation*, edited by Elizabeth Jacoway and David R. Colburn, 15–41. Baton Rouge: Louisiana State University Press, 1982.

Jacoway, Elizabeth, and David R. Colburn, eds. *Southern Businessmen and Deseg-regation*. Baton Rouge: Louisiana State University Press, 1982.

Jackson, Kenneth T. *Crabgrass Frontier: The Suburbanization of the United States*. New York: Oxford University Press, 1985.

Jones, Maxine. "No Longer Denied: Black Women in Florida, 1920–1950." In *The African-American Heritage of Florida*, edited by David R. Colburn and Jane Landers. Gainesville: University Press of Florida, 1994.

Kallina, Edmund F., Jr. *Claude Kirk and the Politics of Confrontation*. Gainesville: University Press of Florida, 1993.

Kelly, Alfred H., and Winfred A. Harbison. *The American Constitution: Its Origins and Development*. 5th ed. New York: Norton, 1976.

Key, V. O., Jr. *Southern Politics in State and Nation*. New York: Vintage, 1949.

Killian, Lewis M. *Black and White: Reflections of a White Southern Sociologist*. Dix Hills, N.Y.: General Hall, 1994.

Klein, Kevin N. "Guarding the Baggage: Florida's Pork Chop Gang and Its Defense of the Old South." Ph.D. diss., Florida State University, 1995.

Kluger, Richard. *Simple Justice: The History of Brown v. Board of Education and Black America's Struggle for Equality*. New York: Random House, 1977.

Kruse, Kevin M. *White Flight: Atlanta and the Making of Modern Conservatism*. Princeton and Oxford: Princeton University Press, 2005.

Lassiter, Matthew D. *The Silent Majority: Suburban Politics in the Sunbelt South*. Princeton and Oxford: Princeton University Press, 2006.

Lawson, Steven F. *Black Ballots: Voting Rights in the South, 1944–1969*. New York: Columbia University Press, 1976.

———. *In Pursuit of Power: Southern Blacks and Electoral Politics, 1965–1982*. New York: Columbia University Press, 1985.

Lawson, Steven F., David R. Colburn, and Darryl Paulson. "Groveland: Florida's Little Scottsboro." *Florida Historical Quarterly* 65 (July 1986): 1–24.

Lewis, John. *Walking with the Wind: A Memoir of the Movement*. In collaboration with Michael D'Orso. New York: Harcourt Brace, 1998.

Lowry, Rich. "Bush: The Next Generation." *National Review*, October 24, 1994.

Lublin, David. *The Republican South: Democratization and Partisan Change*. Princeton: Princeton University Press, 2004.

Lucoff, Manny. "LeRoy Collins and the National Association of Broadcasters: Experiment in the Public Interest." Ph.D. diss., Florida State University, 1971.

MacManus, Susan A. "Aging in Florida and Its Implications." In *The Graying of Florida: A Report on the 2000 Meeting of the Reubin O'D. Askew Institute on Politics and Society*, 8, 9, 18. Gainesville, Fla.: Reubin O'D. Askew Institute on Politics and Society, 1999.

———, ed. *Reapportionment and Representation in Florida*. Tampa: Interbay Innovation Institute, 1991.

———. *Targeting Senior Voters*. New York: Rowman and Littlefield, 2000.

MacManus, Susan A., with Patricia Turner. *Young vs. Old: Generational Combat in the Twenty-First Century*. Boulder, Colo.: Westview Press, 1996.

Manley, Walter W., II, and Canter Brown Jr. *The Supreme Court of Florida, 1917–1972*. Gainesville: University Press of Florida, 2006.

Mathews, Donald R., and James W. Prothro. *Negroes and the New Southern Politics*. New York: Harcourt, Brace, and World, 1966.

McCally, David P. *The Everglades: An Environmental History*. Gainesville: University Press of Florida, 1999.

McClenahan, Heather C. R. "Florida in Black and White: Newspapers, Race, and the 1968 U.S. Senate Campaign." Master's thesis, University of South Florida, 1994.

McCollough, David. *Truman*. New York: Simon and Schuster, 1992.

McGill, Ralph. "A Decade of Slow, Painful Progress." *Saturday Review*, May 16, 1964.

McWhiney, Grady. *Cracker Culture: Celtic Ways in the Old South*. Tuscaloosa: University of Alabama Press, 1989.

Miller, Donald. "Postdenominational Christianity in the Twenty-First Century," 558 *Annals 57*, American Academy of Political and Social Sciences (July 1998): 183-87.

Mohl, Raymond. "Asian Immigration to Florida." *Florida Historical Quarterly* 74 (Winter 1996): 261–86.

———. "Elizabeth Virrick and the 'Concrete Monsters': Housing Reform in Postwar Miami." *Tequesta* (2001): 5–38.

———. "Miami: The Ethnic Cauldron." In *Sunbelt Cities*, edited by Richard Bernard and Bradley R. Rice, 58–99. Austin: University of Texas Press, 1983.

———. "Race and Space in the Modern City: Interstate 95 and the Black Community in Miami." In *Urban Policy in Twentieth-Century America*, edited by Arnold R. Hirsch and Raymond Mohl, 100–158. New Brunswick, N.J.: Rutgers University Press, 1993.

Moore, Deborah Dash. *To the Golden Cities: Pursuing the American Jewish Dream in Miami and Los Angeles*. New York: Free Press, 1994.

Mormino, Gary. "Florida's Year of Reckoning, 1973." *Forum: The Magazine of The Florida Humanities Council* 27 (Winter 2003): 18–19.

———. "G.I. Joe Meets Jim Crow: Racial Violence and Reform in World War II Florida." *Florida Historical Quarterly* 74 (July 1994): 23–42.

———. "A History of Florida's White Primary." In *Sunbelt Revolution: The Histori-*

cal Progression of the Civil Rights Struggle in the Gulf South, 1866–2000, edited by Samuel C. Hyde Jr., 133–50. Gainesville: University Press of Florida, 2003.

———. *Land of Sunshine, State of Dreams: A Social History of Modern Florida.* Gainesville: University Press of Florida, 2005.

———. "Miami Goes to War, 1941–1945," *Tequesta* 57 (1997): 5–52.

———. "Trouble in Tourist Heaven." *Forum: The Magazine of The Florida Humanities Council* 17 (Summer 1994): 11–13.

———. "World War II." In *The New History of Florida,* edited by Michael Gannon, 344–72. Gainesville: University Press of Florida, 1996.

Mormino, Gary, and George E. Pozzetta. *The Immigrant World of Ybor City: Italians and Their Latin Neighbors in Tampa, 1885–1985.* Gainesville: University Press of Florida, 1998.

Morris, Edmund. *Dutch: A Memoir of Ronald Reagan.* New York: Modern Library, 2000.

Nolan, David. *Fifty Feet in Paradise: The Booming of Florida.* New York: Harcourt Brace Jovanovich, 1984.

Nordheimer, Jon. "Florida's 'Supersquare'—A Man to Watch." *New York Times Magazine,* March 5, 1972.

Novak, Robert. *The Agony of the GOP 1964.* New York: Macmillan, 1965.

Novak, William J., and Julian E. Zeliser, eds. *The Democratic Experiment: New Directions in American Political History.* Princeton: Princeton University Press, 2003.

Ortiz, Paul. *Emancipation Betrayed: The Hidden History of Black Organizing and White Violence in Florida from Reconstruction to the Bloody Election of 1920.* Berkeley and Los Angeles: University of California Press, 2005.

Padgett, Gregory B. "Push for Equality: A Bus Boycott Takes Root and Blossoms." *Forum: The Magazine of The Florida Humanities Council* (Winter 1994): 14–17.

———. "The Tallahassee Bus Boycott." In *Sunbelt Revolution: The Historical Progression of the Civil Rights Struggle in the Gulf South 1866–2000,* edited by Samuel C. Hyde Jr., 190–209. Gainesville: University Press of Florida, 2003.

Parks, Arva, and Gregory Bush. *Miami: The American Crossroad.* Needham Heights, Mass.: Simon and Schuster, 1996.

Paterniti, Michael. "America in Extremis: How Florida Became the New California." *New York Times Magazine,* April 21, 2002, 28–35, 66, 74.

Paulson, Darryl. "Campaign Finance in Florida: Who Gave It, Who Got, Who Knows?" In *Money, Politics, and Campaign Finance Reform Law in the States,* edited by David Schultz, 213–37. Durham, N.C.: Carolina Academic Press, 2002.

Paulson, Darryl, and Paul Hawkes. "Desegregating the University of Florida Law

School: *Virgil Hawkins v. the Florida Board of Control.*" *Florida State University Law Review* 12 (1984): 59–70.

Pepper, Claude Denson. *Pepper: Eyewitness to a Century.* With Hays Gorey. New York: Harcourt Brace Jovanovich, 1987.

Phelts, Marsha Dean. *An American Beach for African Americans.* Gainesville: University Press of Florida, 1997.

Phillips, Kevin P. *The Emerging Republican Majority.* Garden City, N.Y.: Anchor Books, 1970.

Pierce, Charles W. *Pioneer Life in Southeast Florida.* Coral Gables: University of Miami Press, 1970.

Pierce, Robert N. *A Sacred Trust: Nelson Poynter and the St. Petersburg Times.* Gainesville: University Press of Florida, 1993.

Pleasants, Julian M. "Claude Pepper, Strom Thurmond and the 1948 Presidential Election in Florida." *Florida Historical Quarterly* 76 (Spring 1998): 49–73.

———. *Hanging Chads: The Inside Story of the 2000 Presidential Recount in Florida.* New York: Palgrave Macmillan, 2004.

———. *Orange Journalism: Voices from Florida Newspapers.* Gainesville: University Press of Florida, 2003.

Porter, Gilbert L. "The Status of Educational Desegregation in Florida." *Journal of Negro Education* 25 (1956): 246–53.

Portes, Alejandro, and Alex Stepick. *City on the Edge: The Transformation of Miami.* Berkeley and Los Angeles: University of California Press, 1993.

Prior, Leon O. "Nazi Invasion of Florida!" *Florida Historical Quarterly* 49 (October 1970): 129–39.

Putnam, Robert. *Bowling Alone: The Collapse and Revival of American Community.* New York: Simon and Schuster, 2000.

Rabby, Glenda Alice. *The Pain and the Promise: The Struggle for Civil Rights in Tallahassee, Florida.* Athens: University of Georgia Press, 1999.

Raper, Arthur Franklin. *The Tragedy of Lynching.* Montclair, N.J.: Patterson Smith, 1969.

Ray, Janisse. *Ecology of a Cracker Childhood.* Minneapolis: Milkweed Editions, 1999.

Reed, John Shelton. *One South: An Ethnic Approach to Regional Culture.* Baton Rouge: Louisiana State University Press, 1982.

Reed, John Shelton, James Kohls, and Carol Hanchette. "The Dissolution of Dixie and the Changing Shape of the South." *Social Forces* 69, no. 1 (September 1990): 221–33.

Rehnquist, William H. *The Centennial Crisis: The Disputed Election of 1876.* New York: Knopf, 2004.

Reeves, Richard. *The Triumph of Imagination.* New York: Simon and Schuster, 2005.

Rieder, Jonathan. *Canarsie: The Jews and Italians of Brooklyn against Liberalism.* Cambridge: Harvard University Press, 1985.

Roady, Elston E. "The Expansion of Negro Suffrage in Florida." *Journal of Negro Education* 26 (1957): 297–306.

Rogers, William W. "Fortune and Misfortune: The Paradoxical Twenties." In *The New History of Florida,* edited by Michael Gannon. Gainesville: University Press of Florida, 1996.

———. "The Great Depression." In *The New History of Florida,* edited by Michael Gannon. Gainesville: University Press of Florida, 1996.

Rogers, William W., and James M. Denham. *Florida Sheriffs: A History 1821–1945.* Tallahassee: Sentry Press, 2001.

Rosenbaum, Walter A., and James W. Button. *The Aging and Florida's Local Governments: A Report from Cities and Counties.* Gainesville: Department of Political Science, University of Florida, 1987.

Rymer, Russ. *American Beach: A Saga of Race, Wealth, and Memory.* New York: Harper Collins, 1998.

Sabato, Larry J., ed. *Overtime: The Election of 2000 Thriller.* New York: Longman, 2002.

Sale, Kirkpatrick. *Power Shift: The Rise of the Southern Rim and Its Challenge to the Eastern Establishment.* New York: Random House, 1975.

Sanders, Randy. *Mighty Peculiar Elections: The New South Gubernatorial Campaigns of 1970 and the Changing Politics of Race.* Gainesville: University Press of Florida. 2002.

Saunders, Robert W., Sr. *Bridging the Gap: Continuing the Florida NAACP Legacy of Harry T. Moore 1952–1966.* Tampa, Fla.: University of Tampa Press, 2000.

Schulman, Bruce J. *The Seventies: The Great Shift in American Culture, Society, and Politics.* New York: Free Press, 2001.

Schnur, James Anthony. "Cold Warriors in the Hot Sunshine: The Johns Committee's Assault on Civil Liberties in Florida, 1956–1965." Master's thesis, University of South Florida, 1995.

Sherrill, Robert. "Can Miami Save Itself?" *New York Times Magazine,* July 19, 1987, 18–24.

———. "Florida's Legislature: The Pork Chop State of Mind." *Harper's,* November 1965.

———. *Gothic Politics in the Deep South: Stars of the New Confederacy.* New York: Grossman, 1968.

———. "The Power Game: George Smathers: The Golden Senator from Florida." *Nation*, December 7, 1964.

Shofner, Jerrell H. "Communists, Klansmen, and the CIO in the Florida Citrus Industry." *Florida Historical Quarterly* 71 (January 1993): 300–305.

———. "Custom, Law, and History: The Enduring Influence of Florida's 'Black Code.'" *Florida Historical Quarterly* 55 (January 1977): 277–98.

———. *Nor Is It Over Yet: Florida in the Era of Reconstruction, 1863–1877*. Gainesville: University Presses of Florida, 1974.

Sicius, Francis. "The Miami-Havana Connection: The First Seventy-five Years." *Tequesta* 58 (1998): 5–46.

Smith, Charles U., ed. *The Civil Rights Movement in Florida and the United States: Historical and Contemporary Perspectives*. Tallahassee, Fla.: Father and Sun, 1989.

Sugrue, Thomas J. *The Origins of the Urban Crisis: Race and Inequality in Postwar Detroit*. Princeton: Princeton University Press, 1996.

Tebeau, Charlton W., and William Marina. *A History of Florida*. 3rd ed. Coral Gables: University of Miami Press, 1999.

Thomson, H. Bailey. "Orlando's Martin Andersen: Power behind the Boom." *Florida Historical Quarterly* 79 (Spring 2001): 492–516.

Toobin, Jeffrey. *Too Close to Call: The Thirty-Six-Day Battle to Decide the 2000 Election*. New York: Random House, 2001.

Wagy, Thomas R. *Governor LeRoy Collins of Florida: Spokesman of the New South*. Tuscaloosa: University of Alabama Press, 1985.

———. "Governor LeRoy Collins of Florida and the Little Rock Crisis of 1957. *Arkansas Historical Quarterly* 38 (Summer 1979): 99–115.

Waring, Thomas R. "The Southern Case against Desegregation." *Harper's*, January 1956.

Watts, Stephen. *The Magic Kingdom: Walt Disney and the American Way of Life*. Boston: Houghton Mifflin, 1997.

White, Theodore H. *The Making of the President 1960*. New York: Atheneum. 1961.

Whitfield, Stephen. "Blood and Sand: The Jewish Community of South Florida." *American Jewish History* (1982): 73–96.

———. "Florida's Fudged Identity." *Florida Historical Quarterly* 71 (April 1993): 413–35.

Wilkins, Roger. *A Man's Life: An Autobiography*. New York: Simon and Schuster, 1982.

Wilkinson, Alec. *Big Sugar: Seasons in the Cane Fields of Florida*. New York: Knopf, 1989.

Williams, Juan. *Thurgood Marshall: American Revolutionary.* New York: Times Books, 1998.

Williamson, Joel. *The Crucible of Race: Black-White Relations in the American South since Emancipation.* New York: Oxford University Press, 1984.

Winkler, Allan. *Franklin D. Roosevelt and the Making of Modern America.* New York: Pearson Education, 2006.

Woodward, C. Vann. *The Strange Career of Jim Crow.* New York: Oxford University Press, 1954.

Index